THE DEPUTY INTERVIEWS

THE DEPUTY INTERVIEWS

THE TRUE STORY OF J.F.K. ASSASSINATION WITNESS

AND FORMER DALLAS DEPUTY SHERIFF

ROGER DEAN CRAIG

BY

STEVE CAMERON

Published by Steve Cameron Productions
Front cover and book design by Steve Cameron

Cameron, Steve
The Deputy Interviews: The True Story of J.F.K. Assassination Witness, and Former Dallas Deputy Sheriff, Roger Dean Craig -1st ed.

First edition 2019.

stevecameronproductions.com

Dedicated to Army Staff Sergeant Clay Allen Craig

May 19, 1985 – April 29, 2008

FOREWORD

BY DAVID T. RATCLIFFE

I obtained a copy of Roger Craig's unpublished manuscript *When They Kill A President*, from Tom Davis in the mid-1980s. I was living in Santa Cruz, California and had been listening to Mae Brussell's weekly radio program, World Watchers. Tom was another first-generation assassination researcher; a friend of Mae's, he ran Tom Davis Books, fulfilling all of Mae's book orders. After first mail-ordering books, in time I was able to visit Tom at his office-warehouse. He had researched fascism in the United States from the early 20th century before Hitler's rise to power in 1933. Mussolini's definition of fascism was when the corporation becomes the state and the state becomes the corporation. The banking houses and Wall Street lawyers had been hyper-focused on their Manichaean Devil, Communism, since the 1917 Russian Revolution, and Tom was very well read on this history as well as having a significant knowledge of authors and books chronicling its development. He began selling books in 1970 with the byline "The largest selection of political conspiracy books in the United States." Through his own network he had acquired Roger's manuscript and mentioned it in passing while we were discussing people who had stood up to the usurped power of the national security state apparatus. I asked him for more details and he offered one of the few copies he still had. In the early 1990s I began posting text files to newsgroups of out-of-print books and articles on the health costs of nuclear technology and the assassination of JFK, and in March 1992 I posted *When They Kill A President*. In 1994 I began building ratical.org, launching it on the Autumnal Equinox in 1995. The first hypertext version of *When They Kill A President* was published in late 1998.

The fundamental significance in all this is reclaiming and promulgating the living history of our single, indivisible human family. The history of the life of our times belongs to all of us. It is the foundational record of our world and how it actually operates given what has occurred previously, leading up to this moment. Author of The Society of the Spectacle, Guy Debord wrote in 1988, "Spectacular domination's first priority was to eradicate historical knowledge in general; beginning with just about all rational information and commentary on the most recent past. With the destruction of history, contemporary events themselves retreat into a remote and fabulous realm of unverifiable stories, uncheckable statistics, unlikely explanations and untenable reasoning "

A martyr is a witness to truth. *When They Kill A President* is Roger Craig's witness to the reality of the extra-constitutional firing of the 35th President by elements of our national security state's high-level military intelligence networks. It is his martyrdom lived out and never compromised. In so doing, he gave his all, eventually sacrificing everything he had—in the end, his life—for the sake of principle, for the truth of a seminal turning point in our history.

Roger Craig's martyrdom reflects John Kennedy's. Jim Douglass, author of *JFK and the Unspeakable: Why He Died and Why It Matters*, gave the Keynote Address at the 2009 Coalition on Political Assassinations (COPA) Conference. Near the close he summed up the meaning of the assassination:

> "Because John Kennedy chose peace on earth at the height of the Cold War, he was executed. But because he turned toward peace, in spite of the consequences to himself, humanity is still alive and struggling. That is hopeful. Especially if we understand what he went through and what he has given to us as his vision.
>
> At a certain point in his presidency, John Kennedy turned a corner and he didn't look back. I believe that decisive turn toward his final purpose in life, resulting in his death, happened in the darkness of the Cuban Missile Crisis. Although Kennedy was already in conflict with his national security managers, the missile crisis was the breaking point.
>
> At that most critical moment for us all, he turned from any remaining control that his security managers had over him toward a deeper ethic, a deeper vision in which the fate of the earth became his priority. Without losing sight of our own best hopes in this country, he began to home in, with his new partner, Nikita Khrushchev, on the hope of peace for everyone on this earth—Russians, Americans, Cubans, Vietnamese, Indonesians,

everyone on this earth—no exceptions. He made that commitment to life at the cost of his own. What a transforming story that is.

And what a propaganda campaign has been waged to keep us Americans from understanding that story, from telling it, and from re-telling it to our children and grandchildren. Because that's a story whose telling can transform a nation.

But when a nation is under the continuing domination of an idol, namely war, it is a story that will be covered up. When the story can liberate us from our idolatry of war, then the worshippers of the idol are going to do everything they can to keep the story from being told.

From the standpoint of a belief that war is the ultimate power, that's too dangerous a story. It's a subversive story. It shows a different kind of security than always being ready to go to war.

It's unbelievable—or we're supposed to think it is—that a president was murdered by our own government agencies because he was seeking a more stable peace than relying on nuclear weapons.

It's unspeakable. For the sake of a nation that must always be preparing for war, that story must not be told. If it were, we might learn that peace is possible without making war. We might even learn there is a force more powerful than war. How unthinkable! But how necessary if life on earth is to continue.

That is why it is so hopeful for us to confront the unspeakable and to tell the transforming story of a man of courage, President John F. Kennedy. It is a story ultimately not of death but of life—all our lives. In the end, it is not so much a story of one man as it is a story of peacemaking when the chips are down. That story is our story, a story of hope....

The fact that we are still living—that the human family is still alive with a fighting chance for survival, and for much more than that—is reason for gratitude for a peacemaking president, and to the unlikely alliance he forged with his enemy.

So let us give thanks this Thanksgiving for John F. Kennedy, and for his partner in peacemaking, Nikita Khrushchev.

Their story is our story, a story of the courage to turn toward the truth. Remember what Gandhi said that turned theology on its head. He said truth is God. That is the truth: Truth is God. We can discover the truth and live it out. There is nothing, nothing more powerful than the truth. The truth will set us free."

Concerning Douglass' book, Marty Schotz, author of *History Will Not Absolve Us: Orwellian control, public denial, and the murder of President Kennedy* (1996), has observed: "What Jim did was to resurrect the JFK in each of us, and thus to set before us the task of carrying on the work he was doing. Jim was able to do this because he saw and was able to render JFK's story as a gospel tale." Since 1963, the cover story of the assassination of President Kennedy is that it is a mystery. As Schotz wrote in the Introduction to his book, "The murder of the President is not a mystery. The nature of the conspiracy that took President Kennedy's life was from the outset quite obvious to anyone who knew how to look and was willing to do so. The same holds true today. Any citizen who is willing to look can see clearly who killed President Kennedy and why." In his 1998 COPA address, lawyer and high school teacher Vincent Salandria presented a nonpareil critical analysis in his talk, "The JFK Assassination: A False Mystery Concealing State Crimes." The quintessential distillation of this historic watershed event is Salandria's summation that, "The Kennedy assassination is a false mystery. It was conceived by the conspirators to be a false mystery which was designed to cause interminable debate. The purpose of the protracted debate was to obscure what was quite clearly and plainly a coup d'état. Simply stated, President Kennedy was assassinated by our U.S. national security state in order to abort his efforts to bring the Cold War to a peaceful conclusion."

Deputy Sheriff Roger Craig's recounting of his bearing witness to many key events on Friday, November 22, 1963 is an instance of a member of our human family who lived up to one of the greatest potentials each of us can manifest. That he never relinquished his steadfast devotion to the truth of what he saw is a shining light and example for all who learn of his experiences and testament, revealing what each of us can realize in our own lives. Our living history has been buried, classified, stolen, omitted, and distorted. To see the world as it actually is and liberate the truth of our living history is profoundly sacred work. All of us in the United States are the ones best positioned to challenge the destructiveness of the three-pronged sickness Dr. King called out— militarism, racism, and extreme materialism—that is destroying the exquisite and irreplaceable eons of Life exploring itself here on Mother Earth. We can and must change direction towards affirming Life in all its infinite variations and sacredness. To live with A Sacred Regard For All Living Things is the way we must go if we are to survive. We have choices and power here that the majority of humanity do not enjoy. The choice and the power resides with us. And the choice to recognize that power, and take responsibility for it to make this into a world where all of us can live together in peace and fellowship sits right here. In doing so, we honor the supreme sacrifices made by people like President Kennedy and Roger Dean Craig and, standing on their and so many others shoulders, we serve the needs of Life on Earth and the future of all yet unborn that will follow us here.

"It's that everything [in the Cold War in 1962-1963] was totally out of control and then, through a kind of incredible process where these two men were communicating secretly with each other over the year previous [Sept. 1962-63] and smuggling letters back and forth to each other, in the midst of this conflict, they were beginning to trust each other.   It's a remarkable process. And it's all beneath the surface. But so are all the things that count as Merton understood.   And that's why I have some hopes that if we are willing to go deeply enough into the darkness—and Kennedy was, and Khrushchev was—anything can happen for the good. But if we don't go into the darkness it doesn't happen."
-Jim Douglass at Elliot Bay Books, Seattle, May 6, 2008.

—David T. Ratcliffe, March 2019
editor and publisher
rat haus reality press (ratical.org/rhrPress.html)
Assistant Director
Museum of Hidden History (hiddenhistorycenter.org/MoHH)
Archivist, Board member
Committee for Nuclear Responsibility (ratical.org/radiation/CNR)

PREFACE

BY PHIL SINGER

On Friday, November 22nd, 1963, many people woke up pretty much knowing what their day was going to be like. Or so they thought. Go to work or school, shop, have lunch, dinner, go to a party, meet with friends, etc. Looking forward to the weekend. Thanksgiving next week. And so on. However, at 12:30 p.m. Central Standard Time, things changed dramatically for a number of people. Essentially, they got thrown into history. Was it fate? Was it coincidence? Some of these people were witnesses to a murder on Elm Street in Dealey Plaza of Dallas, Texas. They were there to see President Kennedy and his wife. Some of these people were doctors and nurses at Parkland Memorial Hospital in Dallas, where the mortally-wounded president was brought.

Some were Dallas Police Department officers. Some were reporters. Some were young military men in the Washington, D.C. area that ended up carrying the dead president's body in a casket over a four-day period. And some were Navy personnel at the Bethesda Naval Hospital in Bethesda, Maryland that were involved in the autopsy of J.F.K. Their plans were altered that day. And essentially, their lives were changed forever.

They all got thrown into history. They didn't ask for it. They didn't plan on it. But it happened alright. One of the people that got thrown into history that day was Roger Craig, a young deputy sheriff in Dallas. He was standing on Main Street as the motorcade with President Kennedy drove by. It was approximately 12:28 p.m. It was sunny and bright. The limousine turned right onto Houston Street and headed north for a short block. Then it turned left onto Elm Street. And shortly after that a number of shots rang out. Roger Craig instinctively ran west into Dealey Plaza. And became a witness to history.

He saw and heard a number of things that afternoon. Very important things. As a trained law enforcement officer, Craig observed and took note of several critical events in Dealey Plaza. He heard a shrill whistle. And saw a man leaving the scene of the crime get in a vehicle. Bullet shells on the 6th floor of the Texas School Book Depository Building. A German Mauser rifle being found on that same floor between some cardboard boxes. And more. Later that afternoon he identified the man in custody [Lee Harvey Oswald] at the Dallas Police Department Station as the same person that he saw getting into the vehicle at around 12:40, heading west on Elm toward the triple underpass. Suddenly, it wasn't so sunny and bright anywhere. Everything seemed dark and sad across the nation.

Sheriff Bill Decker told Roger Craig, his deputy sheriff, to keep his mouth shut about what he saw and heard that fateful afternoon. But his story had already hit the newspapers. And had been reported on television. Craig's testimony pointed to a conspiracy — evidence of more than one person being involved in the assassination of the president in broad daylight. And Craig's story pointed to a cover-up as well. Eventually, he got fired from his job. But he continued to share his recollections about the events of November 22nd, 1963. Roger Craig showed a tremendous amount of courage and integrity, even as attempts were made on his life. Sadly, he died under some very mysterious circumstances in 1975.

While some other people that day were also thrown into history, many of them kept quiet about things that they saw and heard. Roger Craig felt compelled to tell the truth. And he paid a deep price for his honesty. And bravery. As a long-time J.F.K. assassination researcher, I've known about him and his story for many, many years. I never did meet him. I wish that I did though. Just to shake his hand and say, "Thank you, sir!"

Regardless of how Roger Craig tragically died, he was a witness to history, having been thrown into it. He didn't ask for it. He didn't plan it. It just happened. And while some others chose to alter their stories or keep silent, Roger Craig, at great personal risk, spoke the truth. He showed immense bravery and integrity under incredible pressure. And for that, I consider him one of the real heroes of this case.

Lastly — thank you, Steve Cameron, for bringing Roger Craig's story to all of us so that we can learn more about this great American patriot and deputy sheriff.

CONTENTS

Dedication   v

Foreword by David T. Ratcliffe   vii

Preface by Phil Singer   viii

1. INTRODUCTION   1

2. ABOUT ROGER CRAIG   5

3. ROGER DEAN CRAIG JR.   9

4. DALLAS COUNTY SHERIFF'S DEPT. INSIDER   71

5. DENNIE DARNELL WOOD   83

6. ROBERT GRODEN   105

7. PHIL SINGER   137

8. J. GARY SHAW   187

9. ACKNOWLEDGMENTS   229

10. ROGER CRAIG'S 1971 MANUSCRIPT: 233
WHEN THEY KILL A PRESIDENT

THE DEPUTY INTERVIEWS

INTRODUCTION

There's never been a time in my life, that I've grown so much as a human being, since the day I began learning about the life of former Dallas Deputy Sheriff, Roger Dean Craig. But before I explain how that came to be, I would like to go back a few years. Actually, quite a few years.

It was 1984. I was given an assignment by my sixth-grade teacher, to write a report about the 35th President of the United States of America, John Fitzgerald Kennedy.

I didn't know much about the man. I'd seen him in photographs, and I read about him in school books. But what I didn't know about him, could have filled an ocean. So, I went down to the public library, to read as many books about him that I could, to learn more about the man and his presidency. And with the help of my mother, we spent hours at the library, and at home researching his life, and his times. The following words are some of the things I wrote about him in my report:

> "John Kennedy believed… that progress was only possible, if the young people of the world faced the future with hope and enthusiasm…
>
> He believed that every child should have a full opportunity to develop their talents, without being held back by prejudice, or poverty…
>
> John Fitzgerald Kennedy's work was cut short by a tragedy, but the goals he set are still before us.
>
> His words challenge all of us to get in the fight, to keep our country beautiful, and to give each American a full opportunity to excel, and to achieve."

I received a ninety-seven on that report, which pleased my mother very much. But at the time I wrote it, I did not realize, that the tragedy that cut short John Kennedy's work, was something that I would be writing about, and thinking about, to this very day.

The first time I remember hearing that President Kennedy was killed by more than one person was in 1991, when I was flipping through cable TV channels, and I landed on a documentary called *The Men Who Killed Kennedy*. It talked about multiple shooters, and how people in the government were possibly involved in the assassination, and helped to cover it all up. And at the time, I just could not understand why I had never heard about any of this information before. Why had I not learned about this in school?

After watching this for a while, my father walked into the room. And he stood there next to me, in complete silence, listening to some of the things being said. And then, after a few minutes, he yelled, "Turn that crap off!" I immediately felt like I had done something wrong, but I didn't know what. I could see the anger on his face, and what I can only describe as a fear in his eyes. I had never seen an expression on my father's face like this before. So, I asked him, "What's wrong, Dad? What did I do?" I'll never forget what he said. His exact words to me were, "I'll never believe my government had anything to do with that, and I don't want you to believe it either." And then he stormed out of the room. After he left, I reluctantly got up and shut off the television, just as he had ordered me to do. I walked away from it, and then tried to forget about what had just happened. My father and I never spoke about it again.

Admittedly at the time, I allowed that documentary to do most of my thinking for me. But as years went by, I began investigating things for myself, and what I found would forever change the way that I viewed the world.

And now when I think back to when my father became so upset that day, I can't help but wonder, was he just trying to protect me, out of concern that I might lose hope, and enthusiasm for my country's future? Unfortunately, I can no longer ask him if that was the case. He died in 2012. But if it was, he failed in his attempt. Because the country that I was taught about in school, is sadly not the country that I've learned about since, and that I now see before me.

The year 2012 was the same year that I was introduced to Roger's story, by way of a documentary called *Evidence of Revision*. I stumbled upon it, while researching cases of strange deaths. The reason being, my father had recently died, from what was quickly ruled a suicide. At the time, my mother had just died from a cancer-related illness. She passed away about ten days before my dad was found dead. So, suicide seemed plausible to me, at the time. He loved that woman immensely, and he missed her terribly after she was gone, as did I.

However, before the ink had dried on his death certificate, new information began emerging. Information that contradicted the official story, and the coroner's suicide conclusion. And so, like a son would, I began investigating the circumstances of my father's death with another close family member. And soon, we both came to the unsettling conclusion, that my father had been murdered.

My father was found shot to death in his home, that was located in a small town in the Florida Panhandle, where he was living alone. He was shot multiple times in his chest, and his hands. But for reasons unknown, his death was ruled a suicide. And the case was closed.

It was during this period, while researching my father's death, that I found the remarkably tragic story of Roger Dean Craig.

This is where my father's story ends, for now, and Roger's begins…

After researching the life of Roger Dean Craig for several years, I found many dead ends concerning his life, and his death. The internet was littered with rumors about the man. So, in 2016, I decided to reach out to several members of his family, and others who personally knew him, to try to find the truth.

What follows is in-depth research and interviews, that I conducted from 2016 to 2019, to try to finally get to the bottom of who Roger Dean Craig was, and what he died for. This is my personal journey, deep down into the memory hole, to learn the truth about someone that I've never met. Someone heralded by those who knew him, as being one of the greatest unsung heroes that the United States has ever seen, who ultimately paid the highest price for trying to tell it like it was. This is his story…

ABOUT ROGER CRAIG

BY ROGER CRAIG

I was born in the small town of Cornell, Wisconsin, on May 12, 1936. I was curious about life and living things from the very start of my own. I always had a lot of energy and was an excessively ornery young man. My family moved to Minneapolis when I was about seven or eight years of age. One of my favorite past-times (much to the chagrin of my parents), was climbing the tall cliffs overlooking the Mississippi River. These adventures many times ended in near disaster. For instance, I once fell in excess of fifty feet straight down into the river — but lucky me — I was brought out by a fisherman who caught a small boy. I was curious about places as well, places I had never seen nor been and at the age of thirteen, I hopped a freight train which took me to Miles City, Montana. I took various odd jobs (one has to eat, you know) and from there I went from town to town and state to state. Over the next two years, I traveled entirely seven states, working on farms and ranches.

At age fifteen I made a gigantic decision. The exciting part of the world was somewhere else. So, I joined the Army. Very shortly, Uncle Sam caught up with the fifteen-year-old renegade and ended my very brief military career at Fort Smith, Arkansas.

After that, I decided to find my parents for a visit and discovered that they had moved to Dallas, Texas. I stayed with them a short while and took a job in a local factory until I became seventeen years old. I was then drafted by the military, sent to Korea where I served my thirteen months. When my time was up, I returned to Dallas and took a job with the Purex Corporation in 1956. Three years later, I went to work as a Deputy Sheriff in Dallas County — it is now October, 1959. In 1960, I was privileged to receive the honor as Officer of the Year for the Sheriff's Department. I was with the Department for eight years (or until July 4, 1967) at which time I was terminated by Sheriff Bill Decker — no explanation, no reason given. But *I* know why and here begins my story… [Continuing Inquiry newsletter, Jan. 22, 1983, Volume VII, Number 6, p. 12]

"If you pursue the assassination and its aftermath, be sure you are willing to pay the full price."

-Roger Dean Craig

Roger Dean Craig Jr.
(Photo courtesy of Nita Edwards)

Steve Cameron: Hi. I'm calling for Roger Craig Jr.

Roger: This is Roger Dean Craig Jr.

Steve: Mr. Craig, how are you doing? This is Steve.

Roger: Hi Steve. I'm doing well.

Steve: Alright, great. Thanks for taking this call today. Today is May 4, 2017. We spoke on the phone earlier, and we scheduled this interview to ask you some questions about your father, Roger Dean Craig Sr.

Roger: Yes.

Steve: Before we do that, I want to ask you a little about yourself?

Roger: Okay. Well, I was born to my mother, Juanita Fern Cooper, and my father Roger Dean Craig in Oklahoma. My father was in the army at the time. Shortly after that we moved to Dallas, and I lived there up until I was ten years old. And then we moved to Corpus. Then I moved back to Dallas when I was around eleven or twelve, and moved in with my father.

Steve: What year did you say you were born, Roger?

Roger: March 22, 1954.

Steve: When did you first move to Dallas?

Roger: I was eighteen months old when we moved from Oklahoma to Dallas. I was supposed to be born in Dallas, at Parkland Hospital. But my father was in the military, and he came in on leave at Fort Sill Oklahoma. So, my mother being nine months pregnant decided she was gonna make a car trip up to Fort Sill Oklahoma and see my father. Well, that trip from Dallas to Fort Sill, I was born. In other words, the ride was rough on her, because back then in 1954, the cars weren't that luxurious. And I think she went up there in a '36 Chevrolet. The springs weren't that good.

Steve: Yeah, that must have been a little bumpy.

Roger: So, I was born in Oklahoma instead of Parkland Hospital. And that's how that went.

Steve: Okay. When I first met you in person you told me you had spent some time in the military, is that correct?

Roger: Yeah, I went in in 1972. I got a draft notice. And so, I went down and joined. I figured I was going in anyway. Now, I didn't go to Vietnam, but several guys from my basic training unit did. I went to Fort Hood instead. Why, I don't know. I had a couple of friends that were in basic with me that got killed over there in Vietnam. I went through Fort Polk for basic. Tiger Land. Which was to get you ready for Vietnam. They called our names out. They sent me over to Fort Hood, and sent them wherever.

Steve: Before your military experience, did you ever have weapons training?

Roger: Oh yes. My father used to take me out to the junkyards, and I remember one time – this is after him and my mother got divorced – I was about eight or nine. We went out there, and they had some old cars, and old washing machines. And he had gone to the property room at the Sheriff's Department and got a Russian Burp gun, with a fifty-round drum on it. That's a nine-millimeter, or close to it. And we just shotup everything out there. He taught me how to shoot from the hip. Taught me how to shoot a rifle. All that stuff. He told me I was a natural at it. He bought me my first .22 rifle when I was nine years old. My father was also an expert archer. He won several trophies and medals for that. And he could hit them targets. He taught me how to shoot a bow out in the backyard, and I got pretty good at it. And my grandfather took me squirrel hunting and rabbit hunting all the time. So yeah, I was pretty familiar with weapons.

Steve: Okay. I think you had mentioned to me, that when you were in the military, you had some experience as a sniper, or had sniper training?

Roger: Well, it was advanced long-range shooting, is what it was. I qualified expert in it. I learned how to take the M-16 and shoot from the hip, and shoot the targets, and hit them and everything. In other words, not aim, just shoot. It was advanced weapons training. I guess you could call it sniper. It wasn't sniper training like they have now. It was just long-range shooting. We'd go out to the Rod & Gun Club there on Fort Hood and we'd shoot the targets out there. That's where all the big NCOs (Non-commissioned officers), and the colonels would go, and everybody. I was pretty good with a rifle. And a pistol too.

Steve: Around what year did you leave the military?

Roger: I left the military in 1975. At the time, I was going through a bad divorce. I got custody of my kids. And it was during that divorce when I got notice that my father died.

Steve: Okay. Before we talk about the day your father died, can you please tell me about your time with the Dallas Sheriff's Department?

Roger: Well, I always wanted to be a deputy sheriff. You know, because of my father. And hanging around Bill Decker, and the rest of them. That was one of my life long dreams, to be a deputy sheriff. So, I went down there, and I was sworn in after all the physicals and everything, on February 14, 1978. Some of the other deputies almost fell over when I first came in there, like they had just seen a ghost, because of how much I looked like my father back then (laughter).

Steve: How many years did you spend at the Sheriff's Department?

1978 photo of former Dallas Deputy Sheriff, Roger Craig Jr.

Roger: Seven years I believe. My father was there eight years. He was there from 1959 to 1967.

Steve: How would you describe your relationship with your father when you were a child?

Roger: Well, we had a good rapport together, like a father and son would. By the time of the Kennedy assassination, he had already divorced my mother, and had already married Molly.

Steve: What year was their divorce?

Roger: 1961 I believe.

Steve: And you would have been about seven?

Roger: I was six, not quite seven. It was right after my sixth birthday. And we lived on Leroy Street at the time.

Steve: Can you tell me about their relationship, if you don't mind?

Roger: My mother and father were both headstrong people. And when you get two headstrong people together, it's gonna be a little chaotic at times.

Steve: They were very young when they met, I would imagine.

Roger: They were fifteen, or sixteen years old when they met. Then by the time she was not quite eighteen, I was born. And he was in the army, and was like seventeen going on eighteen. They were very young. And he was having a hard time finding a job after he got out of the military. He got a job at the Purex plant over here off 175. He worked there for a little while, until he joined the Sheriff's Department. He tried three times to join the Sheriff's Department, and he kept flunking the physical, because he didn't weigh enough.

Steve: Oh really?

Roger: Yeah (laughter).

Steve: I want to hear more about that, but first, can you tell me what your dad's family life was like when he was a child, and what led him on the path that he ended up traveling on?

Roger: He was close to his brothers. Real close. All of his brothers, even his half-brother. But his father, that was strained. Because his father as a very stern person. His father was in the navy during World War II. He had what I guess they would call PTSD today. He was in the South Pacific in the navy as far as I know. And that wasn't a nice place to be. Especially if you were on a ship. So, he was very stern, and very strict, and very boisterous with his voice. His mother, she was kind of, not timid, but very restrained. She didn't want to get too close to you, because she might get hurt emotionally. So, I can understand why he ran away at thirteen.

Steve: At thirteen he ran away from home?

Roger: Yeah. He went to Montana to go work on a ranch. When I was fourteen, I had a little spat with a girlfriend, so I ran way from home and went to go work on a ranch (laughter).

Steve: Apple doesn't fall too far away from the tree I guess (laughter). What were the circumstances of that?

Roger: My girlfriend broke up with me. I got upset. And I wasn't doing good in school. So, I hitchhiked to Arkansas.

Steve: What year was this?

Roger: 1968. I went to work for Chapman Ranches Incorporated. I told them I was eighteen. Used my own social security number. Worked there two days, and made twenty-four dollars. And the sheriff come in there in the middle of the morning, and hauled my ass to the Arkansas County Jail, and held me until my mother or father picked me up. And that's the last time I ran away from home. I was living with my father at the time.

Steve: What were your father's thoughts at that time?

Roger: He thought I'd been kidnapped.

Steve: Why, because of his involvement with the J.F.K. assassination investigation?

Ex-Deputy Reports Son, 14, Missing

MIDLOTHIAN, Texas (AP)— Roger Craig, former Dallas County deputy sheriff, reported Tuesday night that his 14-year-old son has been missing since 8 a.m. Monday and is feared kidnaped.

Craig said the boy was slim, weighed about 130 pounds and had green eyes. He was wearing a yellow shirt and brown pants when he left his home for school Monday morning.

The elder Craig has been called "the most important live witness" in the investigation of the John F. Kennedy assassination by New Orleans Dist. Atty. Jim Garrison.

He testified before the Warren Commission that he saw a man who looked like accused assassin Lee Harvey Oswald run from the area of the Texas School Book Depository Building, up the grassy knoll and into a station wagon near the building.

He left the Dallas County sheriff's department in 1967 after being with the department about nine years.

Craig said his son had been absent from school once or twice and that he at first thought he was "playing hooky.

"But it's been so long now," a Craig friend said, "that we are afraid something else has happened. He's never been gone more than a few hours before."

1968 AP article about Roger Craig's missing son, Roger Jr.

Roger: Yeah, and that's how the sheriff knew where I was at, because it was in the news. Funny story, though. When the sheriff woke me up, he was walking me down the stairs, and out to the squad car, and he says, "Do I have to cuff you? If I don't, are you gonna try to run? Because I don't want to have to shoot you." And I thought to myself, "I'm a runaway, not Bonnie and Clyde."

Steve: He was messing with you?

Roger: Oh yeah. He was trying to scare me.

Steve: Who came and got you?

Roger: My father, my mother, and my step-father.

Steve: There was some information I came across, that when your dad ran away, at some point he joined the military.

Roger: He did at fifteen.

Steve: Would you say to get away from that family life he was living?

Roger: Right. At fifteen he went through basic and everything. And then he got put on a base with his brother. The same one he was using his name and social security number to get in the army with.

Steve: Which brother?

Roger: I believe that was Donald. He was the oldest. He was a half-brother. And then Dwayne. Then my father. Then Jimmy. He was the baby.

Steve: So, he used Donald's name to enlist?

Roger: Right. He was like seventeen.

Steve: How did all that unfold?

Roger: I used to have an album that had a picture of them standing on the front porch of the barracks in their uniforms, with their arms on each other's shoulders. And I think that's around when they got caught.

Steve: So, Donald was aware of it?

Roger: Oh yeah. He thought it was funny. When my dad got out of the army the first time, he joined the civil air patrol, and learned how to fly a little one-engine plane.

Steve: So, he was sent home by the army, is that correct?

Roger: Right. He was sent home, because he was only fifteen years old. This was during the Korean War. He got sent home. And then when he was of age, and didn't need consent, which I think is the age of seventeen, he joined and went back in the military. And since he already had basic, he didn't have to go back through basic, so he was immediately sent to Korea. I think in '53.

United States Army, Private First Class, Roger Dean Craig.

Steve: What kind of career did he have in the military?

Roger: Oh, he was just an infantryman. There was a story, and I don't know how true it was. But he had scars on his chest, and I asked him how he got them. They looked like knife marks on his chest. The story he told was that he got captured by the Red Chinese, and they tortured him with bayonets. They were trying to get information out of him. But then they got overrun, and he was saved. And he went right back to fighting, because the cuts weren't that deep, but it left scars, little light scars all over his chest. Anyway, that's the story I was told.

Certification of
Military Service

★★★★★★★★★★★★★★★

This certifies that	Roger D. Craig 17 353 002
was a member of the	Army of the United States
from	October 9, 1953
to	September 30, 1955
Service was terminated by	Honorable Release from Active Duty
Last Grade, Rank, or Rating	Private First Class
Active Service Dates	Same As Above

Date of Birth: 05/12/1936   Place of Birth: Madison, WI

Service records provided by Nita Edwards.

Steve: When he left the military, do you know what the circumstances were?

Roger: Just discharged after two years. After your enlistment is over with, then you're out, unless you want to re-up. Well, evidently, he didn't want to re-up, because I think I was born by then. So, I guess my mother got pregnant with me the day he left to go into the military, or overseas.

Steve: What year did he join the Sheriff's Department?

Roger: 1959.

Dallas Deputy Sheriff Roger Dean Craig.

Roger: He had a friend over there that was a dispatcher. And he told my father he could get him into dispatch. So, he tried the physical at least twice, and he couldn't pass it because he didn't weigh enough. So, his friend told him, "If you can't pass the physical, just eat ten pounds of bananas, before you go in for your physical." So, my father ate ten pounds of bananas, went in for the physical and passed, because he weighed the amount of weight he was suppose to weigh according to his height.

Steve: Do you have a memory of that, of him eating those bananas?

Roger: I remember him eating bananas, but I didn't know why he was doing it. I remember I wanted a banana, but he was eating them all (laughter). Anyway, he got on the Sheriff's Department, and he worked dispatch for I think a year. Right there at the old, what we call the old Decker jail. Or the old hanging jail there on Main Street.

Steve: Speaking of Decker, did he know Sheriff Bill Decker before he joined?

Roger: No. He just knew a couple of guys who worked at the Sheriff's Department. And after he was there for about six months or so in dispatch, he brought me into work with him.

Steve: What was that like?

Roger: Oh, it was great. See, back then, everybody who worked at the Sheriff's Department had fedoras on, because Decker always wore a fedora, with the front brim down and all that. Well, my father brought me in there, and I had a pair of slacks on, shined shoes, a white shirt buttoned at the collar, and a grey fedora on. So, when my father came in to go to work, he brought me in, and Decker saw me and grabbed me by the hand and took me to his office, set me down in front of the typewriter, put a piece of paper in there, and said, "Type me a letter." I was only five or six years old. I didn't know how to type, so I just sat there and played on the typewriter.

Steve: So, I guess he unofficially deputized you then?

Roger: I guess so. Either that or made me the clerk (laughter). My father went in the dispatch office, and come out about an hour later, wanting to know if I was bothering anybody, and Decker said, "Go back to work." So, he went back in the dispatch office, and I sat there until my father got off work.

Steve: What was your impression of Decker when you first met him?

Roger: I thought he was wonderful. He was a very friendly man. He was nice to me. And he was nice to my father. There was another time my father took me there and Decker grabbed me by the hand and said, "Roger, you go to work. We're going somewhere."

Steve: Where'd you guys go?

Roger: Well, we went to a place they used to call "Cowboy Town" in West Dallas, where they acted out saloon fights, and shootouts, and putting people in jail, and all that. Rode the stagecoach together. Went to the saloon. I ordered a root beer float. He ordered a sarsaparilla, which was a red-looking drink with a cork in it. Got to go to the sheriff's office there. I got to put a guy in the jail. At five or six years old, that was pretty good. We stayed out there all day, and came back at the end of my father's shift, and then we went home.

Steve: So, he treated you like his own son?

Roger: Oh yeah. He treated me just like a son. He used to take me up there in the officers' mess hall, and have lunch. I'd get my favorite, meatloaf and mashed potatoes. That was my favorite. Showed me around the courthouse. It was just one of those things. He wanted me to have fun and enjoy myself. And I think that was important to him.

Steve: How would you and others in the Dallas area, at that time, describe Sheriff Decker's reputation?

Roger: Well, he wasn't that tall, but he was a mighty man. He didn't have any children. I found that out later when I got older, that he and his wife didn't have any children. But if a child came up missing, or abused, or anything, he would turn the whole Sheriff's Office out on horseback and in squad cars, until that child was found, or was safe. There was no abusing a child and getting away with it, because if you did, you were gonna spend some time in the county jail if Decker found out about it.

Steve: What were your father's feelings about Bill Decker? Before the assassination.

Roger: Before the assassination? He thought the man walked on water. He really did. He thought that Sheriff Decker was the greatest man that ever was, or ever will be. And he just wanted to do the best he could to impress, or please Sheriff Decker.

Steve: Was that due to the reputation that preceded Decker?

Roger: Oh yeah. He was a legend. Back during the Bonnie and Clyde times, Decker was Chief Deputy under Sheriff Smoot Schmid.

Former Dallas County Sheriff Richard "Smoot" Schmid.

Roger: Schmid sent Decker to Louisiana, to assist Texas Ranger Frank Hamer's hunt for Bonnie and Clyde. The story I heard was that before he left, Decker went down to the property room and got a weapon to go down there with him. A B.A.R. (Browning Automatic Rifle), because the B.A.R. was Clyde Barrow's favorite weapon.

Steve: Decker wanted to do them in using Clyde's favorite weapon?

Roger: That's right.

Steve: Was he a part of the ambush that killed them?

Roger: I think he was, but I'm not sure.

Author's note: According to an article published in the New York Times, following the death of Dallas County Sheriff Bill Decker on August 29, 1970, he was credited for setting up the ambush that, "ended the careers of Bonnie Parker and Clyde Barrow on May 23, 1934, beside an east Louisiana swamp road. He told officers where to wait for the desperadoes, and later would only admit 'somebody told me' where to set up the ambush." At the time that the couple was killed, the F.B.I. estimates, that they were responsible for at least thirteen murders during their crime spree that began in 1932.

Images of Bonnie Parker and Clyde Barrow.

Bonnie and Clyde's lifeless bodies are seen hunched over in the front seats of their stolen 1934 Ford Deluxe V-8, after being ambushed by a posse led by Texas Ranger Frank Hamer.

Interview continued…

Steve: I've seen the picture. There's a famous picture showing Decker standing over the corpse of Bonnie.

Roger: Yeah, they brought Bonne back to Dallas, because she was going to be buried here in Dallas in the family plot, or cemetery. They took that picture at the morgue there at the old Parkland Hospital off Oak Lawn, which is a Sheriff's Department training academy now. That's where they took that picture with everybody standing around Bonnie.

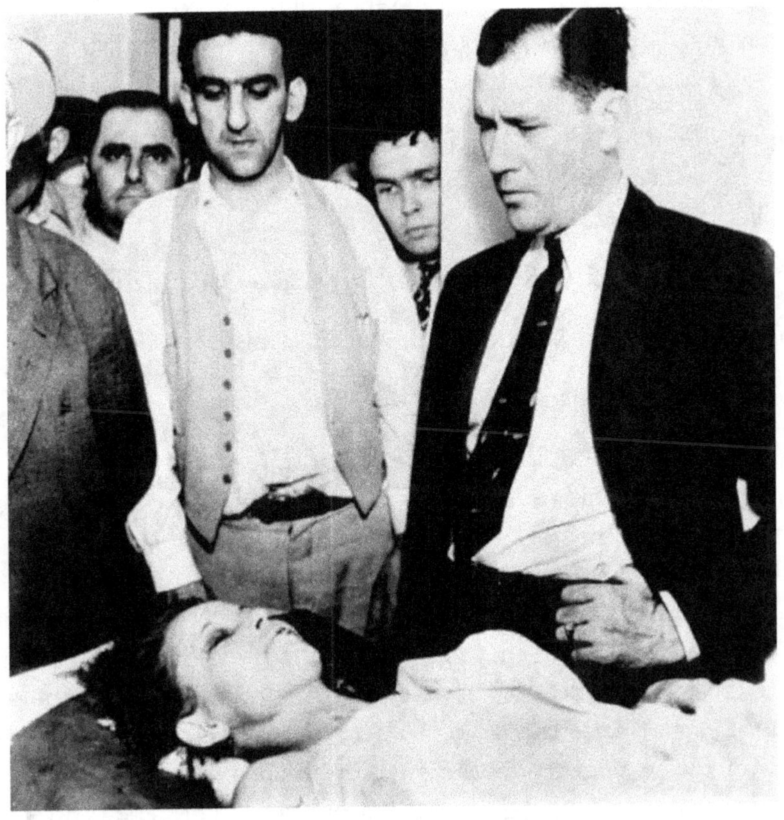

Bill Decker (right) stands over the corpse of Bonnie Parker (1934).

Steve: Do you think the Bonnie and Clyde situation cemented Decker's fame in Dallas, and led to him becoming Sheriff?

Roger: Oh yeah. He won his election in 1949 hands down, and never faced another opponent. He died in office in 1970. Decker was a very determined man. And when he got something in his head, he didn't stop until it was finished. Let me tell you a story. While I was working the jail at the Dallas County Sheriff's Department, we got a release form for a prisoner. I pulled his information, and it had a big red stamp on it, that said, "Decker Hold." And Sheriff Carl Thomas had to okay it before we could release that guy. That's how much power Decker had. He was dead. Been dead for years. And we couldn't release a guy because it had a red stamp on it, that said, "Decker Hold."

Steve: So even from the grave he still had power? That's very interesting. Let's go back to your father, after he left dispatch. That would have been around 1960?

Roger: Right. About 1960 he got out, and went to patrol in the southeast, which was the Seagoville area, because Seagoville didn't have a police department.

Steve: What was one of his first highlights as a Dallas deputy sheriff?

Roger: I would say the riot in Seagoville was his first one.

Steve: What happened there?

Roger: Well, my father got dispatched to a disturbance in the city of Seagoville. Upon his arrival, he saw numerous black males in the middle of the street. So, he got out of his car to find out what was going on, and to talk to them. See, Decker believed if you had a problem, just send one deputy, and if more is needed, he can call for them. Well, they attacked my father, and they got him on the hood of the car, and they nearly beat him to death. They were beating on him. Well, some how or another he got to the radio, and gave a distress call. Then they got him on the ground, and beat on him some more. When the other deputies got there, they got the guys off my father. Then, my father pulled out from the front seat of his squad car, that Russian Burp gun with the fifty-round drum. He leveled the weapon towards the crowd, yanked the bolt back, and yelled, "Disburse!" And according to the way he told it, and the way the other people told it, the people rioting kind of left like a covey of quail out of a bush. Because when you're looking down the barrel of a fully automatic machine gun, you do not want to stay there (laughter).

Steve: Your father didn't have to pull the trigger?

Roger: No. He didn't have to pull the trigger or nothing.

Steve: He came in and upheld the peace.

Roger: Right. He upheld the peace without taking any lives. That's just the way it was back then with Decker. If you can avoid killing somebody, avoid it. You're out there to protect the public, and to arrest the perpetrator, and that's it. Decker believed that you always treat people, whether you're arresting them or not, with respect. The Sheriff's Department is a symbol of trust, respect, and honor. It's been that way since the first Sheriff's Department here in Dallas in 1846.

Steve: Some of these police departments around the country could learn a lesson from that, with some of the violence that's happening on our streets every day.

Roger: Oh yes.

Steve: Do you know what set that disturbance off?

Roger: I think it was racial tension, due to what was going on in the late fifties, early sixties.

Steve: From your perspective, what was the relationship between the Sheriff's Office and the Dallas City Police Department, when your dad was working in law enforcement?

Roger: The relationship between the city police and Dallas county was like two stepbrothers. Neither one of them liked each other. And neither one wanted the other around. And they were always arguing over jurisdiction. Which, the county has jurisdiction over the city, because the city is in the county. And they wouldn't share information. Because each one wanted the credit.

Steve: If the Sheriff's Department's motto was trust, respect, and honor, what was the motto of the Dallas City Police, if they had one?

Roger: Well, their unofficial motto was, and I hate to say this, because it's racist, and I'm not a prejudice person at all, but it was, "Whoop that N-word." And their second unofficial motto was, "If they do not have a D.P.D. shield, beat their ass and put 'em in jail."

Steve: Oh my. Would it be safe to say then, that they were corrupt during that time?

Roger: My opinion now – especially since I've been through law enforcement and everything – back then yes, they were corrupt. That's just my opinion.

Steve: Have you heard stories about Dallas City Police taking bribes?

Roger: Yeah, I've heard stories, but I couldn't confirm anything, because it would just be hearsay.

Steve: But it would be safe to say, that many of them knew Jack Ruby, and spent time in his clubs?

Roger: A bunch of them knew Jack Ruby. They treated him like a friend. A lot of them were in and out of his clubs.

Steve: Who was in charge of the Dallas city police in 1963?

Roger: Captain Will Fritz. The chief of police was Jesse Curry.

Steve: Were Captain Fritz and Sheriff Decker at odds?

Roger: Yes. Definitely. Because Decker didn't hire him. What I heard was, before Fritz went to the Dallas police, he tried to get on the Sheriff's Department. Decker wouldn't hire him. Decker saw something in him. See, Decker could read people. He really could. You could walk in his office, and he could tell you what you were thinking. I don't know how he got that knack, but he was just that way. And Decker only wanted to do what was right in his mind. If you came in and said, "You really need to do this," and he didn't think it was right, he'd tell you to get out of his office.

Author's note: In the following F.B.I. report, dated November 29, 1963, just days after the assassination of President Kennedy, former

Dallas attorney Travis Kirk was interviewed by Special Agents of the F.B.I., concerning Kirk's knowledge of past acquaintances and activities in Dallas, during his twenty-three years of practicing law there. In their report, the agents detail Kirk's animosity toward the Police Department, and especially Captain Will Fritz, and how Kirk revealed to them that Fritz and Ruby were "close friends," and that he thought it was "entirely possible and probable," that Captain Fritz deliberately arranged for Jack Ruby to shoot and kill Lee Harvey Oswald, while Oswald was being escorted through the basement of Dallas Police headquarters, during his transfer to the city jail. According to the agents, Kirk also told them that Jack Ruby was "allowed a complete run of the Police Station, and particularly the Homicide and Inspectors Bureau," in spite of his reputation as being a member of the Dallas underworld:

2 (Rev. 3-3-59)   FEDERAL BUREAU OF INVESTIGATION

KEY PERSON

Date _____ 11-29-63 _____

1

    Mr. TRAVIS KIRK was interviewed on the street at 400 California Street, San Francisco, California. He was questioned regarding his knowledge of the activities and acquaintances in Dallas, Texas. Mr. KIRK said that he had practiced law for 23 years in Dallas, Texas, and was very well acquainted with the District Attorney's Office, the Police Department, and the Sheriff's Office. He said that he had worked in the District Attorney's Office for about six years, and then went into private practice as a defense attorney.

    His clients included a great many prostitutes and other unsavory characters in the area. In conjunction with many of his cases, he had had occasion to go into the night club owned by JACK RUBY, and he was personally acquainted with JACK RUBY only as a night club owner. He did not recall ever having actually met RUBY, but felt that RUBY would probably know him by name because of his reputation as a defense attorney.

    He remarked that in his years of practice he had developed quite an animosity toward the Police Department, particularly toward Mr. FRITZ who was the Head of the Homicide Detail of the Dallas Police Department. He advised that FRITZ was the type of character who would stop at nothing to make his point. He remarked that he believed that it is entirely possible and probable that FRITZ had deliberately arranged to have OSWALD shot in order to close the case. Mr. KIRK based this on the fact that FRITZ and JACK RUBY were very close friends, and that JACK RUBY, in spite of his reputation of being a "hood," was allowed a complete run of the Police Station and particularly the Homicide and Inspectors Bureau.

    Mr. KIRK said that he had not heard anything from any of his acquaintances in Dallas regarding this particular incident, and based his opinions solely on his knowledge of methods used by Mr. FRITZ.

CR 84

11-29-63   San Francisco, California   File # _____ DL 44-1639 _____
    at   EWING H. RAUCH, JR., & FRANCIS J.   ~~44-494~~
cial Agent COLLOPY, JR.:mhb/md.   Date dictated _____ 11-29-63 _____

Interview continued…

Steve: Okay. Let's go back to the incident in Seagoville for a moment. That happened when your dad was a rookie?

Roger: Yeah. He had just got out onto patrol. He spent one year as dispatcher, and then Decker put him on patrol and gave him the southeast quadrant.

Steve: Did he have other career highlights, that you can think of, before the Kennedy assassination in 1963?

Roger: Well, I think the next thing was, he noticed this guy casing a bunch of jewelry stores in downtown Dallas. So, my father got with a couple of investigators, and they ended up arresting the guy. Turned out, he was an international jewel thief. And my father won officer of the year that year.

Steve: Yeah, I read about that. There's a J.F.K. assassination researcher and historian named Edgar Tatro, who began corresponding with your father a few months before he died. And sometime after he died, he wrote an article about him called "Roger Craig and 1984," and in the article, I think Tatro writes about your father's arrest of that Jewel thief. I have it here somewhere, if you don't mind holding on for a moment?

Roger: Sure, I'll hold on.

Steve: Okay, here it is, and this was published in Penn Jones' Continuing Inquiry newsletter in 1983. Tatro writes, "Craig's previous claim to fame as a deputy sheriff had been his apprehension of a fugitive, Harry Day, based upon Craig's recollection of Day's face seen on a wanted poster two years prior to the time of the arrest. Amazingly, Craig had picked out the right man. Craig was no slouch as a lawman." [Excerpt from "Roger Craig and 1984" by Edgar F. Tatro, The Continuing Inquiry, May 22, 1983, Volume VII, Number 13, pp. 6-7]

Roger: That was real nice of him.

Steve: Yeah, and I have those correspondence letters between him and your father. I'll try to get them to you, so you can read them. They're available on the internet. So, after your father was named Officer of the Year, do you remember if there was an award ceremony him?

Roger: Oh yeah. They had a big banquet, and gave him a certificate. And my father received a very fancy watch, and my mother also received a very fancy watch, with inscribing on the back, that said, "Officer of the Year," and, "Wife of Officer of the Year." It was a big hoop-dee-doo.

Steve: Who presented the award?

Roger: I believe it was Bill Decker. I believe he presented it, and the watches. I remember being there with my tweed coat on, slacks and shoes, and my fedora.

Steve: So, did you kind of see your dad as a hero at that time?

Roger: Oh yeah, at that time, he was the greatest thing that ever walked on the face of the earth. Everybody loved him. Everybody thought he was the greatest thing in the world. And he'd have helped anybody, or do anything for them. But the law was the law. That's just the way it was. Sometimes I believe he'd have arrested his own mother if she broke the law (laughter).

Steve: Did he ever second guess himself, like maybe he thought he saw something, but he didn't?

Roger: No. He was very observant. When he saw something, he saw something.

Steve: That kind of goes back to the jewel thief, how he spotted him. Let's forward a couple of years to November 22, 1963. What role did the Sheriff's Department play in the investigation after the assassination? Did they take a backseat to the Dallas City Police Department?

Roger: Yes. Decker had told his deputies not to talk about it, not to interfere, and do not investigate anything. Because it was strictly on the city of Dallas. And you do not disobey Decker. If you did, you got on his bad side.

Steve: Then, what do you think was your father's motivation was, for disobeying him? Because, he did continue to investigate the assassination after it happened, and he did talk to others about what he witnessed, including reporters.

Roger: Because somebody told him to shut up, and don't say anything, and he said, "I know what I know. I saw what I saw. And if anybody asks me, I'm gonna tell 'em." And that's his words, not mine.

Steve: So, these are conversations that you overheard as a child?

Roger: Yep.

Steve: Okay, let's go over some of the things your dad witnessed. According to his 1971 manuscript *When They Kill A President*, Kennedy's motorcade drove past your dad while he was standing in front of the Dallas County Court House at 505 Main Street.

Roger: Right. Decker ordered his deputies to not participate in the security of the motorcade, because the Dallas city police had jurisdiction. So, Decker ordered my father and his other deputies to just stand outside in front of the Sheriff's Office, while the motorcade drove through there.

Steve: So, he saw the President's limousine drive past him, and make the right turn onto Houston, before making the left turn onto Elm Street?

Roger: Oh yeah, it passed right by him.

Steve: And then according to his manuscript, he heard the shots a few seconds later, and began running towards the limo when the President was shot.

Steve: And when your father got to Elm, he saw an officer run behind the picket fence on top of the knoll, where a parking lot and rail yard was located. And so, your father followed him.

Roger: Yes.

Steve: And while behind the fence, he saw a woman driving a brown Chevy attempting to leave the lot, but before she could, your father jumped in front of her car, and stopped her. That's when Deputy Sheriff Lewis arrived and said he would handle it.

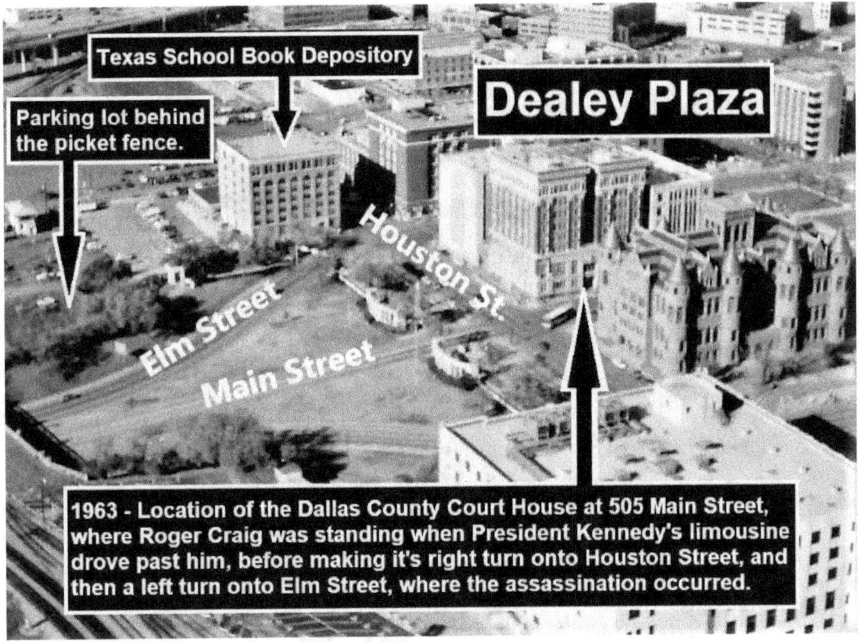

Photo of Dealey Plaza courtesy of Phil Singer.
(Descriptions added by Steve Cameron)

Author's note: According to Craig's description of this incident in his manuscript, the woman was in a parking lot that was reserved for deputies:

"I noticed a woman in her early thirties attempting to drive out of the parking lot. She was in a brown 1962 or 1963 Chevrolet. I stopped her, identified myself and placed her under arrest. She told me that she had to leave and I said, "Lady, you're not going anywhere." I turned her over to Deputy Sheriff C. I. (Lummy) Lewis and told him the circumstances of the arrest. Officer Lewis told me that he would take her to Sheriff Decker and take care of her car. ...Let us examine this parking lot. It was leased by Deputy Sheriff B. D. Gossett. He in turn rented parking space by the month to the deputies who worked in the court house, except for official vehicles. I rented one of these spaces from Gossett when I was a dispatcher working days or evenings. I paid Gossett $3.00 per month and was given a key to the lot. An interesting point is that the lot had an iron bar across the only entrance and exit (which were the same). The bar had a chain and lock on it. The only people having access to it were deputies with keys. Point: how did the woman gain access and, what is more important, who was she and why did she have to leave? This was to be the beginning of the never-ending cover up. Had I known then what I know now, I would have personally questioned the woman and impounded and searched her car. I had no way of knowing that an officer, with whom I had worked for four years, was capable of losing a thirty-year-old woman and a three thousand pound automobile. To this day Officer Lewis does not know who she was, where she came from or what happened to her." [*When They Kill A President*, pp. 6-7]

Interview continued…

Steve: Then your father turned his attention to where people had gathered on top of the grassy knoll, who were telling him that shots were fired from behind the picket fence. Then a man named Arnold Rowland came up to your father, and told him that while he and his wife were waiting for the motorcade to drive through Dealey Plaza, they noticed two men standing inside the sixth-floor windows of the Texas School Book Depository. One of them was holding a gun, and the other was pacing back and forth.

Author's note: According to the Rowlands, they thought these men were a part of the President's security team, so they didn't report what they witnessed until after the President had been shot:

"Mr. Rowland and his wife were standing at the top of the grassy knoll on the north side of Elm Street. Arnold Rowland began telling me his account of what he saw before the assassination. He said approximately fifteen minutes before President Kennedy arrived, he was looking around and something caught his eye. It was a white man standing by the 6th floor window of the Texas School Book Depository Building in the southeast corner, holding a rifle equipped with a telescopic sight and in the southwest corner of the sixth floor was a colored male pacing back and forth. Needless to say, I was astounded by his statement. I asked Mr. Rowland why he had not reported this incident before and he told me that he thought they were secret service agents—an obvious conclusion for a layman. Rowland continued. He told me that he looked back at the sixth floor a few minutes later and the man with the rifle was gone so he dismissed it from his mind." [*When They Kill A President*, p. 7]

Interview continued…

Steve: Your father then handed the Rowlands over to Deputy Lewis, who had once again approached him, and told your father that he would take their statements. After handing the Rowlands over to Deputy Lewis, your father ran into Deputy Sheriff Buddy Walthers. And it was at this time, approximately ten minutes after the assassination, and perhaps the most crucial thing that your father witnessed, he saw Lee Harvey Oswald, or someone who looked a lot like him, exit the front of the school book depository…

Roger: And run down the hill towards the Rambler.

Steve: And that car was a Rambler station wagon?

Roger: Yes. Now it could have been the light green, or the white. It was a light color. Back in those days they had this light-colored green, and in the sun it might look white. It could have been green. It could have been white. But it was a Rambler.

Author's note: This is how Craig described the Rambler incident in his 1971 manuscript:

"The time was approximately 12:40 p.m. when I ran into Buddy Walthers. The traffic was very heavy as Patrolman Baker (assigned to Elm and Houston Streets) had left his post, allowing the traffic to travel west on Elm Street. As we were scanning the curb I heard a shrill whistle coming from the north side of Elm Street. I turned and saw a white male in his twenties running down the grassy knoll from the direction of the Texas School Book Depository Building. A light green Rambler station wagon was coming slowly west on Elm Street. The driver of the station wagon was a husky looking Latin, with dark wavy hair, wearing a tan wind breaker type jacket. He was looking up at the man running toward him. He pulled over to the north curb and picked up the man coming down the hill. I tried to cross Elm Street to stop them and find out who they were. The traffic was too heavy and I was unable to reach them. They drove away going west on Elm Street. In addition to noting that these two men were in an obvious hurry, I realized they were the only ones not running TO the scene. Everyone else was running to see whatever might be seen. The suspect, as I will refer to him, who ran down the grassy knoll was wearing faded blue trousers and a long-sleeved work shirt made of some type of grainy material. This will become very important to me later on and very embarrassing to the authorities (F.B.I., Dallas Police and Warren Commission). I thought the incident concerning the two men and the Rambler Station Wagon important enough to bring it to the attention of the authorities at the command post at Elm and Houston." [*When They Kill A President*, pp. 11-12]

Interview continued...

Steve: Your father also described a scene inside of Captain Fritz's office, where Fritz was interrogating Oswald after he had been arrested at the Texas Theater for allegedly shooting Dallas Police Officer J. D. Tippit. And it was inside Captain Fritz's office where your dad identified Oswald as being the man that he saw running away from the depository and get into the Rambler.

Roger: Yes, that's correct.

Author's note: The following is Craig's description of the events that occurred in Captain Will Fritz's office, after he was personally invited there by Fritz, to see if Oswald was the same man he saw get into the Rambler station wagon, with another man at the steering wheel, before they both sped away from Dealey Plaza:

"Later that afternoon I received word of the suspect's arrest and the fact that he was suspected of being involved in the President's death. I immediately thought of the man running down the grassy knoll. I made a telephone call to Capt. Will Fritz and gave him the description of the man I had seen and Fritz said, "that sounds like the suspect we have. Can you come up and take a look at him?" I arrived at Capt. Fritz office shortly after 4:30 p.m. I was met by Agent Bookhout from the F.B.I., who took my name and place of employment. The door to Capt. Fritz' personal office was open and the blinds on the windows were closed, so that one had to look through the doorway in order to see into the room. I looked through the open door at the request of Capt. Fritz and identified the man who I saw running down the grassy knoll and enter the Rambler station wagon—and it WAS Lee Harvey Oswald. Fritz and I entered his private office together. He told Oswald, "This man (pointing to me) saw you leave." At which time the suspect replied, "I told you people I did." Fritz, apparently trying to console Oswald, said, "Take it easy, son—we're just trying to find out what happened." Fritz then said, "What about the car?" Oswald replied, leaning forward on Fritz' desk, "That station wagon belongs to Mrs. Paine—don't try to drag her into this." Sitting back in his chair, Oswald said very disgustedly and very low, "Everybody will know who I am now." At this time Capt. Fritz ushered me from his office, thanking me. I walked away saddened but relieved that it was the end of the day and I could go home, where I could try—at least for a little while—to put the tragedy and the day's events out of my mind. I was soon to find out that my troubles had only begun—for I had seen and heard too much that fateful day. [*When They Kill A President*, pp. 18-19]

Over the years, while studying this case, I've often been asked, "Who do you think was driving the Rambler?" And I've asked myself that same question, many times. And after researching all of the possibilities that I've come across for who it might be, it is my opinion based on that research, that the "husky looking Latin" man Craig saw driving the Rambler station wagon, may have been Lawrence John Howard Jr. of Los Angeles, California.

I also believe that the man Craig thought was Lee Harvey Oswald running from the school book depository, may have actually been William "Tex" Seymour of Arizona, who looks very similar to Oswald, and was accused by Richard Monroe Margeson of being a known hitman, who introduced himself as "Harvey Lee" from New Orleans. Margeson also claimed that Seymour indicated that he worked with the C.I.A., and showed him a piece of paper with "the name E. H. Hunt and a phone number on it." Hunt, a convicted Watergate conspirator and career C.I.A. spook, would later "confess" to his son during an audio recording made in 2004, that he played a "benchwarmer" role in the plot to assassinate President Kennedy. Hunt referred to this plot as "the Big Event," and named numerous individuals with ties to the C.I.A. and anti-Castro operations, as being involved in the assassination.

Margeson originally came forward to authorities in 1975, years after the J.F.K assassination. His information was turned over to the F.B.I., and then the HSCA followed up by interviewing him for their investigation on May 14, 1977. Margeson claimed that his suspicions grew immediately after the assassination, when he began seeing pictures of Oswald on television, because he looked identical to the man who he worked with in California in 1962. Margeson said that he eventually came forward after watching a documentary about the Warren Commission, that said Lee Harvey Oswald was in Russia at the time Margeson was working with the man in California resembling Oswald. According to the official timeline of Oswald's movements, he was not in California during the time Margeson claims to have known this Oswald impostor, who he says that he later learned was William "Tex" Seymour.

Margeson explained to authorities that Seymour was first introduced to him while working in East Los Angeles, through his friend Lawrence

Howard in 1962, while the men were working for a man named Jack Casey, who supposedly hired them "to paint and refurbish the Old Union Temple." Margeson also told authorities that he was "very close friends" with Howard from 1960 to 1963, and that Howard "did not show up for work" for an extended period leading up to the J.F.K. assassination. Margeson also revealed, that Howard owned "a 1959-60 light blue or green Nash Rambler," and that Howard told Margeson, "they were going to do something very bad that will make the U. S. invade Cuba."

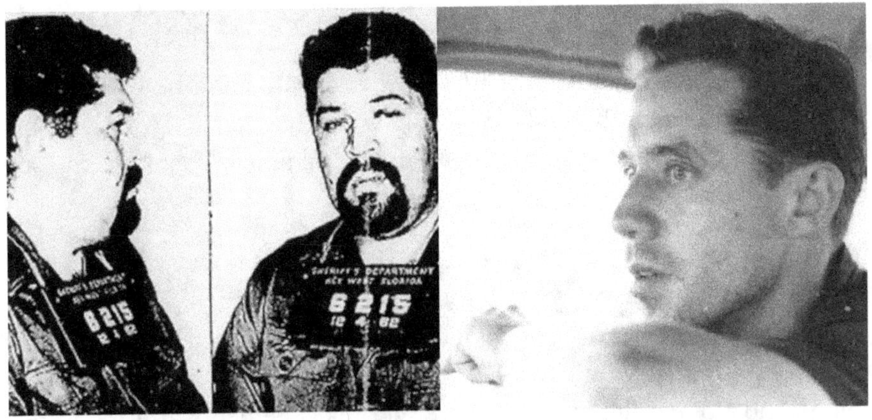

Lawrence John Howard Jr. (left), and William Seymour (right).

The links between Howard and Seymour to the assassination of President Kennedy were first investigated by the F.B.I. and the Warren Commission in 1964, and then by New Orleans District Attorney Jim Garrison during his investigation and trial of Clay Shaw in the late 1960s, and also during the HSCA hearings of the 1970s.

Howard and Seymour were members of a group called INTERPEN (Intercontinental Penetration Force). The group consisted of several experienced soldiers who were involved in training members of anti-Castro groups, that were being funded by the Central Intelligence Agency in the early 1960s, in an effort to undermine Fidel Castro's communist regime in Cuba.

In September of 1963, a woman named Silvia Odio was visited at her home in Dallas by three men. Odio, a Cuban exile, claimed that the third man was introduced to her as "Leon," and that he was an American sympathizer who wanted to participate in an assassination attempt of Fidel Castro.

Two of the men who reportedly visited Odio, were Lawrence Howard, and another member of INTERPEN named Loran Hall, who told the F.B.I. in 1964, that he had accompanied both Lawrence Howard and William Seymour to Odio's home in September of 1963, and also confirmed to them, that Seymour was "similar in appearance to Lee Harvey Oswald."

Richard Margeson also identified Loran Hall as being one of the men who he worked with, while working with Lawrence Howard, and William Seymour at the Old Union Temple building in East Los Angeles during late 1962, and early 1963.

The following report, dated October 2, 1964, details how both Lawrence Howard and William Seymour were interviewed by the F.B.I. regarding the allegations made by Loran Hall, and Silvia Odio. However, both men claimed to have no recollection of meeting her in September of 1963. And Loran Hall would later retract his statements after being re-interviewed by the F.B.I., telling them that he no longer recalled having any contact with Odio:

UNITED STATES DEPARTMENT OF JUSTICE

FEDERAL BUREAU OF INVESTIGATION

Reply, Please Refer to
No.

Miami, Florida
October 2, 1964

LEE HARVEY OSWALD

It is recalled that SYLVIA ODIO has advised that on an evening in the latter part of September, 1963, she was visited at her apartment in Dallas, Texas, by two Cubans or Mexicans, accompanied by an American whom she believed to be LEE HARVEY OSWALD.

LORAN EUGENE HALL, upon interview on September 16, 1964 at Johnsondale, California, stated he had been in Dallas, Texas in September, 1963 in the company of LAWRENCE HOWARD and WILLIAM SEYMOUR, and has contacted many Cubans in the Dallas area, including a Cuban woman, a Mrs. ODIO, who lived in apartment A, located on Magellan Circle, Dallas in the same building with a Cuban friend of HALL, named KIKI FERROR. During a second interview on September 20, 1964, HALL stated that during his visit in Dallas in September, 1963, he was accompanied by LAWRENCE HOWARD and a Cuban whom he knew as "WAHITO," and was not accompanied at that time by WILLIAM SEYMOUR. He also said he recalled no contact with ODIO.

Upon interview at Los Angeles, California on September 20, 1964, LAWRENCE JOHN HOWARD advised that he accompanied HALL to Dallas, Texas in September, 1963 with a Cuban refugee named CELLIOS ALBAS who was also known by the name "QUARITO." HOWARD recalled no contact with a Cuban woman named ODIO at an apartment on Magellan Circle in Dallas.

WILLIAM SEYMOUR of Phoenix, Arizona, during interview on September 18, 1964, stated he and LAWRENCE HALL were in Dallas, Texas in October, 1963, rather than September, 1963, and SYLVIA ODIO was unknown to him.

L. Howard (left), Loran Hall (left of center), Billy Seymour (far right).

On page 324 of the *Warren Report* are details of Loran Hall's confession to the F.B.I., that he visited Silvia Odio's home with Lawrence Howard, and William Seymour in September of 1963:

> On September 16, 1964, the FBI located Loran Eugene Hall in Johnsondale, Calif. Hall has been identified as a participant in numerous anti-Castro activities. He told the FBI that in September of 1963 he was in Dallas, soliciting aid in connection with anti-Castro activities. He said he had visited Mrs. Odio. He was accompanied by Lawrence Howard, a Mexican-American from East Los Angeles and one William Seymour from Arizona. He stated that Seymour is similar in appearance to Lee Harvey Oswald; he speaks only a few words of Spanish, as Mrs. Odio had testified one of the men who visited her did. While the FBI had not yet completed its investigation into this matter at the time the report went to press, the Commission has concluded that Lee Harvey Oswald was not at Mrs. Odio's apartment in September of 1963 [*Warren Report*, p.324].

It's my belief, that these men were somehow involved in a plot to not only assassinate President Kennedy, but to also setup Lee Harvey Oswald leading up to it, so he would later be blamed for the killing.

Whether or not Oswald was the person who Roger Craig and others saw get into the Rambler is debatable. However, the links between INTERPEN, the C.I.A., and the assassination of J.F.K. are undeniable to me, and have been thoroughly established throughout the years, by numerous J.F.K. assassination investigators long before I ever put these dots together, so my conclusions and opinions about these links are certainly not groundbreaking. But I do believe more attention should be put into this area of investigation by researchers, to help us learn more about the players who were actually involved in the "Big Event," that occurred on November 22, 1963.

Interview continued…

Steve: The things your father witnessed and investigated that day, where did all that information go?

Roger: He had already turned in that information on the day of November 22nd. He had turned over several incidents over to other people, and it went nowhere. And that's what frustrated him. Nobody was taking his information seriously. It was like, "Oh, we know what happened, we know what happened. We don't need your information. Have a nice day. Bye." Stuff like that. So, he took it upon himself. He was a stickler for wanting to know everything about either what he seen, what he found. Anything to do with law enforcement or investigation, he wanted to know everything.

Steve: Is it fair to say he was stepping on some toes to try to find out that information?

Roger: Oh, definitely. He was stepping on some big toes. We're talking sasquatch toe.

Steve: Would Captain Fritz have been one of those toes?

Roger: Yes.

Steve: Because Fritz went on to testify to the Warren Commission, and said that he didn't recall your father coming into his office that day, and that your father never told him he saw Oswald get into a Rambler and flee Dealey Plaza with another man.

Roger: I don't know why.

Steve: So, after the assassination, who do you think was your father's biggest obstacle when he tried following up on things he investigated that day?

Roger: Decker told everybody to stay out of it. As far as preventing my father from researching things, other than the order Decker gave, my father was finding roadblocks at a lot of places, but he would go around them. He had a knack for finding things that other people couldn't find out.

Steve: So, he may have been going through some files that he didn't have permission, or official access to?

Roger: Right. Like pull files and put them to memory, or jot stuff down. He also had spy cameras. He had wiretapping stuff for telephones.

Steve: So, he was invested in this then. He wanted to solve this.

Roger: Oh definitely. And like Sheriff Decker, once my father started something, he didn't give up until he finished it.

Steve: There was an incident when your father was shot at, is that correct?

Roger: Which time?

Steve: This particular incident I'm referring to, is when he stepped off a curb just before a bullet grazed his head. Do you recall your father talking about this?

Roger: Oh yes. I was staying the weekend with him, and my father got a call on the phone, and was asked to meet a guy at a diner over there on Carroll Street.

Steve: Do you remember who called him?

Roger: I don't really remember, be he was a friend of my fathers I think, and he told him, "I need to talk to you, can you meet me over here." So, my father went over there. And on the way, he noticed another guy in a car following him. Well, he gets to the restaurant, and him and his friend are there having coffee. And then my father sees the man who was following him come in there, and sit down across from them. After they finished their conversation, they got up to pay their bill and leave. But before they could, the other man got up and walked out. Well, my dad and his friend paid their check and left. They walked out toward the street where they had parked their cars, and when they got to the curb, his friend fell down to the ground. My father thought he tripped, so he was about to help him up, when he stepped off the curb, and at the same time he said he heard a crack, and felt a burning pain on the side of his head. Well, he had just been shot at, and it missed him because he stepped off the curb. And then his friend jumped up off the ground, got in his car, and drove off.

Steve: So, his friend just got up and left?

Roger: Yes. He got up off the ground and left immediately. Like, "Whoops, they missed. Bye!" Well, when my father got home, he came in the door, and we were all siting around there, and he said, "The sonofabitch set me up," and showed us the burn mark on the side of his head, just above his ear. There was no blood, but there was a streak there on the side of his head. Then after a couple of days, he had an interview with a news deal here in Dallas, and he come in the door and said, "Turn on the T.V.," and we sat down there and watched the interview. And he told the whole story, about how he stepped off the curb and everything. And not long after that, Paul Harvey came by the house to interview him.

Steve: Paul Harvey, the radio personality?

Roger: Yes. He came to the door, and I answered it, and he said, "Hi, I'm Paul Harvey. I'm here to interview your father, Roger Craig." So, I told my father Paul Harvey was there to see him. And I knew it was Paul Harvey just by the sound of his voice, because I used to listen to the radio all the time back then.

President George W. Bush presents the Presidential Medal of Freedom to legendary radio personality, Paul Harvey, on November 9, 2005.

Steve: He was pretty famous back then, right?

Roger: Oh yeah. And Paul Harvey coming to interview my father, that was great! So, my father told Molly, "Take the kids and y'all go out somewhere and stay gone for a while." And she said, "Okay, we'll go look at some garage sales." She loved garage sales. That woman would make a U-turn on a busy highway if she saw a sign that said "Garage Sale."

Steve: What year were your father and Molly married?

Roger: I think 1961.

Steve: Did they have a good relationship?

Roger: Yeah.

Steve: Did things change after he was shot at?

Roger: Well, he got more distant, and more secluded.

Steve: From Molly?

Roger: From everybody. He'd get agitated at the slightest provocation. Not from within the family, but from outside provocations. If something outside happened, it was like, "Y'all need to get in the back room and stay there," you know? I guess you could call it paranoia.

Steve: But it sounds like he had a good reason to be paranoid.

Roger: Oh yes, definitely. I mean, they only tried to kill him five times. And the fifth one got him!

Steve: So, you were about twelve or thirteen when your father was shot at this first time, and it would have been around 1967?

Roger: Yes, I think that's about right. It was a few months after Decker had fired him.

Steve: What other changes in your father's behavior were there after he was shot at?

Roger: Well, he was looking out the windows a lot, and messing with the telephone. Doing some wiring. Setting up a reel-to-reel. Doing stuff like that. And I found out later what he was doing with the telephone.

Steve: What was that?

Roger: He was bugging it. I got up in the middle of the night. Couldn't sleep. I kind of called this girl I knew. And we were kind of talking, like young teenagers do. And the next day, my father calls me in, and says, "You got up in the middle of the night and talked on the telephone for an awful long time." I was going to deny it at first, but then he turned on the reel-to-reel, and it was me talking to her, and her talking to me (laughter).

Steve: Busted (laughter).

Roger: I couldn't call her, or see her for a week, except when I was at school.

Steve: That's a funny story. But I'm sure your father wasn't bugging the phones so he could catch his son having late-night phone calls.

Roger: Oh no.

Steve: What do you think his reasoning was for that?

Roger: To record phone calls to him, or somebody calling him for dubious purposes. He had been getting threats over the phone. Or people wanting to rendezvous with him that he didn't know, so he was recording them. And he was also using the reel-to-reel to record what he knew.

Steve: So, he was doing it for insurance purposes?

Roger: For in case anything happened to him, so it would be there for a record. I saw him one time rolling the reels up and putting them into a box. And it was a big box.

Steve: How did your own relationship change with your father after as you grew older?

Roger: It was strenuous. It was almost like he was a different person, but not really. He didn't want me around as much. Especially when my first daughter was born. When I brought her over to see him, he acted like he didn't want us to be there. He was still married to Molly then, and Molly wanted to see the baby, and he said, "No!" And so, we left. I was seventeen at the time. Me and my wife left, and took the baby with us. I couldn't figure out what was going on, you know?

Steve: But now that you look back on it…

Roger: Now that I look back on it, he didn't want us around him, because it was like, "I'm an I.E.D. (Improvised Explosive Device), and if you stick around, something's gonna happen.

Steve: That must have been hard on you back then.

Roger: It was. But now I understand why he was like that.

Steve: Can you describe the other times that your father had attempts made on his life?

Roger: The second one, I think was when his car blew up. And the third time, they ran his car off a cliff.

Steve: Is that the incident that happened in the Davis Mountains?

Roger: Yeah. The fourth time, he opened the front door, and someone shot him in the chest and shoulder with shotgun.

Steve: Was the person who shot him ever apprehended?

Roger: No. He said he heard a knock at the door. So, he walked up to the door, opened it, and then, "Boom!" He woke up in the ambulance going to the hospital.

Steve: Okay. I want to switch gears here a little, and ask you about your dad and his involvement with Jim Garrison's investigation. Sheriff Decker wasn't too happy about that, and from reading your father's manuscript, Decker fired him over it. What do you think his reasons were for that?

Roger: Well, he told everybody to stay out of it. Don't talk to nobody, and to let the feds, and Dallas handle it. And Decker didn't like you disobeying an order. If he gives you an order, he expects you to follow it. My father didn't, so therefore, he suffered the consequences.

Steve: What was the final straw?

Roger: I think it was after Decker confronted him about talking to Garrison. He asked him if he'd been talking to him, and my father said no. But I don't think Decker believed him. And the next thing I know, my father was fired.

Steve: Was this around 1967?

Roger: Yes. It was July 4th, 1967.

Steve: That brings me back to a something you told about me during one of our previous conversations, having to do with a warning that Deputy Sheriff Buddy Walthers gave your father. You said your father knew Buddy very well, and that he contacted your father not long after he left the Sherriff's Office. Can you please tell me more about that?

Roger: At the time, we were living in Midlothian, Texas. And Buddy called my father, and told him to meet him at the county line. When he did, Buddy warned him not to come back to Dallas.

Steve: Not to come back?

Roger: Yeah. And that was in 1968. Then, not long after that, Buddy got a subpoena to go to the Garrison deal in Louisiana.

Steve: Right. Because Jim Garrison wanted Buddy to testify at his trial of Clay Shaw, that was set to begin in February of 1969 I believe.

Roger: Right.

Steve: But unfortunately, in January of 1969, Decker sent Buddy and another officer to a motel room in East Dallas, to apprehend an escaped prisoner named Walter Cherry. And when they went into the motel room, they were both shot during a confrontation with the escaped prisoner. Buddy was killed, and the other officer (Al Maddox) was shot in the foot. Buddy was also in Dealey Plaza with your father in 1963 when Kennedy was killed. He investigated a bullet that had ricocheted off the curb over on Main Street near the triple underpass, and was also seen investigating a manhole cover on the south side of Elm Street where one of the bullets reportedly hit, and where a bullet, or bullets had also hit the grass next to it. And while investigating that scene, according to Buddy, an F.B.I. man picked up one of the bullets from the grass and walked away with it in his hand, which was never entered into evidence.

A .45 slug according to Buddy. He told your father about this, and at least a few others. And then sometime in 1967, while Jim Garrison was being interviewed on television about his case against Clay Shaw, he showed a photo of Buddy, and another man who looked like an F.B.I. agent, bending over and picking up what appeared to be a bullet from the grass. But after this interview aired, Buddy began telling people that it wasn't true, and that he never saw a bullet lying in the grass. But there were people that said Buddy told them there was a bullet in the grass, including your father, and Buddy's partner Deputy Sheriff Al Maddox, as well as Buddy's wife Dorothy. And there was also a patrolman by the name of J.W. Foster who testified before the Warren Commission, and told them that he saw where a bullet hit the corner of the manhole cover on the south side of Elm Street. And other witnesses also said they saw where multiple bullets had hit the grass near that same manhole cover, and that their original F.B.I. reports had been altered (Wayne and Edna Hartman). So, this is evidence of a cover-up, and proves to me at least, that there was more than one shooter. Because the official story is that Oswald only had time to fire three shots, which had all been accounted for. And one of those shots was the Warren Commission's magic bullet theory, that supposedly caused seven wounds in both President Kennedy, and Governor Connally. It's just so ridiculous. And I think Buddy changed his story, because he was afraid. And I think he warned your father, because he knew that they were both over the target so to speak, for what they witnessed on November 22, 1963. And unfortunately, Buddy never got a chance to testify at Garrison's trial, because he was killed just a couple of weeks before it started.

Roger: But my father did give his deposition, and testified at the trial.

Steve: And your father had multiple attempts on his life leading up to that.

Roger: Oh yeah.

Steve: When Buddy had that conversation with you father, warning him to not come back to Dallas, it wasn't too long after that, that Buddy met his fate inside that motel room.

Roger: Yeah. About six months later.

Steve: Did you go to New Orleans with your father for Garrison's trial?

Roger: Yes. I think we went to give the deposition first. I remember us staying in a motel room. And Jim Garrison had somebody come pick up my father and take him over to Garrison's office. We did have a chance to walk around the streets in New Orleans a little bit. But we always had a couple of people with us. I don't know who they were. We were only there for a couple of days.

Steve: And then in 1969 your father testified at Garrison's trial in New Orleans, is that correct?

Roger: Yes. After he got fired in '67, we went to go live in Midlothian where Penn Jones had gotten us a house to live in. And my father became city judge of Midlothian, and county judge at Ellis County, Precinct 6.

Steve: So, he tried to go on with his life after leaving the Sheriff's Department?

Roger: Yeah. He married people. He was J.P. (Justice of the Peace) in both the city and the county while we were living in Midlothian. He also worked as a private investigator. But he was pretty torn up about losing his job with Sheriff's Department, because he believed in the law. He believed in honesty. And he believed in integrity. He tried to go back in '69, but they wouldn't hire him back.

Steve: I want to forward a few years now, to May 15, 1975, the day that your father died. The Dallas County Coroner ruled that he committed suicide. From previous conversations with you, I'm aware that you don't agree with his ruling. So, if you don't mind, can you explain why you don't think your father took his own life?

Roger: Because he loved life too much, and I don't believe he would do it. I really don't. He tried too hard to stay alive. After he died, I saw his driver's license, and he had just renewed it on his birthday, which is May 12th, three days before his death. He just had his thirty-ninth birthday party. You don't go renewing your driver's license if you're planning to go kill yourself. So, I don't believe it, especially when I went in and got the body from the morgue, and saw the bruises on his wrists, and the abrasions on his knees.

Steve: Can you explain some of the circumstances of his death? In a previous conversation, you mentioned that you've seen the autopsy report, and it didn't make sense either.

Roger: Yeah. Well, it didn't jive with me, because the one I saw when I went up to the coroner's office, it said the gunshot was from right to left, in a downward motion.

Steve: Like someone standing above him?

Roger: Yeah. And standing slightly to the front, and to the side of him. That's what it sounded like to me, and it didn't jive with it being a suicide.

Steve: The report I think I read, said the entrance wound was at the upper right side of his chest, and at a downward angle into his chest.

Roger: Right. And how are you gonna do that? Hold the rifle up over your head?

Steve: And why would you do it to the right side of your chest, and nowhere near your heart?

Roger: And he had a .45 Magnum laying on the dresser next to the door to the bedroom.

Steve: Was the rifle that he supposedly took his life with, was that found next to him?

Roger: It was found on the bed. That's what the original report said. I don't know what they did with it after that. But what I saw, it said he was laying in the middle of the bedroom on the floor, that he bled out, and that the rifle was laying on the bed. The bed was up against the wall longways.

Steve: Do you know if prints were ever taken off that rifle?

Roger: I don't know. But I bet there wasn't.

Roger: After I had gotten my father out of the morgue, and put him in the funeral home, I went over to my Grandmother's house. And I had put all of my father's stuff in the back bedroom. Well, that night we went to the rodeo, and when we come home from the rodeo, all that stuff was gone. Every bit of it. The house had been broken into.

Steve: Can you please give me a little more detail about that?

Roger: Okay. When I went to the morgue to get my father, there were several boxes, about six or eight boxes. And they were plumb full of stuff that was taken out of my grandfather's house, that was my father's. I don't know why the Dallas Police Department boxed up everything of my father's and took it to the morgue, but that's where it was at. And when I signed for the body, they showed me all the boxes, and I loaded them up in the vehicle, and took them to my grandmother's house. Put them in the back room. That was on a Friday. We went to the rodeo Saturday night. When we got back, all that stuff was gone. His books. His papers. His bank statements.

Steve: Were your father's reel-to-reels in those boxes?

Roger: No. I don't know who got them. But all of his papers were in there. His stuff that he had accumulated for evidence. Newspaper clippings. Handwritten letters.

Steve: Did your dad keep a diary?

Roger: If there was a diary in there, I never got to read it.

Author's note: I asked Roger about the diary, because before I met him, I discovered information that his father did keep a diary. According to researcher Harold Weisberg, a woman named Rita Musgrove, who was friends with Roger Craig, and helped him edit his 1971 manuscript, *When They Kill A President*, contacted him by phone a few months after Roger died in 1975. She told Weisberg that she was in possession of Roger's diary, and some of his other materials. Here are excerpts from Weisberg's typed notes from their telephone conversation:

She quotes Penn as saying Roger suicide four months ago (all this from memory-taped when I saw what she was going into).

Roger kept a diary. She has it, Penn wants it, and Roger wanted him not to have it and regarded it as cause for his own killing. She read parts to me, the reason being the way I come accross in my writing. She is on our mailing list.

I told her how to check out with Paul Rothermel whether or not Roger is dead. She has duplicated the diary out of her possession.

Roger also stole police radio tapes-three channels. 18" reels.

Many details about police, sheriff inside, irrelevant Ruby details after hailing, Decker and what Craig says happened to him and how, with names and dates.

Craig appears to have started keeping this diary for his son the day before JFK was due to arrive simply because it was so unusual to see a President.

Her reading of some of the early passages is entirely consistent with his testimony: excpt for what was omitted and what he did not add when he "corrected" it as printed at Maggie Field's.

What struck me as most important were new details of the finding of the shells and rifle and the time those at the TSBD learned about the Tippit killing. Roger looked at his watch. it was 1:06. This is entirely consistent with the Bowley affidavit, ignored by the Commission/Belin in person and particular.

Different Buddy Walthers story than I get from Hudkins;inference he was killed by partner rather than man he was sent to pick up. Repeats what logs show, first Tippit shell (he says all) automatics. Rifle shells all lifted up as found, suspicious to him at time.

In a January 1983 issue of Penn Jones' Continuing Inquiry newsletter, Rita Musgrove wrote an article about Roger Craig's diary, and explained that it would be published in full over the course of a few months. However, it apparently never was, and the newsletter only printed the first instalment of the diary (which I shared on page 5: About Roger Craig, by Roger Craig). Here is an excerpt from the newsletter:

INTRODUCTION

TO

DIARY OF AN EX-DALLAS DEPUTY - ROGER CRAIG

By Rita Musgrove

I was priviledged to meet Roger Craig for the first time in the summer of 1970 when my husband, daughter and I came to Dallas on vacation from our mid-western home. I was introduced to him at the home of Mr. Penn Jones, whom I had gone to visit while in Dallas. I did not know that Roger would also be visiting there that same evening.

Even though I was thrilled to meet him, the thrill itself paled in comparison to the admiration and respect I felt almost immediately for this soft-spoken, proud man who was truly to later become one of our nation's classic unsung heroes.

I made every effort that evening to meet Roger in his ballpark and on his terms. Apparently and thankfully it was a warm and successful meeting with no aggressiveness nor pinning him to the wall with questions on my part. Within a few days, Roger and I were spending hours on the telephone in conversation, once again at his pace. I came to Dallas frequently after that first meeting at Penn's house and spent several days each time with the Craig family. There developed a bond and a trust between the two of us specifically that remains unbroken --- to this very hour.

I was here, either by telephone across the country, or in person, or by letter, and I saw first-hand his inability to even feed his small family; I saw the pain; I sensed the anger and unbearable frustration; I felt his feelings of injustice and indignation at the price he was being forced to pay even then ---- and all for telling the truth. I believe this is called PERSECUTION. Had it not been for Penn Jones and a small handful of others, I shutter to think how much worse life might have been for Roger and his family.

The Roger Craig story, which will follow in this newsletter over the next few months, I trust will give you a true and honest insight into Roger Dean Craig, the man I came to know so very dearly --- the same man I would wish all of you reading this newsletter could have known as well and as personally as a very small group of us were honored to have known him.

The words, all of them, in these next few issues of The Continuing Inquiry are his words, not mine. He was meticulous in his record keeping. When he was told that the President was coming to Dallas, he began to keep daily (and sometimes even hourly) notes as to what was taking place through those incredible days and their aftermath of several years. These hundred-plus pages of notes and records *Contu*

12

THE CONTINUING INQUIRY

were given to me in 1971 and the only changes that I have made are grammatical, punctuational, spelling, etc. I do not claim journalistic expertise but he trusted me to put in it it's proper edited form -- and, I am greatly honored.

And, to Roger, I say to you I have done the best I can, my friend, and wherever you are, God keep you.

Remember ---- we believe.

[Penn Jones' Continuing Inquiry newsletter, Jan. 22, 1983, Volume VII, Number 6, pp. 11-12]

From reading this, Rita Musgrove was clearly very fond of Roger Craig, and felt that she needed to share his diary with the public. But what's unclear, is why the rest of her installments were not published. I searched every issue following it, until the newsletter ended its run in July of 1984, and I could not locate any additional installments.

In November of 2018 I was informed by a prominent J.F.K. assassination researcher while attending a conference in Dallas, and according to him, Rita was murdered several years ago, and it was related to her involvement with Roger Craig and her research into the J.F.K. assassination. However, I haven't been able to verify this information. But I also have not been able to find anything else published by Rita Musgrove after 1983.

Interview continued...

Roger: Now this is the funny part. I tore out one of the checks from of the checkbook that was in there before everything got stolen. Stuck it in my billfold. Went to the bank. It was called Lakewood Bank in east Dallas. And I asked them about my father's account there. The bank told me that the account number never existed. And I said, "There was over sixty-thousand dollars that was put in here, and there were no withdrawals, and this is the account number on the check." And Lakewood Bank said, "That account never existed, we don't know what you're talking about."

Steve: Your dad's account?

Roger: Yes. And he had checks. Deposit slips. Stamped and everything. And he had bank statements. I looked at them before all his stuff was stolen.

Steve: And how long was this after he died, that you went to the bank?

Roger: About a week.

Steve: Is it possible someone closed it, and they didn't have it on record, or any records of it?

Roger: You got to have records. If it was closed, it would be on microfiche.

Steve: Yeah, you would think that they had some kind of a record of it.

Roger: But they said the check I gave them for that account, that there was no such account number, and there never was a Roger Craig with an account at that bank. Now, you figure that one out.

Steve: What do you think happened?

Roger: I think it was just like I heard what happened in Trauma Room 1 at Parkland hospital in 1963. Do you remember what they did there?

Steve: What did they do?

Roger: What I heard was, the Secret Service came in there and they took the tiles off the wall, and the tiles off the floor, and every piece of equipment in there.

Steve: Scrubbed it.

Roger: Oh yeah. And how hard would it be for an organization to scrub a bank account back in 1975?

Steve: Did you pursue any legal action, or hire an attorney, or have an investigator look into it, to find out how that account could have just disappeared like that?

Roger: I went to an attorney, and I told him everything about the account. And I also asked him to look into a documentary that Mark Lane made about my father (Two Men In Dallas), that hadn't come out yet, so I asked him to look into that too. I paid him seventy-five dollars upfront for his services. And then three days later he called me back and said he couldn't take the case, and hung up on me.

Steve: What happened after that?

Roger: Well, I went back to Fort Hood. I was getting ready to get out of the military, and I had other things to take care of, like my family. I had two girls at the time, and I was raising them as a single father. I guess I just kind of forgot about it, and said, "Oh well, that's life." I was only twenty-one years old at the time.

Roger Craig Jr., with his daughters, Nita and Renee.

Steve: Is that bank still around?

Roger: No, they closed their doors not long after. Maybe a few years after that. Not sure why.

Steve: There's an F.B.I. report that I read, that was filed by your dad's ex-wife Molly, about being followed after your dad's death, and she wanted to know if they were surveilling her movements, because she believed she was being followed, and that her phones were possibly being tapped. Did you know about that?

Roger: Oh yes. And I was followed too. When I first got out in patrol in 1980, I was given the Seagoville area just like my father, and there was a dark-colored Crown Vic that followed me everywhere I went. This went on for about a year, and then one day, it just stopped.

Author's note: The following excerpts are from a publicly available F.B.I. report, regarding an inquiry that was made on February 9, 1976, by Roger Craig's ex-wife Molly, concerning her belief that she was being monitored by federal agents, over eight months after Roger had died. At the time this report was made, Molly was married to another man, and she had been divorced from Roger for approximately two years before his death:

UNITED STATES DEPARTMENT OF JUSTICE

FEDERAL BUREAU OF INVESTIGATION
Dallas, Texas
February 9, 1976

ASSASSINATION OF PRESIDENT
JOHN FITZGERALD KENNEDY
NOVEMBER 22, 1963
DALLAS, TEXAS

On February 4, 1976, Mr. ▓▓▓▓▓▓▓▓▓▓▓▓▓ Attorney at Law, Main Bank Building, Dallas, Texas, Telephone Number ▓▓▓▓▓▓ appeared at the Dallas FBI Office accompanied by ▓▓▓▓▓▓▓▓▓▓▓▓▓▓▓▓▓▓ ▓▓▓▓▓▓▓▓▓▓▓▓▓▓▓▓▓▓▓▓▓▓▓▓▓▓, Dallas, Texas, and his wife, ▓▓▓▓▓▓ The Hahns reside at ▓▓▓▓▓▓▓ Dallas, Texas, Telephone ▓▓▓▓▓▓ The ▓▓▓▓ desired to ascertain if the FBI was surveilling them or otherwise investigating ▓▓▓▓▓▓▓

▓▓▓▓▓▓▓ identified herself as the widow of Roger Dean Craig, a former Deputy Sheriff of Dallas County, Dallas, Texas, at the time of the assassination of President Kennedy. She advised that her former husband had allegedly committed suicide, but before doing so he had written a book regarding his part in the investigation of the assassination which had never been published and that she has the manuscript of this book in her custody. She remarked that this manuscript did not portray the FBI in a favorable light. She indicated she had no intentions at this time of having the manuscript published. She remarked that Craig had apparently testified before the Warren Commission and also in the Clay Shaw trial in New Orleans, Louisiana.

Mrs. ▓▓▓▓▓ notes reflect that on Monday, January 26, 1976, at 9:00 p.m., she was followed home from the Hope Lutheran Church by an automobile with two occupants. On Thursday, January 29, 1976, at 2:00 p.m., she went to a K-Mart discount department store in Dallas with a neighbor and was followed by a man unknown to either of them, who stayed within two feet and closer to them for about 30 minutes. Mrs. ▓▓▓▓ and her neighbor split up in the store, and the man followed Mrs. ▓▓▓▓ to the record department, while an unknown woman followed the neighbor to the toy department. As Mrs. ▓▓▓▓ was about to confront the man following her, he disappeared. She described this man as 40-45 years of age, 5'10" tall, slender build, dark complexion, possibly of another nationality, with a large pointed nose. He was wearing a white jacket and dark slacks. The woman following the neighbor was in her 20's, approximately 5'3" tall, dark hair in pageboy style, slender with nice appearance.

Mrs. ▓▓ continued that on Thursday, January 29, 1976, at 8:00 p.m., a woman called her on the telephone asking for "Mrs. ▓▓" When she insisted that the woman calling give her name, she replied that it was "Mrs. Gertz" with "Air Temp." This woman indicated she was selling air and heating equipment. Mrs. ▓▓ considered this call unusual because her telephone number had been changed to an unlisted number on Tuesday, January 27, 1976. She stated that her husband called the company for whom this woman supposedly worked, but there was no one employed there by the name of Mrs. Gertz.

She continued that on Saturday, January 21, 1976, (apparently January 31, 1976), while at the Llove Recreation Center at Dallas, a gray-haired man was in front of her at the roller skating rink and had been several other places where she was on that day. He had two women with him and took a photograph of Mrs. ▓▓ from about three feet in front of her. Mrs. Hahn claims she made two photographs of this man, but the only one which developed was one which did not show his face.

On Tuesday, February 3, 1976, Mrs. ▓▓ claims she was cut off two times on the telephone just as she answered it. She claimed her attorney, ▓▓▓▓▓, called her new home telephone number on a Friday, no date indicated, and a male voice intercepted the call saying, "This is not a working number."

Mr. ▓▓ notes reflect that on Monday, January 26, 1976, he requested the Bell Telephone Company to change the telephone number at their residence and to continue it on an unlisted basis due to an obscene telephone call on Sunday, January 25, 1976. This number was changed on Tuesday, January 27, 1976, and the line was immediately cleared of static and popping noises. He requested the telephone company to check the line for a possible wiretap and was to be called at his office on Thursday by Mrs. Beach of the telephone company. He states he also requested that the old telephone number have a recording to the effect, "This number is no longer in service." Mr. ▓▓ states that someone, apparently from the telephone company, called his 12-year old stepdaughter on Wednesday, January 28, 1976, and told her the telephone was not tapped. On Thursday, January 29, 1976, Mrs. Beach of the telephone company did not call him as she had said she would and on that evening the call from "Mrs. Gertz" was received. He states he

called the telephone number of the company Mrs. Gertz represented and received no answer. He also learned that the telephone company changed the old telephone number recording back to "At the customer's request, the number is unlisted."

On Friday, January 30, 1976, Mr. ▓▓ called Mrs. Beach at the telephone company, at which time she apologized to him for not having called him personally.

Mr. ▓▓▓ and Mr. and Mrs. ▓▓ were advised that the FBI was not surveilling them nor conducting any investigation concerning them whatsoever.

The report of SA Robert P. Gemberling dated November 30, 1963, at Dallas, Texas, in captioned matter reflects interviews with Roger Craig on November 22, 1963 (page 69), and November 25, 1963, (pages 71 and 72). In the first interview, Craig, who was employed as a Deputy Sheriff of Dallas County, Texas, stated shortly after the assassination, he saw an individual run down the grassy area from the direction of the Texas School Book Depository; that this individual whistled and a white Rambler station wagon driven by a Negro male pulled over to the curb, picked up the individual and headed toward the Dallas-Fort Worth Turnpike. Craig stated that later that day he was given the opportunity to observe Lee Harvey Oswald at the Dallas Police Department, and he was positive Oswald was identical to the individual he observed getting into the station wagon.

When reinterviewed on November 25, 1963, Craig again reiterated the above information but described the driver of the station wagon as a white male, stating that since he had previously been interviewed, he had decided the driver was a white male.

The testimony of Craig before the Warren Commission to the foregoing information is set forth in Volume VI, Pages 260-273, of the Warren Commission report.

The "Dallas Times Herald" newspaper on November 2, 1967, carried an article captioned "Garrison Probe Figure Claims Shot." This article stated that Roger Craig, former Dallas County Deputy Sheriff, who resigned from the Dallas County Sheriff's Office in July, 1967, to become a private investigator, had stated someone shot at him on November 1, 1967, in a parking lot in East Dallas. The article continued that Craig said he believed his going to New Orleans the previous week for interrogation by District Attorney James Garrison was probably connected with the attempt on his life. This article also stated that Craig had indicated he was "tailed" while in New Orleans on October 25 and 26, 1967, and was still being "tailed" in Dallas.

An article in the New Orleans Times Picayune on February 14, 1969, indicated Craig testified as a prosecution witness in the Clay Shaw trial at New Orleans, again reiterating the information about observing a man believed to be Oswald getting into a station wagon shortly after the assassination.

A newspaper article in the Dallas Morning News on May 16, 1975, reflects that Craig had apparently committed suicide at his father's home on May 15, 1975, while his father was in the back yard working on a lawn mower. It was indicated that Craig left a note saying he was sorry for what he had to do, but he could not stand the pain. According to Craig's father, Craig had been taking pain killing medication for injuries from a car wreck two years before and for a gunshot wound in the shoulder which he had received at Waxahachie, Texas, about six months before. The article stated that Craig had reported to Waxahachie police that a stranger appeared at the door of a house where Craig was waiting for a woman friend and shot Craig with a shotgun when Craig answered the knock on the door.

The entire F.B.I. report is available on the Mary Ferrell Foundation website (maryferrell.org).

There was indeed a note found at the scene of Roger Craig's death, that could be interpreted as being a suicide note written by him.

However, when I asked his son Roger Jr. about it, he told me that he believed this note was an apology note, that was written inside of a greeting card, that he never gave to his children regarding his divorce to Molly, and that the police found the card inside of a desk drawer in his bedroom, long after he wrote it. Roger Jr believes that his father wrote this note as an apology to the children, while he was going through a divorce with their mother.

Whether or not this is the case, I do not know. But I do believe Roger Craig did not commit suicide. And whether or not he wrote a suicide note, I still believe that he did not take his own life, based on everything that I've researched regarding the circumstances of his death.

Three years before Roger died, he had also expressed fear of publishing his 1971 manuscript, *When They Kill A President*. The following is a letter that he wrote to Penn Jones about his concerns, and his wishes to not publish the manuscript at the time he wrote the letter. Craig also mentions Rita Musgrove, and her involvement with the manuscript:

January 7, 1972

Mr. Penn Jones, Jr.
Midlothian Mirror
Midlothian, Texas

Dear Penn:

I've given a lot of thought and consideration as to
whether I should or should not allow the "Craig Manuscript" to be printed in any way - i.e.; book form,
newspaper excrpts, serials, etc. and have come to the
conclusion that it would not benefit me or my family
in any good way, therefore, my decision is that I do
NOT want it printed in any manner. In addition to the
fact that I don't think it would help my situation, my
belief is that it would endanger my family and I feel
that they've already been through enough; also I have
the feeling that it wouldn't help my health. Don't
get the issues confused and think that I'm"selling
out" because we both know that I'm not. I believe
in my country, I have done nothing except tell the
truth, which I will continue to do. However I feel
that I have been exploited to a stopping point.

The manscript will be given to my children and will
be more valuable historically in the future than it
could possibly be at this time. It it were printed
now it could only hurt my family. Personally, I
sincerely believe that if the material was printed
at this time that you would have another "death"
to write about - mine. I may not be the smartest
person in the world, but, on the other hand, I'm
not the dumbest either. I feel that my family
should have a chance to lead a "normal" life and
I'm going to do everything that I can to see to
it that they have that chance.

Rita Musgrove has done a great job in editing the
manuscript and she knows that I appreciate the work
that she done on it. I would like to have the copy
of the manuscript that she put in plastic, to preserve
for the kids, it was the copy that you took home with
you last summer, the typed carbon. I understand that
several copies have been made of the manuscript and
I don't expect that I will recover all of them.

                              Continued..

-2-

In all probability the manuscript will be put into
book form in future years, but this is not the time
to do so. I'm using copies of this letter, as shown
below, to inform other interested persons of my decision.

Also, I regret that I was not informed of Rita's
visit to Dallas in September of 1971, since I
understand that she had planned to work on the
manuscript at that time, but there was a last minute
change in plans. Maybe we can all get together at
another time.

Sincerely,

Roger Craig

Source: Harold Weisbergs Archives: jfk.hood.edu

Interview continued...

Steve: Do you recall any other harassment in the days and weeks following your dad's death, besides the break-in at your grandmother's house, and the theft of his belongings?

Roger: There was phone calls, and hang ups, and stuff like that. And Parkland had called me while my father was still in the morgue, down there at the county morgue, and said he had outstanding bills and they needed to skin him to pay for his bills. And I said, "No! Not under any circumstances are you gonna skin him." At the time, my fear was they were trying to get rid of evidence. Because of the gunshot wound to the upper right part of his chest, and the wounds on his wrists and knees. And the best way to get rid of the evidence is to take the skin off. If you skin him, and then later on if the body is exhumed, all the evidence is gone.

Steve: So, the hospital called you to do this?

Roger: Yes. The hospital called me before I went down there to get the body. They wanted to skin him. And the next day when I went to get the body, I saw all the abrasions and everything, because he still had his skin.

Steve: So, they wanted to skin him for unpaid bills?

Roger: Yes. See, Parkland's a burn center also. So, they wanted the skin to pay for the bills that he owed. Well, Parkland is a county hospital. And if you're indigent, you don't have to pay. The county picks it up. So, I don't know what their reasoning was. And I'm not even sure that the person who called me was from Parkland. They said they were. And then at the funeral home, his brother Dwayne started to jump on me, saying, "You let them skin him," because I guess somebody told him they skinned my father. And I told him, "No I didn't! I told them not to skin him."

Steve: Did you tell somebody that they called you, and maybe that's how his brother heard about it?

Roger: No. I didn't tell nobody.

Steve: So, why do you think he thought you had authorized it?

Roger: Because legally, I was the only one who could authorize it, because I was his first son. And I didn't give them permission.

Steve: Did you ever confirm if they did?

Roger: No. We didn't look.

Steve: I don't blame you. That must have been a horrible experience to even have to imagine that. Especially at a time like that, when you were still grieving over the loss of your father. If it's okay with you, I'd like to talk about some happier times that you shared with your father. Do you have any funny stories that you'd like to share about your dad, from when you were growing up?

Roger: The night he brought the turkey home. That's a funny story.

Steve: Sure, let's hear it.

Roger: He come in one night with his coat over something. And it was a turkey (laughter). Thanksgiving was coming up, and we didn't have money for Thanksgiving dinner. But he had found a turkey on the backroads, just running through the brush. So, he captured it and brought it home. We fed it for two or three days, and then we had turkey dinner for Thanksgiving.

Steve: Can you tell me your fondest memory of your father?

Roger: Yes. It was Easter Sunday. We were standing in front of the house on Leroy Street. My mother had her Easter dress, and bonnet on. My father was dressed in his suit. I had on my fedora, white shirt, and slacks. And I was holding an Easter bunny rabbit that he gave me. That was my fondest memory. Because that's when everything was happy, and everything was going good.

Roger: We rode horses every day. We lived next door to my uncle Frank, and Danny, and Mike. The lady down the street was teaching me how to play the piano. And my father liked to play the guitar, and make up songs. He used to sing me a song he called Rudolf the Red-Nosed Cowboy.

Steve: Oh really? Do you remember how it went?

Roger: "Rudolf the Red-Nosed Cowboy, had two very shiny guns. And if you ever saw him, you'd say, 'let's run!' Then one night the Sheriff came, and he said, 'Rudolf with your guns so bright, won't you guide my posse tonight?'" That was one of his made-up songs.

Steve: Did your father lean towards country?

Roger: Oh yes. He loved country, and he loved Hank Williams, and I'm not talking about junior (laughter). And he liked John Henry, the steel-driving-man. And my father could sure play that guitar, and sing them songs. That was the best time.

Steve: Is there anything else about your father that you would like the world to know?

Roger: Before the J.F.K. assassination, he was a very happy person. Full of life, and optimistic about the future. And afterward, it was like his world came to an end. And he had to fight for every day.

Roger Jr. with his parents Roger & Juanita, on Easter Sunday, 1960.
(Photo courtesy of Roger Dean Craig Jr.)

Steve: Well, he's definitely one of my heroes. And I know many others who feel the same way about him. I wish I could have sat down with your dad and talked to him about what he went through, and the things he investigated concerning the case. But talking to you has been the next best thing. Thank you for agreeing to do this interview, and for speaking to me so candidly about your father, and what you experienced growing up as his son, and your relationship with him, and what you've learned about him as you've grown older since his passing. Right now, I want to give you an opportunity to speak on anything else you'd like. Anything at all.

Roger: I'd like to talk about my son Clay, if that's alright?

Steve: Of course. Is that your son who died during the Iraq War?

Roger: Yes. Clay was born May 19, 1985. He was killed by an Iranian sniper, according to his squad, on April 29, 2008. And his 23rd birthday would have been May 19th.

Steve: I've read a little bit about Clay online. There's a really nice memorial for him. A memorial page.

Roger: He's my hero. That boy was my hero. When he was twelve, he put my uniform on to go to school, with my black beret and everything.

It was Veteran's Day, and he wore it to school. And he said, "Dad, I'm gonna carry on the legacy." Because he knew about my father in Korea, and my father's father was in the Navy in the pacific during World War II, and he knew about me when I enlisted during the Vietnam War. And he said, "If I have a son, I'm gonna teach him just like you've taught me." I taught him how to shoot and everything. I started him with a .22 rifle that my father gave me when I was nine years old. A single shot, model 63.

Clay Craig, with his father, Roger Craig Jr.

Roger: At five years old, Clay could put a hole in the center of the "D" on a Dr. Pepper can, from fifty feet away. And then when he went in the military, he did so good on the firing range, they made him a sniper with the 101st Airborne. That's pretty good shooting if they make you a sniper.

Steve: It sure is.

Roger: Then they made him Staff Sergeant, and gave him a squad. The 502nd Infantry Regiment, Charlie Company. And they were in this little town, and they were told to check buildings, to make sure the doors were locked. Well, they found one door open. Clay went into the courtyard with two of his men. He turned around, and told his men to go back inside the building. And when he started back inside, a sniper shot him in the back of the head and killed him. Then four of his men picked him up, and put him in a Humvee, but when they rounded a corner, they hit an I.E.D., and it killed all four of them. So, there was five soldiers lost that day. My son was already dead. But they were still gonna try to get him to a Dustoff. On the day of Clay's funeral, we were at the Anderson Clayton Funeral Home, and Clay had a bandage on top of his head, and forehead. The whole top of his head was covered in bandages. I think to hold it together. So, I told the Sergeant first class and the Staff Sergeant there, that I didn't want people seeing him like that, and I asked them if they had an extra beret. And they did, so we put it on his head to cover the bandages. And then when they closed up the coffin to take him to the burial, I went out there to stand by the hearse, and the guys from the 1st Cavalry Division, which is my old Division, came outside with Clay. And there were four people standing out there in civilian clothes, and one of them walked up and said, "The Sheriff's Department is here. The four of us are all deputies with the Sheriff's Department. And Roger, we want you to know that you still have friends at the Sheriff's Department." And I said, "Thank you."

Steve: That was really nice of them to come there and tell you that.

Roger: Yeah. It really was. And then they put Clay in the hearse, and we went to the graveyard. And I've got the gravesite right behind him, out there at Dallas Fort Worth National Cemetery.

Steve: Did Clay have a family of his own?

Army Staff Sergeant Clay Allen Craig.

Roger: Yeah. He had a wife, and a little girl. And he loved that little girl. Soldiers have to write a letter, before they go out on maneuvers in a combat zone. They have to write a letter home, for just in case. His wife informed me, that in his letter, he said, "If anything happens to me, I want my daughter raised exactly the way my father raised me."

Steve: When was the last time you saw your son?

Roger: I saw him just before his third hitch over there. And I asked him, "Is everything okay with you?" Because I was concerned with PTSD, because this was his third tour over there. And he said, "Dad, I love it, and I'm gonna make a career out of it." And then, on April the 27th, I get a phone call. See, my son went over there on that hitch as a Sergeant, the same as I was when I got out. And this is how the phone call went. I answered the phone and I said, "Hello?" The voice on the other end said, "This is Staff Sergeant Craig, I'd like to talk to Sergeant Craig." And I recognized the voice, and knew it was Clay. So, I said, "Okay, this is Sergeant Craig." And he said, "I outrank your ass now," (laughter). And we talked, I guess for about an hour and a half. But evidently, it was his last minutes on his card or whatever, because I lost him, and the phone hung up. But I always told him, and this is what I told him every time, "I love you. I'm proud of you. Take care of your men." Because he was a Sergeant. And if you take care of your men, your men will take care of you. And that's what I tried to instill in him. And evidently, I did a pretty good job.

Steve: What do you think Clay would say about your dad, if he were alive today?

Roger: Oh, he read everything I had on him. He thought he was wonderful.

Steve: I have a feeling he's up there right now with your dad, and everything's been revealed to them.

Roger: Oh yeah.

Steve: Thank you for telling me about your son, Roger.

Roger: You're welcome.

"Suddenly the motorcade approached, and President Kennedy was smiling and waving, and for a moment I relaxed and fell into the happy mood the President was displaying… I was soon to be shocked back into reality."

-Roger Dean Craig

Dallas County Sheriff's Department Insider

Steve Cameron: Thanks a lot for doing this. I really appreciate it. Tell us a little bit about yourself.

Dallas County Sheriff's Department Insider: Well, I am a native Texan. I was born in Dallas, at the old Parkland hospital, not the one where J.F.K. died, but the old one. We moved to the suburbs when a major highway was put through the home where we lived. I married a sailor, and moved from Texas, to San Diego. Then we moved to Mountain View, which is south of San Francisco. I was living there when J.F.K. was shot.

Steve: If we can just flash forward a little, after you had left California, and moved back to Dallas, I guess permanently, what year would that have been?

DCSD Insider: We moved back here in 1967.

Steve: Okay. Let's forward to when you began working at the Sheriff's Department. What year was that?

DCSD Insider: I began working there in 1977. I went to work in communications, and spent twenty-five years there. I don't know about communication centers at other law enforcement agencies, but ours was a like a home away from home for officers out in the field. If they didn't have anything to do, or if they brought a prisoner in to book them, they'd come by and speak with us, and sit and chit chat. And on the weekends and holidays, that's where they spent their time, so we had a lot of time to sit around and talk.

Steve: Would you ever sit around and talk about what happened on November 22, 1963?

DCSD Insider: Well, yes. And especially because my first sergeant, that I had when I went to work at the Sheriff's Department, who was incidentally married to my best friend from the sixth grade, was actually on duty the day Kennedy was shot.

Steve: Is that **** ******?

DCSD Insider: It is **** ******. Yes, it is.

Steve: Okay.

DCSD Insider: Most communications centers now are manned by six different people. But **** did it all. Someone was sitting in teletype, but he was the dispatcher, and the telephone operator. And he said things were absolutely a zoo that day.

Steve: Has he divulged anything that could be considered insider information? Or did anyone else at the department have firsthand information, or personal views about it being something more than what the official story was said to be?

DCSD Insider: I don't think that anybody in the Sheriff's Department, well maybe there were some, because you never find anybody that agrees one hundred percent, but the general consensus at the Sheriff's Department when I was there, when we would sit around and talk about it was, "There's no way." They did not believe that Oswald had killed him.

Steve: So, that was the sentiment there in the office?

DCSD Insider: To my knowledge it was. Yes. There was when I went to work there. I think, that because it was fifteen years later, the talk was more freely spoken, and there was less trepidation of retaliation, than there probably was in those ten or fifteen years before I got there.

Steve: Before you joined the Sheriff's Department, had you ever heard Roger Craig's name in the past?

DCSD Insider: No. I had not.

Steve: He passed away in 1975, so I believe by the time you joined the Department…

DCSD Insider: Junior was there.

Steve: Right. I think Junior joined around the same time you did.

DCSD Insider: Yes, probably.

Steve: When I met Roger Jr., I met him in Dallas. I met him on February 14, 2017. And he told me when we met, that it was thirty-nine years to the day, that he was sworn in.

DCSD Insider: Oh, wow.

Steve: So, it would have been 1978 that he became a Dallas County deputy sheriff.

DCSD Insider: I don't think I ever met Roger Sr., maybe I did, but I do remember Roger Jr. coming in. I think he might have come in to pick up some booking papers, or something, but I really don't remember what it was. And he was talking about his dad, and some of the things that his daddy had done. And it was shortly after that, I can't give you a timeframe, but I came into work one day, and the sergeants were in there talking, and there were some other personnel in there, that actually knew Roger Jr., and they were saying, "Did you hear about Roger's dad?" And I just stopped, and my little ears went up, and they were talking about his dad killing himself. And I said, "Oh that's horrible." And they said, "Yes it was." And it was a general thing, and a sad fact, that some police officers do that. And in that room, at that time, it was believed that he probably had committed suicide. And then another time, Junior came in the radio room, and it had to have been a couple of years later, I can't remember exactly when, but somebody was talking about his dad, and what a good man he was, and someone asked, "Why would he do that?" And Junior just looked at him and said, "My dad didn't kill himself." And then he went on to explain some of the discrepancies about

1978 - Roger Dean Craig Jr., while out on patrol in Sunnyvale, Texas.

DCSD Insider: the crime scene. And he said, "Other than the fact that my daddy would never, ever have killed himself," he said, "There were marks on his body. And there's no way, with the weapon that was used, there's no way he killed himself, the way they said he did." Then he said, "He was murdered."

Steve: Yeah, the conversations I've had with him, he stands by that. He had access to the original autopsy report, and police report, and when he went to pick his father up from the morgue, he saw his dad's body, and it had marks on the wrists, like he'd possibly been handcuffed, or had his hands tied up. And he had markings on his knees, like he had possibly been forced down onto his knees. The trajectory of the bullet appeared to be from a slightly downward angle, without hitting his heart. The bullet entrance was up high, at the right top portion of the chest, just below his clavicle and first rib. And I believe the report that I read, also said the cause of death was due to a severed artery, and he bled out. And he was found in the middle of the room on the floor lying face-down, and the rifle he supposedly shot himself with was a .22, that was found lying longways on the bed.

DCSD Insider: To have shot yourself like that, you would have to have been a Houdini. And when Junior was talking about it, to me it sounded like it was an execution style killing.

Steve: There was reportedly a suicide note. But what I found out from Roger Jr., it was written on a card, like a Christmas card, or some kind of a greeting card.

DCSD Insider: I remember him saying that.

Steve: He said he thinks the note his dad wrote on that card, was something that he wrote to his children, when he was going through a divorce with his wife Molly. And he wrote stuff in it, like he can't take the pain, or words to that effect. And then it was put into an envelope, and then into a drawer of a dresser or desk, where other cards were found. And so, Roger thinks that when the police came and investigated the scene, they pulled a stack of cards from that drawer, and they determined that was the suicide note. And maybe it was what Roger thinks it was. And maybe it's not. But I don't think it was a suicide note written by Roger on that day, unless he was forced to write it. There are just too many inconsistencies that I've found, for me to believe Roger took his own life that day.

DCSD Insider: Some of the people that law enforcement deal with, sometimes it can be overwhelming. And I have known officers that have committed suicide. But they did it with their service revolver, and put it in their mouth, and did it that way. And I believe if he had indeed committed suicide, and this is just my opinion, that would have been the only logical way he would have done it. And certainly not with a .22 rifle.

Steve: Yeah, I agree with you. And especially not from that angle. And not aiming at any of his vital organs. Yeah, it just doesn't make sense.

DCSD Insider: That last time I saw Junior when he came into the radio room, there was a look in his eyes. You could see the hurt in his eyes.

Roger Craig Jr., at the 6th Annual J.F.K. Assassination Conference in Dallas, Texas, held in November of 2018.
(Photo courtesy of Peter Hymans)

Steve: Yeah, even to this day, it's still very fresh with him. The first phone call I made to him, it was in 2017, and he hung up on me. I had told him a little bit about my interest in his dad's story, and how I would like to discuss it with him, and before I could get five seconds out, he said, "Not interested," and hung up the phone.

DCSD Insider: Maybe, because he'd been living with the pain of that memory for so long.

Steve: Oh yes. Of course.

DCSD Insider: And maybe he didn't want to reopen that scar.

Steve: Yeah, and I don't blame him.

DCSD Insider: I don't either.

Steve: As you know, I lost my father in 2012, to what was ruled a suicide, and I know how painful talking about it can be at times, and thinking about all of that stuff again. But I called him right back, and said, "Please sir, just hear what I have to say, and decide from there if you want to talk about it with me." And then he said, "You know what, Steve? I have been thinking a lot about my father lately." And then, we had a pretty decent conversation. And at that point, he started opening up to me. So, I flew to Dallas to meet with him about a week later, to discuss his father's story in person some more, and about a movie project that I wanted to develop about his father. And during our meeting, he gave me his blessing. And we're still friends to this day. At that point, after getting Roger's consent, I held some meetings with a professional filmmaker, and screenwriter named Stephen C. Sepher, to write the script with me, along with our co-producer and mutual friend, Frank Lyon, who first introduced me to Stephen a few months before I met Roger. And when I first approached him with the idea to make a film centered around the assassination, Stephen told me he was a big fan of the 1973 film *Executive Action*, a conspiracy film about the assassination, starring Burt Lancaster, and written by Dalton Trumbo.

Artwork from original *Executive Action* lobby card.
(Courtesy of Chris Gallop)

Steve Cameron & Frank Lyon, 2017 ARPA International Film Festival.

Steve: And so, I gave Stephen all the information I had about Roger Craig, and he became very excited to write about his story. He also wrote and produced a film called *Heist* a couple years back, that starred Robert De Niro, Jeffrey Dean Morgan, and David Bautista from *Guardians of the Galaxy*. And Heist dealt with underworld mob figures, and police corruption. And so, after I watched it, I knew Stephen C. Sepher was the right person for this project. So, we partnered up to develop Roger Craig's story into a film script, that we've named *The Deputy*. And he did a fabulous job with it.

DCSD Insider: That's great!

Steve: Thanks. Okay, well I think we can stop the interview at this point, unless there's anything else you'd like to add?

DCSD Insider: Well, at the time the president was assassinated, my mother was working for a dress manufacturer called "Jennifer Juniors," which was in the building directly across Houston Street, from the Texas School Book Depository. Her boss was a gentleman named Abraham Zapruder.

Steve: Oh, no kidding?

DCSD Insider: Yes. And she said he was one of the nicest, and sweetest men. She said that he was the nicest person she ever worked for. And he came in early that morning, and called everyone who worked there together, and he said, "We're not going to work this morning. I want you all to do whatever you need to do, but this is probably going to be your only chance to see a living president." And he said, "You just find you a place where you can have a good view, of all that's going to go on." And Mother said most of the people went down there. But my mother and two of her friends stayed upstairs. I think it was on the fifth floor. And they opened the windows, so they could smoke up there, while watching the motorcade go by.

Steve: It was probably a good view.

DCSD Insider: It was. It really was a good view. And she said, when they turned the corner, she said that Jackie was so pretty, and she said the President was so handsome. And she said, "We heard a pop, pop, but we thought it was the motorcycles backfiring." And she said, "Then we saw the back of Kennedy's head being blown off."

Steve: Which would indicate a shot from the front.

DCSD Insider: Yes. And she said then the motorcycle cops dropped their bikes and ran toward the grassy knoll.

Steve: Which was located to the front and to the right of Kennedy's limo.

DCSD Insider: Yes. And she said they just stood there in that window in disbelief and just watched. But she said about fifteen minutes later, she went back down to her floor, and there she heard a noise. Her work station was all the way across the room. You could see all the way across that room. And she said there was a man walking towards her, and he walked right past her work table. And she swore, until the day she died, that it was Lee Harvey Oswald. And she said she locked eyes with him, and he walked all the way back, to the back of her floor in the building, and then he took the freight elevator down.

Steve: And this would have been the building that Zapruder worked out of? The Dal-Tex Building I believe?

DCSD Insider: Yes. It was. She said she watched him get in the elevator and go down. She said, "I don't know what happened to him, or who he was at that time?" But she said, "It chilled me to the bone." And we talked about it, off and on over the years, and I said, "You know what? It would be nice, since you were an eyewitness to all of this, if you would write down what you saw, what your reactions to it were, and how it affected you and the people around you." And she looked and me and said, "What, do you think I'm stupid?" And I said, "Well, no." And she said, "Look, I would like to live to see my grand children grow up." And she said, "You've got to stop and think. Everyone who's talked, or been vocal about what happened that day, is dead." And she said, "I will talk to you, but I will not talk to anybody else."

Steve: Yeah, there's a list. I think it's over a hundred people, last I checked, that had very close ties to this, whether they saw something, or had information, or were scheduled to testify, who died under very mysterious circumstances, including Roger Craig. But, let's go back to the fifth floor, that your mom and her friends were looking out of. If there would have been proper security that day, there would have been no one allowed to be in those open windows. And about fifteen minutes after the shots, she said that she saw somebody that looked like Oswald walk right past her? Yeah, maybe. It's possible. But there were also lookalikes involved.

DCSD Insider: Yeah, I was getting ready to run that through my mouth.

Steve: So, possibly it was one of Oswald's lookalikes. And I believe they were being used to frame him, like going to gun ranges, and creating incidents, so people would remember him, like shooting at other people's targets, and getting into arguments with people at the range. So, I think there were definitely lookalikes being used to set him up along the way.

DCSD Insider: Yeah.

Steve: Okay, thank you for sharing that story, and for agreeing to do this interview. We'll go ahead and end it here, if that's okay?

DCSD Insider: Yes. That's fine. And you're very welcome.

"I have been asked to lie. I have been told to say nothing... I have not changed nor will I change. I have to live with myself and this is most important to me."

-Roger Dean Craig

Dennie Darnell Wood

Steve Cameron: Can you please state your name?

Dennie Darnell Wood: Lena Darnell Wood.

Steve: And your friends call you Dennie?

Dennie: Yes.

Steve: Then I'll call you Dennie throughout the interview, if that's okay?

Dennie: That's fine.

Steve: And if you have any questions, or want to cut me off, just ask. And if there's any questions that I forgot to ask you, I'll give you some time at the end to add anything that you think might be important.

Dennie: Okay.

Steve: First off, can you tell me a little about yourself?

Dennie: I'm from Colman Oklahoma. And I switched off from Coleman to Dallas. I'd say a quarter of my life was spent in Dallas, and the rest in Oklahoma. When I got married, my husband and I moved from Oklahoma to live with his daddy in Dallas, Texas.

Steve: And who was your husband?

Dennie: Donald Wood. He was Roger Craig's half-brother.

Steve: Okay. Was Donald blood related to Dwyane, one of Roger's other brothers?

Dennie: Yes.

Steve: So, Donald was his half-brother as well?

Dennie: Yes. He was a half-brother to all three Craig boys.

Steve: And how did you and Donald meet?

Dennie: Before we got married, I lived with my dad in Dallas, Texas. My dad worked as a mechanic for a car dealership. And my husband had bought a car there. And his ex-wife worked there as a secretary and would bring their daughter there. And he would come and pick his daughter up, or make his car payments. And I was always walking over to the car lot to talk to daddy, and I met Donald when he was at the car lot one day.

Dennie & her husband, Donald Wood (Courtesy of Ernie Wood).

Steve: And this was in Dallas?

Dennie: In Dallas, yes.

Steve: Do you recall what year that was?

Dennie: In 1974. And we got married March 14, 1975.

Steve: Before you got married, do you remember the first time you met Donald's brother Roger?

Dennie: Yes, I do. We had pulled up in front of his daddy's house, and Don went in to pick up some stuff that he had bought for his daughter, and when he came back out to the car, Roger was with him. And it was basically Donald saying, "This is the girl I'm gonna marry. This is my brother." Just an introduction. But as far as knowing him, I didn't know him until we got married.

Steve: Was Donald Roger's older brother?

Dennie: Yes. It went from Don, to Dwyane, to Roger, and then Jimmy.

Steve: Is Donald still with us?

Dennie: No. He died in 1999.

Steve: Okay. So, when you met Roger, what were your first impressions of him?

Dennie: He seemed like a sophisticated, and knowledged person, but when I got to know him, he was very knowledged, but he wasn't sophisticated at all. Not to me. Maybe to other people, but around me he didn't act like something he wasn't.

Steve: I think during a previous conversation, you said he was funny?

Dennie: Yes, he was. And he was forever pulling tricks.

Steve: What do you mean by that?

Dennie: Well, about ten years ago, the grandkids went through this phase with playing tricks, by fixing the sprayer on the kitchen sink, so it sprays the next person who turns the water on. Well, I had already lived that in 1975. Roger had already done that to me decades ago (laughter).

Steve: So, he invented that trick (laughter).

Dennie: I don't know if he invented it or not, but he sure knew it before my grandkids knew it (laughter).

Home where Dennie Wood first met Roger Craig in 1975.
(Photo courtesy of Google Maps, Street View)

Steve: After your first encounter with Roger, did Donald kind of fill in some blanks for you, about what Roger was going through?

Dennie: Yeah. He filled in a lot, on the way to his dad's after we got married. Because after we got married, we moved in with his daddy and Roger. Donald said, "My brother is gonna say a lot of stuff, and he's gonna rant, and talk about a lot of things." And when we moved in there, Roger was talking about some stuff, and Donald said, "I don't want you to hear this, so get the phone book, and go in the bedroom to hunt for us an apartment." And then after we had lived there a while, he told me the deep and dirty of what it was all about.

Steve: And that was?

Dennie: Roger had been shot. He'd been run off of a mountain. And people were after him, because he wouldn't change his story.

Steve: And that was his story relating to the…

Dennie: The John F. Kennedy assassination. And he said he would not change his story for nobody. And he always said, "One day the truth will come out."

Steve: I don't know if you've had a chance to hear what some of his critics have come out and said…

Dennie: Oh yeah, I have. And I don't appreciate it, but there's nothing I can do about it, because I'm not the next of kin. But if I was, a lot of them would be in libel court, if they couldn't prove what they were saying.

Steve: And you were there. You looked into his eyes, when the words were coming out of his mouth when he was talking about these things.

Dennie: Yes. And I can tell when somebody's lying to me. I have a talent to be able to read people, and can tell if they're being honest and truthful. And that man said the same thing, over and over again.

Steve: If you had a chance to address some of these critics, in a civil way, what would you tell them?

Dennie: I would tell them, the truth should be told, instead of trying to cover it up. And too many people have died trying to tell the truth. And from the time we're born, were taught not to lie. So, what's so big out there, that a man has to die because he's telling the truth?

Steve: And there's no doubt in your mind that Roger was killed for that?

Dennie: I'll never believe he committed suicide. Not ever.

Steve: I'm glad you brought that up, because I would like to ask you more about that. You were one of the last people to see Roger alive, is that correct?

Dennie: Yes.

Steve: And that was on the day that he died?

Dennie: Yes. May 15, 1975. Yes, sir.

Steve: Can you please give me a little background. How did that day start, and when did you see Roger?

Dennie: Well, Don had talked to his daddy the week before. And his daddy had gathered up some things for me, from when I was keeping house. And Don said that we'd be over as soon as we had a morning free. Well, we went over there that morning to pick up some things. And Roger was sitting on the couch. And Pop asked me…

Steve: Who was Pop?

Kristel Albert Craig.
(Photo courtesy of Dennie Wood)

Dennie: Pop was Roger's father, Kristel Albert Craig. He was all of the boys' dad. Not Donald's biological dad, but he was the dad that raised Don from the time he was a baby. Anyway, we had went over there, and Pop told me he had made a fresh pot of coffee, and wanted to know if I wanted some coffee. And I told him that sounded good, and we went in there and drank coffee. And while we were in the kitchen, you could see into the living room, and Roger was sitting on the couch, fully dressed. And that's another thing I don't get, because they said they found him barefooted. Sir, that man never walked across the floor without his house shoes on.

Steve: I've heard some conflicting reports. The autopsy report that I read on the internet, said that he had on a pair of blue trousers, and was wearing jockey shorts. But when I spoke to his son, Roger Jr., he told me that when he went down to the coroners to take him to the funeral home, he read a report that said his dad was found wearing only his boxer shorts.

Dennie: And he was fully dressed when I left there. And he would never have walked across the floor barefooted, because he said the feel of dirt on the bottom of his feet creeped him out. And there was an armory across the road, and anytime that they had training or anything over there, they'd stir up dirt and it blew in the front door. Pop had a screen door, so naturally it would get on that linoleum, and living room floor. And Roger didn't like the feel of it, and he always had his shoes or house shoes on.

Steve: So, while you were there that day drinking coffee, how did the rest of the day go? What was the atmosphere like?

Dennie: It was cheery. It was normal. Everybody was laughing. I was the new kid on the block. So, they pestered a lot. And laughed a lot. Roger asked me if I'd learned how to burn water yet (laughter).

Steve: That day? Did he ask you that, that day?

Dennie: Yeah. That day. That morning. He called me Dee, and he said, "Dee, have you learned how to boil water yet, or have you learned how to burn it?" And I had been cooking for six weeks there already, so he knew I could cook. He was just pestering.

Steve: What kind of shape was Roger in? I'm guessing he was living there with Kristel to recuperate from his injuries?

Dennie: Yes. And whenever I stayed there, I helped take care of the wound on his shoulder.

Steve: So, the wound that you treated when you knew him, was that from the shotgun when he opened the door…

Dennie: Yes.

Steve: What were his thoughts about that? Did he know who did it?

Dennie: He thought the government did it to him.

Steve: He believed that it was the government?

Dennie: The C.I.A., the F.B.I., one of them.

Steve: That they sent someone to shut him up?

Dennie: Yes. And he told me they ran him off of a cliff once, when he was driving in the mountains. He said it was harry being Roger Craig. He said it was a rough life trying to be Roger Craig. He said they wanted him to be a dead Roger Craig.

A stretch of road in the Davis Mountains, located in West Texas.
(Photo courtesy of Google Maps, Street View)

Author's note: During a video-taped interview in 1974, Roger Craig tells interviewer Lincoln Carle about the incident that took place when he was forced off the road, while driving through the Davis Mountains:

Roger Craig: I took a job with a private detective agency… And we had a case to work in West Texas, in the Davis Mountains. My boss sent me out there. He called the client, who was on a three-party line, and told him what flight I was coming into Midland on, where I was going to rent my car, where I would meet him, and what time. So, I flew into Midland, and I rented the car. And I was about two miles from where I was supposed to meet the client… I was supposed to meet him at three o'clock, and it was 2:55 then. I rounded a curve, and there were two men standing outside of a car, that was parked crossways in the road. And there wasn't anything to do, but try to go around them. And I tried, and I missed. And I went over the edge of the mountain, and I rolled end over end for ninety feet or so. I broke my back in two places. I broke my left shoulder. I tore the ulnar nerve, and ligaments out of my left elbow. Crushed my left foot, and my right leg. I spent a year in the hospital. Four major surgeries. Two on my back. And I'm now totally disabled in the back, and partially disabled in the right leg, and unemployed again.

Lincoln Carle: What was this car doing there?

Craig: Blocking the road.

Carle: Who was it?

Craig: I don't know. They left. They didn't stop, they left.

Carle: Did the highway patrolman, or whoever comes to the scene of an accident that investigates this…

Craig: Well, the Sheriff's Department did, down there at Fort Davis. But they're so small, I think they got the sheriff and two deputies working the whole county.

Carle: Don't all accidents go into a state bureau or something?

Craig: Well, it went into the Texas Department of Public Safety, but it was listed as, well not as a hit and run, but they've got another phrase for it that's similar to a hit and run, but somebody got the license number. Somebody saw that car and got the license number. And I traced it to Los Angeles. And it was registered to a vacant lot.

Carle: Did you get a good look at the men?

Craig: Yes. They were Latin. I couldn't give you a good description of them, because they were on the opposite side of the car that I would have hit, had I not tried to go around them.

Carle: And you're convinced that was a setup?

Craig: Definitely, definitely.

Carle: Did you report the fact that the car was across the road?

Craig: Yes.

Carle: That was written down by someone?

Craig: Yes. The Sheriff at Fort Davis, Texas.

Carle: Okay. Certainly, that's illegal. Wouldn't the department of public safety, or someone, had followed that investigation along, because that's got to be criminal when an injury is caused.

Craig: That would be proper procedure.

Carle: Okay. Do you know whether or not the investigation ensued?

Craig: I know it didn't ensue. I know there was a report.

Carle: Do you know why?

Craig: No, I don't know why.

Carle: Did you ask anyone why?

Craig: I was in the hospital for a year, you know.

Carle: Okay. After you were out of the hospital, or recently, have you been able to find out why? Have you been able to find out who?

Craig: No. The only reason I can give for possibly why, is well… I put this on Penn Jones Jr. He is a friend of mine, but every time that I would give him some information that he needed, or would ask me for, which I told him… Every time I told him something, something like this happened.

Dennie Wood interview continued…

Dennie: I remember about a week before he died, I was over at Pop's to spend the day, and was cooking supper for him and Roger. And we had to run to Safeway grocery store to get a couple of things. And on our way back, Roger was turning here, and was turning there. So, I asked him, "What's up?" He said, "I'm losing our tail." I laughed and said, "Well, I'm sitting on mine." And he said, "No. That dark gray car behind us, with no front tag."

Steve: What happened?

Dennie: We lost it. But it spooked me a little bit.

Steve: So, the last day that you saw him he seemed to be in a good mood, and in good spirits? In a previous conversation we had, you told me that he had made plans to go to Oklahoma?

Dennie: We was coming up here to go fishing. That was one of the biggest plans we had made. That morning he asked, "Have you and Donald decided what day we're going to Oklahoma?" And Don told him, "I haven't got a schedule yet, but as soon as I get a schedule, I'll let you know."

Steve: One thing that Roger Jr. told me, was that his dad had reregistered his driver's license three days earlier, on May 12th, because that was his birthday.

Dennie: That's right.

Steve: And Roger Jr. thought that was very strange, because who does that if they're gonna kill themselves?

Dennie: Well, Don asked him, "Are you gonna get an out of state fishing license, or are you just gonna try not to get caught?" And Roger said, "No I'd rather be legal. I don't want to get a ticket as long as my short arm," and made a funny out of that, that morning. And he told Don that he got his fishing license, when he got his driver's license renewed.

Steve: Were you aware of Roger ever using narcotics, or alcohol, or if he ever did drink alcohol, was it to excess?

Dennie: I lived there six weeks, and I never seen the man drunk. But I did see him drink now and again. But he didn't do it in the morning. He didn't do it at lunch. He'd do it in the evening. And that's another thing I didn't like, because I've heard people say he was a drunk. He wasn't.

Steve: And I'm guessing Roger was in some pain from his injuries, so anything he was taking was probably for pain relief.

Dennie: That's the only thing I knew of. Usually he took what they called Bufferin back then. He had bottle of Bufferin sitting on the kitchen table. One day I remember telling him, "You don't need to take too many of them." And he said, "I've only had two today." And he had to be tough, because he didn't take a bunch of drugs.

Steve: So, to the best of your knowledge, you never saw him taking prescription pills?

Dennie: I don't remember that he did, but he could have. But I do know that he took Bufferin.

Steve: Okay. So, the last day that you saw him alive, when you left there, everything seemed normal? Did anything seem strange?

Dennie: It was just like any other day I had seen him.

Steve: Do you recall what time you left the house?

Dennie: It was around ten in the morning. We got over there early that day.

Steve: And about how long were you there?

Dennie: I'd say maybe an hour and a half. Not more than that.

Steve: Can you please tell me how you heard about Roger's death?

Dennie: His daddy and Jimmy, his brother, came over to our apartment about two or three. I really can't remember what time, because that day was horrible. And Pop told my husband, he said, "Donald, they got him." And then all three of them broke down and was crying. Because we all knew what that meant. Because Roger talked about how they're not gonna leave him alone until they get him.

Steve: Did Kristel tell you the circumstances about what happened?

Dennie: He said he was outside working on the lawnmower. And when he went outside to do that, Roger was doing just fine. I think he said he was watching a game show, or something on T.V. And he walked outside to go work on the lawn mower in the backyard. And he said when he came back in, he found him.

Steve: Did he give you an idea of how much time had passed, from the last time that he saw him?

Dennie: About thirty minutes.

Steve: So maybe between a half hour and an hour?

Dennie: Yeah. Pop was very, very hard of hearing.

Steve: Can you explain that?

Dennie: Well, he said that he had the lawnmower going, and he said he didn't hear no gun. He didn't hear nothing. He said, "I could barely hear the lawnmower running," and he said, "Then I went in the house and I found my son." And he had a very hard time. It's like we all knew it, but we didn't want it.

Steve: Did you attend Roger's funeral?

Dennie: Yes. Yes, I did.

Steve: So, after the funeral, was everyone in the family pretty much convinced that he was killed, because of the J.F.K. assassination, that it was related to that?

Dennie: Everybody. Even Molly, and they were divorced at the time.

Steve: At the time of Roger's death, was he seeing anyone?

Dennie: Nope.

Steve: So, he wasn't involved with a woman?

Dennie: If he was, he hid it well.

Steve: While you knew him, he was recuperating from a shotgun wound. Was he able to walk?

Dennie: Yeah. He could walk. It was his shoulder that got blew away. And his back hurt him all the time. But he could still walk. A funny story. When me and Don were living there, you had to walk through our room to get to the bathroom. So, Roger went somewhere and got himself a cowbell, and he would ring the cowbell when starting through the bedroom.

Steve: As a courtesy?

Dennie: Yeah. And when we moved out, Roger moved in that room. And that was the room he died in.

Steve: Did Roger have the same bed that you had, after you moved out?

Dennie: Yep.

Steve: The reason I ask, is because when Roger Jr. described the scene of his father's death, he said his dad was found face-down, in the middle of the room, and the gun, that I believe was used to kill him, was found lying longways on the bed.

Dennie: Well, the man wasn't suicidal the day I left there. No how, no way.

Steve: Did you ever see a rifle in that house, at any time?

Dennie: Nope. Well, I did after Roger died. Because Pop acquired one for protection. It was a J.C. Higgins twelve gauge.

Steve: What did Pop say about the rifle that was found on the bed, in the room where his son's body was found?

Dennie: He had told us a hundred times, that wasn't Roger's gun.

Steve: So, as far as he was concerned, that weapon had never been in the house before the day that Roger died?

Dennie: That's right. He said, "D, I don't know where that gun come from."

Steve: You mentioned earlier, that Kristel was hard of hearing.

Dennie: Yes. They had a thing with a lightbulb at the back door. And if Pop had a phone call, or if anyone needed Pop, they'd turn the light on. Pop said the light didn't get turned on that day at all.

Steve: And the light could be seen during the daytime?

Dennie: Yes. I've seen it before.

Steve: So, that was a signal for him, because he couldn't hear the phone while he was outside, or if someone was calling for him?

Dennie: Yes.

Roger: And so, Roger never signaled for him. That light never came on?

Dennie: No, that light never came on. And that was hard on his daddy. Because, he said, "If Roger could have done anything, he would have turned that light on." And he said, "I could have maybe scared them off." Years later, he told me and Don, that he had Jimmy go in the house, and shoot the same kind of gun while he was in the back yard with the mower going. And he said, "Dennie, I didn't hear it the way you hear it, but I heard a thump." He said, "I believe I should have heard that gun." I don't know anything about silencers, but Pop thought that whoever done it used a silencer. Some way of silencing the gun.

Steve: If it's okay, I'd like to switch gears a little. When Roger was about fifteen, he ran away from home and joined the Army, and he used his brother's name to join, because he wasn't old enough.

Dennie: He used Don's name. My husband.

Steve: Can you tell me that story?

Dennie: He left home and joined the military when he was about fifteen, and he joined under Don's name. Because Don was born in 1932, and that made Roger old enough to not have to have his parent's signature, so he joined the military as Donald Lee Wood. Well, when Don got his papers after they drafted him, and he done his basic over at Fort Leonard Wood, and they got to checking records, they found out they had two Donald Lee Woods, with the same address, the same phone number, the same social security number, and birthday and everything. And so, they pulled them both up, and they were within a mile of each other in Korea, which was a miracle. And Don said when he got his leg broke over there, he was at the infirmary, and he looked out the window, and looked up the road, and here comes his brother. Don said, "Dennie, I was so tickled to see Roger." Then he said Roger said, "Don't get too used to me. They're sending me home." And Don said, "Why? You're not hurt." And Roger told him, "Because, they can only put up with one Donald Lee Wood in the military."

Author's note: The following records are Roger Craig's original military enlistment papers from 1952, when he used his older brother Donald's name and information to join the Army at the age of fifteen. After Roger was caught, Donald's name was crossed out, and "Craig, Roger" was written in place of it:

(Records courtesy of Roger Craig's granddaughter, Nita Edwards)

Steve: Where did the military send Roger after that?

Dennie: They sent him back to his mommy and daddy, but he didn't stay long. He left again. I don't know where he went, and I don't know much about that story.

Steve: I talked to Roger Jr., and he told me that once his father was of legal age, he was drafted into the military under his own name, and sent to Korea.

Roger Craig's military induction papers, dated October 9, 1953.
(Courtesy of Nita Edwards)

Dennie: Yeah, he did. And they wound up over there together again. And that don't happen to brother's every day.

Steve: I believe there was a time when Roger was captured by the enemy, and he spent time as a P.O.W.

Dennie: Yes. And he broke free.

Steve: After Roger left the military, he went to live in Texas with his family. How did Kristel and Roger's mother end up in Texas?

Dennie: I think it was because his uncle Earl and aunt Reba, which was Roger's momma's brother and his wife, and they lived in Dallas. And Uncle Earl told Pop that they had a metallurgy place down there calling his name. So, Pop went to work to a big steel plant down there.

Steve: Where was Donald born?

Dennie: He was born in Wisconsin.

Steve: And how did he end up in Texas?

Dennie: He went with his mom and daddy.

Steve: And at some point, Roger ended up down there with them.

Dennie: Yes.

Steve: Well, I don't have any more questions for you at this time, Dennie. But I would like to give you an opportunity to add anything if you'd like? Any final thoughts that you might have. Anything you might want to add that we didn't touch?

Dennie: Well, Roger told me that, in about twenty-five to fifty years, they will find the truth about everything. And I also want to say, that man did not kill himself. He knew things that they didn't want him to tell, and they wanted nobody else to tell. And the gun was Roger's biggest issue, because they traded the gun. He was in the school book depository, and he knew what gun was found. And it wasn't the one they say Oswald shot the President with. And the deal about Tippit. I want to tell you what he said about Tippit.

Steve: Oh, what was that?

Dennie: Roger walked into a room down at the police station, and overheard them talking about, "Blame it on Oswald. That's the only way we can tie him to being the one who shot Kennedy." Have you heard that before?

Steve: No, I have not. Was this before or after Lee Harvey Oswald had been killed by Jack Ruby?

Dennie: He heard it before, because it was the day they went to the movie theater and got him. He said the radio was going in the background, and it said, "Blame Oswald for killing Tippit."

Steve: Do you know who was saying this?

Dennie: He said it was a bunch of shirts in there. That's what he called them.

Steve: Shirts?

Dennie: Yeah. At the police station. Talking to the head of police.

Steve: Well, it was probably Captain Fritz I would imagine.

Dennie: That's it! That's the name right there.

Steve: Now, when Roger said, "shirts," did he mean feds?

Dennie: Yeah. The feds was talking to Fritz. He didn't say F.B.I., or C.I.A. He said, "shirts." And everybody knew back then, that's what you called the feds.

Steve: Well, I think that's a good place to end the interview.

Dennie: I hope I helped you.

Steve: You did, Dennie. Thank you.

"As for the attempts on my life, I don't know who's behind it. I was shot at in 1967. In 1970 my car was blown up. In 1971 I was run off a mountain road in West Texas… so I have suffered somewhat. And to top it off, my wife left me in 1973. And when I do think I'm getting it together; someone blows my left shoulder off with a shotgun."

-Roger Dean Craig

Robert Groden
(Photo courtesy of Janet Boschock Groden)

Steve Cameron: Hello Robert.

Robert Groden: Hi Steve. How are you doing?

Steve: I'm doing well. For the readers, can you tell me a little bit about yourself?

Robert: Well, my involvement in the Kennedy case began in 1975, when I was given the responsibility of releasing the films of the assassination to the public for the first time on a television show called *Good Night America*, the first national broadcast ever of the Zapruder film. It was Geraldo Rivera's show, back when Geraldo had credibility. And it changed the history of the case, fortunately. It was seen by a lot of people, and it opened a lot of doors. I was then asked to present the photographic and film evidence at various colleges and other venues. As a result of that I was invited to Washington to present the evidence before the House of Representatives.

Geraldo Rivera and Robert Groden backstage during a 1991 taping of
The Geraldo Rivera Show.
(Photo courtesy of Robert Groden)

Robert: And then to my absolute amazement, Congressman Thomas Downing of Virginia introduced legislation just days later to reopen the case, and eventually it passed. And he asked me if I would be willing to be the staff's photographic consultant to the House Assassination Committee. I agreed. And for the next three years, that's what I did. I worked for them. I analyzed films, and photographs. And that's what led to where we are now. The House Assassinations Committee reports that there was a ninety-five percent certainty, a conspiracy to kill the president. And has since been peer-reviewed and found to be ninety-eight percent or greater. And through my publicity with all of that, I got to meet various people who were involved with the case, like Penn Jones Jr., Gary Shaw, Larry Harris. And I worked with them on various issues with the case. And Penn Jones had arranged for me to meet with Roger Craig in May of 1975. And my wife and I were flying down to Dallas to meet with Roger and do some other stuff as well, but the big excitement was to meet Roger. And when the plane landed, we were met by Penn, Gary, and Larry, and we got the news that Roger had deceased.

J.F.K. assassination researcher & author, Penn Jones Jr.
(Forgive My Grief, a four-volume work, 1967-1974. The Continuing Inquiry
newsletter, 1976-1984. Disappearing Witnesses, The Rebel magazine, 1983-1984)

Robert: I've never believed it was suicide. I've never believed it was an accident. But it was so shocking, I couldn't really think of all of that at the time. And then we drove to the funeral home. Roger's wife Molly was there. We found out they were pretty bad off financially, and couldn't really afford to have a decent funeral. So, my wife and I paid fifty dollars toward the funeral, for a man I never met. All I can say is that it's a very sad situation. I wish I had gotten to meet him. And that he had a better, simpler, happier life at the end. A man I admired for his honesty and his courage.

Steve: Do you believe Roger would have been called as a witness to the hearings?

Robert: Oh yeah. Absolutely.

Steve: And that's one of the reasons why you were there to interview him?

Robert: When I went to interview him, it was before the House Committee had been formed yet. We had done the Geraldo show, and the presentations, but the House Committee took a while to form. At the time Thomas Downing introduced legislation, there was another legislation being introduced by Henry González of Texas. And both of those were trying to get passed, but it took years to be finalized.

Thomas H. Downing, Virginia Congressman and Former Chairman of the House Select Committee on Assassinations: "I am sincerely convinced, that more than one person was shooting at President Kennedy in Dallas that day. It is so obvious to me."

Texas Congressman and Former Chairman of the House Select Committee on Assassinations, Henry B. González.

Author's note: Congressman Henry González was seated in the fifth car of President Kennedy's motorcade during the assassination in 1963. In 1976, González joined Congressman Downing's campaign to create a 12-member congressional committee to reinvestigate the assassinations of John F. Kennedy and Martin Luther King.

Interview continued…

Steve: But it was in the air, that there were some investigations that were going to be reopened at the time of Roger's death?

Robert: Yeah. The plans were being made to try to get the House of Representatives to vote on getting the case reopened. But that had not yet happened. One of the people who was involved in this was Tip O'Neill, who I met with in Tom Downing's office for several hours.

Steve: Did you show the Zapruder film to Tip O'Neill?

Robert: Oh yes, absolutely.

Steve: Was that the first time he saw it?

Robert: Yes. The first time he ever saw it.

Steve: What was his reaction?

Robert: His reaction was, "Why weren't we allowed to see this before now?" He was shocked. And he became an immediate supporter of trying to get the case reopened. And that was a good thing. It helped tremendously. He wasn't the only one. But he was the one with the most credibility. The most standing, as it were.

Former Speaker of the House, Tip O'Neill.

Steve: So, leading up to Roger's death, it was definitely in the works that they were going to be reopening the J.F.K. assassination?

Robert: They were going to try, yes. Nothing was definite until it actually happened.

Steve: Right. And a lot of other people died mysteriously leading up to that as well.

Robert: Oh Yeah, quite a few. Quite a few.

Steve: Does one stand out in your mind more than others?

Robert: Of deaths? Lee Bowers, who actually witnessed the assassination and saw the shooting. Dorothy Kilgallen, the only reporter to ever interview Jack Ruby from the time he shot Oswald, until the time he himself died. Those are two of the most famous, but there are literally dozens of them.

Steve: Sam Giancana, not too long after Roger Craig. And Johnny Roselli.

Robert: Yeah, they were both murdered. They knew a lot. They were being subpoenaed to talk before the House Committee, and the Senate Intelligence Committee hearings. And they were silenced so they couldn't talk.

Journalist Dorothy Kilgallen, Chicago Mafia Boss Sam Giancana (center), & influential mobster for the Chicago Outfit Johnny Roselli.

Steve: Do you believe Roger would have been one of the witnesses who would have been called?

Robert: Oh yeah. He would have to have been. The Warren Commission would avoid him like the plague. But the House Committee really wanted to find the truth. At least initially they did.

Steve: Do you believe Roger Craig was killed because of what he knew?

Robert: Absolutely. I'm absolutely convinced of it. And I've always had in the back of my mind the sadness, that perhaps my coming down to interview him may have had something to do with it. It's probably not so, but it's impossible for me to avoid the possibility.

Steve: When you met Penn Jones at the airport, was that the first time you had ever met Penn?

Robert: Oh no. I met him before. We had been friends for quite a while. We had spoken on the phone a lot. Going back a couple of years. Penn was documenting all the, you can call them strange deaths. Convenient deaths. However. And Roger was certainly one of them. I even remember calling Penn, when Sal Mineo the actor was killed. What I found out, Sal Mineo was going to be producing and starring in a film about the assassination of Robert Kennedy. So, the thought crossed my mind, that maybe he was killed because of that.

Author's note: The following is a Press Release from the New York Times, published in 1975 about Academy Award nominated actor, Sal Mineo's upcoming portrayal of Robert Kennedy's assassin, Sirhan Bishara Sirhan, in a film that promised to cast doubt on Sirhan's guilt:

Despite internecine struggles between competing assassinologists, a projected film starring **Sal Mineo** as **Sirhan Sirhan** is scheduled to begin filming this summer. The script has already been written by Donald Freed, who coauthored the novel version of *Executive Action* with Mark Lane, and it similarly constructs a possible conspiracy. Freed further vows that unlike *Executive Action*, which explored the assassination of John F. Kennedy with great box-office success but no political effect, the release of *Sirhan Sirhan* will be keyed to a renewed investigation of the case.

News of the planned motion picture led John G. Christian, another assassination buff, to talk Mrs. Mary Sirhan into dismissing her son's lawyer, Roger Hanson, on the ground that he had no right to discuss a film with Freed. Both Hanson and Freed deny any collaboration on the film; in fact, Hanson claims to have had similar conversations with Christian in the past. "Mrs. Sirhan was very upset," Freed said. "She had been told her son was being exploited. But, rather than paint her son in an infamous or compromising light, the film will show that he was not guilty of the death of Senator Kennedy."

Sal Mineo and Sirhan Sirhan : conspiring to commit art

In his 2010 book *Sal Mineo: A Biography*, author Michael Gregg Michaud quoted Mineo's feelings about the assassinations of both John Kennedy and his brother Bobby Kennedy, and about playing the role of Bobby's accused killer:

> "The Warren Commission is totally bullshit. We know it wasn't Oswald who shot the President… I mean, obviously there can't be one man shooting the president from three different angles… I campaigned for Robert Kennedy because I loved him… It was just horrible when I learned of the assassination. At first, I didn't see how I could ever portray Kennedy's killer. I had always been convinced that Sirhan was the lone gunman who killed Kennedy but now I believe there are grounds for doubt. If the film can influence the courts to reopen the case or force out new facts and answer questions, then it will serve its purpose." [Excerpts from Michaud's *Sal Mineo: A Biography*, pp. 334-335]

In the summer of 1975, Sal Mineo was interviewed about his involvement with a film about Bobby Kennedy's assassination by the St Petersburg Evening Independent newspaper, published just six months before Mineo's murder. Below are excerpts from that interview:

It's a curious acting life for Mineo, playing gun-wielding heavies on TV and likeable guys on dinner theatre stages.

He will take on perhaps his heaviest role to date in October when he begins his role as Sirhan Sirhan, the convicted assassin of Sen. Robert Kennedy, in a film of the same name.

That's a complete turn-around for Mineo, who heavily campaigned for the late senator. Mineo hasn't met Sirhan (who is still appealing his conviction, still maintaining his innocence), but will before filming starts.

"The script raises enough questions to warrant reopening the case, I think," Mineo says now, "and enough question that I'm willing to pursue the role." It's a risky role.

(….)

But he thinks the country is ready for the film "Sirhan Sirhan." The climate is ready for it, he says. "I think more people are ready to believe conspiracy since Watergate."

So Mineo, whose stage and heady film and TV credits go back nearly 25 years, who was nominated for an Academy Award for his role in James Dean's film "Rebel Without a Cause," takes on a lot of TV roles and film roles and dinner theatre roles so he can build up a bank roll for his own film.

"It's a very expensive commitment," he says of his film, "McCaffery." As co-producer, Mineo has had to pay for a scriptwriter, movie rights and pre-production costs, as well as maintain residences in New York and Los Angeles.

(….)

Yet, it is the uncertainties, the vagaries of show business that appeal to Mineo. He's a gambler.

"That's what I love about the business," he says, "not knowing. That's why I love Las Vegas. . . not knowing if my number is going to come up."

Authorities in Los Angeles would eventually charge pizza deliveryman, Lionel Williams for the stabbing-death of Sal Mineo, that occurred on February 12, 1976 during an apparent robbery spree near Mineo's home in West Hollywood. However, Mineo was not robbed, and Williams was an African-American male, which conflicted with statements from the witnesses at the scene, who described the killer as being a Caucasian with long hair. Williams was subsequently found guilty for the murder of Sal Mineo, and was sentenced to 57 years in prison.

Interview continued…

Robert: So, I called Penn to give him that information. I was also fortunate to conduct the very last interview that Penn did before he died in the 1990s. What happened was, I was doing a television show on the assassination, and the producers wanted to talk with Penn. And we were talking about the death of Lee Bowers. So, we went to talk to Penn, but by that time, unfortunately his mind had deteriorated to the point where he couldn't really deal with anything. And it took us about two hours to get thirty seconds of usable footage, sadly. He was a great man. A very brave man. Very honorable man. A personal hero of mine. And I attended his funeral.

Penn Jones pictured with Robert Groden.
(Courtesy of Robert Groden)

Steve: Lets switch gears a little bit. As far as the information that Roger Craig had, and what he had witnessed, have you studied it? I'm sure you have, so could you tell me a little about the Mauser rifle that was identified by Roger Craig, Seymour Weitzman, Eugene Boone, Captain Fritz, the people who were there on scene in the School Book Depository? Can you give me your thoughts on what you think may have happened?

Robert: The fact that you know those names tells me you're very well aware of what I think (laughter). The first rifle that was found up there was a Mauser, and Roger was there and he identified it as such, as did all the others. That was either replaced, or morphed into a Mannlicher-Carcano. Different caliber. The Mannlicher-Carcano would have been a 6.5. The Mauser was a 7.65. Different ammunition. Different rifle.

Steve: Correct. And the weapon seen being escorted from the Texas School Book Depository by Lieutenant Day, that weapon had side sling mounts on it. And the backyard photo that we think is Lee Harvey Oswald holding a rifle, that rifle had bottom sling mounts. And the catalog that he ordered from also had bottom sling mounts.

Robert: There are a lot of questions dealing with that. And they're all legitimate questions. But through the years, a lot of that's become very, very foggy. There clearly was more than one weapon, that's for sure. There was a film taken on the sixth floor of the Depository by Tom Alyea, and one of the scenes on that film has the rifle that we're talking about, one way or the other, is being examined, and there's another rifle lying up against boxes right there next to it. So, I think there was actually more than one rifle up there, and found to be more than one up there. Also, on the roof of the Depository was a British Enfield .303, a totally different weapon. I was able to come across a couple of pictures that are in my latest book *JFK Absolute Proof.* One showing the rifle being examined on Houston Street, by the police, detectives, bystanders, what have you. And another thing I found was a film showing the fire escape on the east side of the book depository. Put two and two together, you've got the fire escape coming down, where the rifle was passed and brought down to the street, and then being examined, and then kind of disappeared. Talk about a magic bullet. We're talking about a magic rifle here, too.

Robert Groden (left), and Gaeton Fonzi (right) during a rifle comparison presentation, while working as staff members for the House Select Committee on Assassinations during the late 1970s.

"Although Garrison's investigation was ridiculed and derided by the media, termed a farce and a fraud, it was later discovered that the C.I.A. maintained an intense interest in its progress and direction… Director Richard Helms ordered that the Agency provide all the help Clay Shaw needed to fight Garrison's case against him. And as a staff investigator for the House Select Committee on Assassinations, I was shocked to learn that the C.I.A. had infiltrated almost a dozen covert operatives into Garrison's staff of investigators. So, Garrison was not only attacked from the outside, but also subverted from within."

— Investigative journalist and author, Gaeton Fonzi.

Steve: Yeah, that's something that's used against Roger Craig at times. He did a newspaper interview in the late '60s, with the Los Angeles Times I believe, and he talked about the rifle that was found on the roof. And then his detractors and critics came out of the woodwork, saying things like, "He changed his story! He's a liar! First, he said there was a rifle found on the roof, and now he's saying there was a Mauser found on the sixth floor!" For all anyone knows Roger Craig could have been misquoted in that article, or purposely misquoted in an effort to damage his credibility. Or maybe he was just confused by the question asked by the person interviewing him? Who knows. But the critics never seem to criticize people like Seymour Witzeman, who changed his story about identifying the rifle on the sixth-floor as a 7.65 Mauser, even though he signed a sworn affidavit that he did.

Robert: Yeah, the other side has always fought back with anything we had.

Former Dallas Deputy Constable, Seymour Weitzman.

Author's note: Deputy Constable Seymour Weitzman signed a sworn affidavit the day after the assassination on November 23, 1963. In it, he describes in-depth how he personally identified the rifle as a 7.65 Mauser, after it was found on the sixth-floor of the Texas School Book Depository:

AFFIDAVIT IN ANY FACT

THE STATE OF TEXAS

COUNTY OF DALLAS

BEFORE ME, _______ Mary Rattan

a Notary Public in and for said County, State of Texas, on this day personally appeared ______
Seymour Weitzman w/m, 2802 Oatés Drive, DA7 6624. Bus. Robie Love, RJ1 1483

Who, after being by me duly sworn, on oath deposes and says: Yesterday November 22, 1963 I was standing on the corner of Main and Houston, and as the President passed and made his turn going west towards Stemmons, I walked casually around. At this time my partner was behind me and asked me something. I looked back at him and heard 3 shots. I ran in a northwest direction and scaled a fence towards where we thought the shots came from. Then someone said they thought the shots came from the old Texas Building. I immediately ran to the Texas Building and started looking inside. At this time Captain Fritz arrived and ordered all of the sixth floor sealed off and searched. I was working with Deputy S. Boone of the Sheriff's Department and helping in the search. We were in the northwest corner of the sixth floor when Deputy Boone and myself spotted the rifle about the same time. This rifle was a 7.65 Mauser bolt action equipped with a 4/18 scope, a thick leather brownish-black sling on it. The rifle was between some boxes near the stairway. The time the rifle was found was 1:22 pm. Captain Fritz took charge of the rifle and ejected one live round from the chamber. I then went back to the office after this.

Seymour Weitzman

In Weitzman's affidavit, he clearly states, "This rifle was a 7.65 Mauser." However, during his deposition to the Warren Commission on April 1, 1964, and after Weitzman is asked by assistant council Joseph A. Ball about his identification of the weapon, Weitzman backpedals from his previous affidavit and claims that he only glanced at the weapon before making his identification:

> Mr. BALL – In the statement that you made to the Dallas Police Department that afternoon, you referred to the rifle as a 7.65 Mauser bolt action?
>
> Mr. WEITZMAN – In a glance, that's what it looked like.
>
> Mr. BALL – That's what it looked like did you say that or someone else say that?
>
> Mr. WEITZMAN – No; I said that. I thought it was one.
>
> Mr. BALL – Are you fairly familiar with rifles?
>
> Mr. WEITZMAN – Fairly familiar because I was in the sporting goods business awhile.

This is very curious, because nowhere in his sworn affidavit did Weitzman say, "I think it was a Mauser." And nowhere does he say, "From at a glance it looked like a Mauser." No. Instead, Weitzman clearly states, "This rifle was a 7.65 Mauser."

Furthermore, below are two excerpts from a November 23, 1963 F.B.I. report describing Weitzman's identification of the rifle being a 7.65 Mauser after he examined it in great detail:

FEDERAL BUREAU OF INVESTIGATION

Date _______11/23/63_______

NOV 30 1963

Mr. SEYMOUR WEITZMAN, Deputy Constable, Dallas County Constable's Office, was interviewed in the presence of Detective C. W. BROWN, Homicide Bureau, Dallas Police Department. He furnished the following information:

At about 12:15 p.m., November 22, 1963, he was assigned to observe the route of President JOHN F. KENNEDY's motorcade through downtown Dallas, Texas. His station was located on the corner of Main and Houston Streets, next to the courthouse, in Dallas. He observed the car in which President KENNEDY was riding to travel north on Houston Street and turn west on Elm Street. Shortly after the President's car turned the corner

Mr. WEITZMAN described the rifle which was found as a 7.65 caliber Mauser bolt-action rifle, which loads from a five shot clip which is locked on the underside of the receiver forward of the trigger guard. The metal parts of this rifle were of a gun metal color, gray or blue, and the rear portion of the bolt was visibly worn. The wooden portions of this rifle were a dark brown in color and of rough wood, apparently having been used or damaged to considerable extent. This rifle was equipped with a four-power 18 scope of apparent Japanese manufacture. It was also equipped with a thick brown-black leather bandolier type sling.

After he had observed this rifle to the extent described above, Captain FRITZ appeared and took the rifle from him. He did not make note of any serial number on the rifle. He observed Captain FRITZ eject one rifle round of ammunition from this rifle. At this point, he discontinued his search of the sixth floor of the building and thereafter became engaged in regular patrol work in connection with investigation being conducted by law enforcement officers from all law enforcement agencies in Dallas County.

In his groundbreaking book *Rush to Judgment*, first published in 1966, attorney and author Mark Lane documents his 1964 testimony before the Warren Commission and how the 7.65 Mauser was cunningly changed to a 6.5 Italian rifle. In it, Lane writes:

"Although the FBI reported on November 23 that Oswald owned a rifle, it was not similar to the one reportedly found on the Book Depository sixth floor. According to the FBI, the rifle Oswald had purchased was a Mannlicher-Carcano 6.5 Italian carbine.... When I first appeared before the Commission, at its request, on March 4, 1964, I asked for permission to examine the rifle. Permission was denied, but on July 2, 1964, I testified again, this time on the condition that I be allowed to examine the alleged assassination weapon. After looking at it and calling attention to Officer Weitzman's affidavit, I told the Commission that, while not a rifle expert, I was able to see that it was a 6.5 Italian rifle because stamped clearly on the rifle were the words 'MADE ITALY' and 'CAL. 6.5'. I suggested that it was unlikely for a police officer to have made such a mistaken identification.... The Commission explained that Weitzman 'did not examine it [the rifle] at close range' and that he 'had little more than a glimpse of it'. The Report stated, 'Constable Deputy Sheriff Weitzman, who only saw the rifle at a glance and did not handle it, thought the weapon looked like a 7.65 Mauser bolt-action rifle.' Later, it said that 'the rifle found on the sixth floor of the Texas School Book Depository Building was initially identified as a Mauser 7.65 rather than a Mannlicher-Carcano 6.5 because a deputy constable who was one of the first to see it thought it looked like a Mauser. He neither handled the weapon nor saw it at close range.' These remarks constitute the entire comment by the Warren Commission Report on this vital issue. The Commissioners did not publish or comment on Weitzman's affidavit in the Report; if they had, they would have had to explain how by a 'glimpse' or a 'glance', and not at close range, Weitzman was able to describe the telescopic sight precisely, as well as the material and color of the sling, not to mention why he swore to an affidavit in the first place if, as the Commission insisted, he could not have known the details he deposed.... Council ought to have shown the Mannlicher-Carcano to Weitzman and asked him if that were the weapon he discovered on the sixth floor, but Weitzman was not permitted to examine the alleged assassination rifle.... Although counsel showed him three different photographs, they were pictures of the area where the weapon was discovered and not of the weapon itself. Weitzman testified that he remained near the rifle until Captain

Fritz had ejected the live round. In addition to his police affidavit, he had given a description of the rifle to FBI agents, and he told Commission counsel that he had described the weapon to them as 'gun metal color . . . blue metal . . . the rear portion of the bolt was visibly worn . . . dark brown oak . . . roughwood'. One may glance at a weapon, perhaps, and determine its color and the type and texture of the wood in the stock, but to determine that 'the rear portion of the bolt was visibly worn' must have required more than a glance. Moreover, in his affidavit Weitzman swore that the rifle had a 4/18 telescopic sight. The Report stated that Weitzman, after 'little more than a glimpse', thought the rifle 'looked like a 7.65 Mauser' but did not disclose that Weitzman swore to the description he gave in substantial detail. It also ignores the fact that his identification of the weapon as a Mauser was supported by the testimony of a number of other officers.... Two men discovered the weapon—Weitzman and Boone—and both of them described it as a 7.65 Mauser. When Captain Fritz arrived he knelt down on the floor to examine the rifle, and he too, according to Boone, declared it was a 7.65 Mauser. Deputy Sheriff Boone testified, 'I thought it was 7 .65 Mauser'. When he was asked, 'Who referred to it as a Mauser that day?', Boone replied, 'I believe Captain Fritz.' Boone said that Fritz had 'said that is what it looks like. This is when Lieutenant Day, I believe his name is, the ID man was getting ready to photograph it. We were just discussing it back and forth. And he [Fritz] said it looks like a 7.65 Mauser.' Boone, unlike Weitzman, was shown the Mannlicher-Carcano rifle, which he was unable to identify as the weapon he and Weitzman had found." [Excerpts from *Rush to Judgment*, pp. 115-120]

Further corroboration that a 7.65 Mauser was found on the sixth-floor of the Depository can be found in Dallas Police Officer Eugene Boone's official report from November 22, 1963, where he describes the events that took place when the rifle was identified:

COUNTY OF DALLAS
SHERIFF'S DEPARTMENT

SUPPLEMENTARY INVESTIGATION REPORT

Name of Complainant   Serial No.

Offense

DETAILS OF OFFENSE, PROGRESS OF INVESTIGATION, ETC.:
(Investigating Officer must sign)

Date Nov. 22, 1963 19___

Mr. Decker;

    I was assisting in th search of the 6th floor of the Dallas County Book Depository at Elm st and Houston St. proceeding from the Northxside East side of the building . Officer Whiteman DPD and I were together as we approched the Northwest corner of the building waxxaxxtha I was the rifle partially hidden behind a row of books with two (2) other boxes of books against the rifle. The rifle appeared to be a 7.65mm Mauser with a telescope sight on the rifle. Capt. Fritz was called to the scene and also someone from the ID ENXXX pictures were taken and then Capt Fritz picked up the rifle. I first saw the rifle at 1:22pm date.

E. L. Boone 240 DSO

Also, this excerpt from a C.I.A. report made on November 25, 1963, claims that Oswald used a Mauser to shoot Kennedy:

> The rifle he used was a Mauser which OSWALD had ordered (this is now known by handwriting examination) from Klein's Mail Order House, Chicago, Illinois. He had the rifle sent to a Post Office Box which Lee OSWALD had rented. In the order for the rifle, OSWALD used the name Alex HIDELL.

Source: The National Archives and Records Administration:
https://www.maryferrell.org/showDoc.html?docId=79544#relPageId=4&tab=page

It would seem that the Dallas Police Department, the F.B.I., and the C.I.A. all couldn't get their stories straight regarding what type of rifle, or rifles were found in the Depository, and which one Oswald supposedly used to shoot the President during the assassination. In an effort to get to the bottom of this discrepancy of rifles that were found, or not found, Lincoln Carle asked Roger Craig about the Mauser, and what happened to it, during a taped interview recorded in 1974:

Lincoln Carle: This Mauser has disappeared?

Roger Craig: As far as I know. I don't know where it is. I don't know what happened to it.

Carle: What do the official records say?

Craig: There are no official records on the Mauser.

Carle: But you said Seymour Weitzman identified it with Captain Fritz as a Mauser?

Craig: Yes.

Carle: Did you not enter this in your report?

Craig: No. Because the investigation was being conducted by Will Fritz.

Carle: Is it in his report?

Craig: I don't know.

Carle: What about Seymour Weitzman's report?

Craig: I've never seen it. I don't know whether he made one. And he's now in a mental institution.

Carle: And that has bothered you I suppose?

Craig: Of course. He was a good friend.

Carle: The fact of the anomalies in the reports, and the situation of the Mauser disappearing, what did you do about it? Did you ask questions?

Craig: No, I didn't ask any questions, because the Dallas police were conducting the investigation, and the F.B.I.

Carle: When it all came out, when it all became published, and you saw that there was at least some great omissions, what did you do then?

Craig: I got sick at first. I just couldn't believe it.

Roger Craig's mention of Seymour Weitzman's treatment for mental illness was confirmed by journalist Michael Canfield after he visited Weitzman in April of 1975 (one month before Craig's death) at one of several federal government facilities he'd been living in since suffering a nervous breakdown in June of 1972. In their 1975 book *Coup D'état in America: The CIA and the Assassination of John F. Kennedy*, authors Alan J. Weberman and Michael Canfield explain, that during Canfield's visit, Weitzman was shown a photograph of Watergate Plumber, Bernard Barker, and he immediately identified Barker as the man that he, and Dallas Police Officer Joe Smith encountered behind the picket fence on November 22, 1963, that claimed he was a U.S. Secret Service agent before showing his credentials, and saying, "Everything is under control."

Convicted Watergate Burglar, Bernard Barker.

Also, according to Canfield, Weitzman made the following remarks after changing his mind to not sign a notarized affidavit about his identification of Bernard Barker:

> "So many witnesses have been killed...and two Cubans forced their way into my house and waited for me when I got home. I had to chase them out with my Service revolver. I fear for my life." [*Coup D'état in America*, p. 57]

Their book goes on to explain that:

> "Weitzman refused to make a tape-recorded statement, but said he would be willing to do it for official investigators." [*Coup D'état in America*, p. 57]

However, in a letter that I managed to track down in the National Archives, that was sent to representatives of the House Select Committee on Assassinations in 1978, and written by Seymour Weitzman's government funded physician, Dr. Charles Laburda, and was supposedly with Weitzman's consent, Weitzman objected to participating in the HSCA's investigation into the assassination of John F. Kennedy:

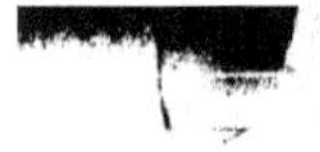

VETERANS ADMINISTRATION
SAM RAYBURN MEMORIAL VETERANS CENTER
BONHAM, TEXAS 75418

IN REPLY
REFER TO: 522/116B

June 1, 1978

TO WHOM IT MAY CONCERN:

This statement is made on behalf of Mr. Seymour Weitzman on his request and with his consent.

Mr. Seymour Weitzman, born January 28, 1922, in his capacity of deputy constable of the Sheriff's Office, personally and from close distance witnessed the events that resulted in the death of former President John F. Kennedy. His testimony and account of what he observed were collected by the Investigators of the Police Department of Dallas, Office of the Sheriff of the Dallas County, and the Warren Commission. His testimony is a matter of record, and he has no new or additional information to add to the statements made at that time.

Since that time Mr. Weitzman was treated for emotional illness for many years, and is presently a member of the Veterans Administration Domiciliary at this Sam Rayburn Memorial Veterans Administration Center in Bonham, Texas. It is of great importance for his welfare and emotional well-being to excuse Mr. Weitzman from participation in any further investigations of the events he witnessed; any information sought from him should be extracted from his testimony and depositions made at that time.

Charles Laburda, Ph.D.
Chief, Psychology Service

Seymour Weitzman was subsequently never interviewed by members of the committee about his identification of the mauser rifle, or his identification of Watergate Plumber Bernard Barker as being the man he encountered behind the picket fence immediately after the assassination on November 22, 1963, who identified himself as a U.S. Secret Service Agent.

Dallas Police Officer Joe Smith, who also encountered this man with Weitzman, was questioned about the incident before the Warren Commission on July 23, 1964 by assistant counsel, Wesley J. Liebeler.

The following are excerpts are from Smith's testimony:

> Mr. LIEBELER. While you were standing here and the motorcade went by, tell us what happened at that point.

Mr. SMITH. I heard the shots… this woman came up to me and she was just in hysterics. She told me, "They are shooting the President from the bushes." So I immediately proceeded up here.

Mr. LIEBELER. You proceeded up to an area immediately behind the concrete structure here that is described by Elm Street and the street that runs immediately in front of the Texas School Book Depository, is that right?

Mr. SMITH. I was checking all the bushes and I checked all the cars in the parking lot.

Mr. LIEBELER. There is a parking lot in behind this grassy area back from Elm Street toward the railroad tracks, and you went down to the parking lot and looked around?

Mr. SMITH. Yes, sir; I checked all the cars. I looked into all the cars and checked around the bushes. Of course, I wasn't alone. There was some deputy sheriff with me, and I believe one Secret Service man when I got there…. I pulled my pistol from my holster, and I thought, this is silly, I don't know who I am looking for, and I put it back. Just as I did, he showed me that he was a Secret Service agent.

Mr. LIEBELER. Did you accost this man?

Mr. SMITH. Well, he saw me coming with my pistol and right away he showed me who he was.

Mr. LIEBELER. Do you remember who it was?

Mr. SMITH. No, sir; I don't--because then we started checking the cars. In fact, I was checking the bushes, and I went through the cars, and I started over here in this particular section.

Mr. LIEBELER. Did you have any basis for believing where the shots came from, or where to look for somebody, other than what the lady told you?

Mr. SMITH. No, sir; except that maybe it was a power of suggestion. But it sounded to me like they may have came from this vicinity here.

Mr. LIEBELER. ...the corner here behind this concrete structure where the bushes were down toward the railroad tracks from the Texas School Book Depository...

Mr. SMITH. Yes.

Photo of the picket fence situated above the grassy knoll in Dealey Plaza, where Police Officer Joe Smith and Deputy Weitzman ran up the knoll, and hopped the fence after witnesses said that shots came from this area. While behind the fence, they encountered a man who claimed to be a U.S. Secret Service Agent, before telling them, "Everything is under control."
(Photo courtesy of Steve Cameron)

An eyewitness to the assassination, Malcolm Summers also encountered a man on the grassy knoll who he thought was there to protect the

President.   The following are excerpts are from an interview with Summers about what he witnessed, that aired on CSPAN in 2002:

> "[The President's motorcade] came around, and I heard what I thought was a firecracker, the first shot... Then the second shot rang out. Then the third was just about where I was [standing on the grass, on the South side of Elm Street watching the motorcade drive past]. I'm standing by the curb there, and I saw Kennedy get hit. I heard [Governor] Connally say, "They're gonna kill us all!" ...And then I heard Jackie Kennedy scream out, "Oh God, no, no, no." It was very sad to hear that... After the car Kennedy was in... it hesitated and stopped there for a second or two... I saw a Secret Service man run up there and slip on the back bumper... I thought he was just trying to dive in the car... And I saw Jackie Kennedy reach for him...

> After the procession cleared out... I immediately ran across the street [Toward the grassy knoll area, approximately forty feet to the right of where Abraham Zapruder was filming]. I was stopped by a guy... he was about 5'10, to 6 ft.... well-dressed, had a tie on, and a coat over his arm. He also had a [Stetson style] hat on. Also, he had a gun under his coat. It wasn't uncovered. I was running straight at him, so I could see the barrel under the coat. And he said, "Better not come up here, you could get shot." I didn't want to argue with him, because he looked like a man of authority. I thought maybe a detective, or an F.B.I. man...

> I described [the gun] to the Sheriff's Department over here... They asked me what did the muzzle look like. When I described the barrel, they said it sounded like an automatic.... The Secret Service came out to my shop to interview me on two different occasions. The first time, it was about three of them that came... I told them about the guy who stopped me and all of that. I told them he looked like an F.B.I. guy, or Secret Service, or a local city detective. They said, "Okay we'll take a report and get back with you." I was wondering why they didn't come back sooner, but about two months later, they told me that they did not have F.B.I. men, or Secret Service, or a city detective that

was in that vicinity where this guy stopped me… They basically told me I didn't see anything, because they said they didn't have anybody there… I was disappointed… because I knew I saw somebody there… It just didn't make sense."

U.S. Secret Service Agent Clint Hill is photographed climbing onto the back of Kennedy's limousine after the President was shot.

In the 1990s researchers showed Malcolm Summers a photo of convicted Watergate burglar Bernard Barker. And like Seymour Weitzman, Summers identified Barker as being the man he saw with the gun under his coat that stopped him on the grassy knoll, and warned him that he could be shot if he didn't leave the area.

Regarding the whereabouts of Bernard Barker on the day of the President's assassination, author Lamar Waldron explains in his 2013 book *Watergate: The Hidden History: Nixon, The Mafia, and The CIA*, that authors Alan J. Weberman and Michael Canfield were party to a lawsuit involving E. Howard Hunt, in which they were able to obtain a sworn deposition from Bernard Barker, and during it he was asked where he was on November 22, 1963:

> **Bernard Barker:** I was working for the agency [Central Intelligence Agency], they know exactly everywhere I was, I reported to them daily.

Waldron writes that Barker also claimed he was home watching television during the shooting, but when asked what he was watching, Barker said he couldn't remember. Waldron goes on to explain, that during Barker's deposition, he was asked if he first learned of the assassination via a news flash. But Barker answered:

> **Bernard Barker:** No… I think I saw the parade, how the whole thing happened.

However, there was no live television coverage of Kennedy's motorcade through Dallas, or of the assassination.

Waldron theorizes in his book, that if Bernard Barker was indeed the person Weitzman and Smith encountered behind the picket fence, and if he was also the man Malcolm Summers encountered on the grassy Knoll a few minutes after the assassination, then Barker likely wasn't one of the shooters, and instead was placed there to keep people away from that area, where snipers were located behind the picket fence near the top of the knoll.

Researcher and author, Penn Jones Jr. wrote about Barker's connections to Clay Shaw, E. Howard Hunt, the C.I.A., and the Bay of Pigs fiasco in his fourth volume of *Forgive My Grief*, published in 1974:

> "In January of this year, former C. I. A. staff member Victor Marchetti revealed that Shaw was a paid contact of the Central Intelligence Agency back in the early 1960s…. Marchetti stated that while Shaw was being investigated by Garrison in 1968, frequent morning briefing sessions were held with high Agency officials in which serious concern was voiced concerning the

possibility of the New Orleans District Attorney uncovering Shaw's CIA contacts and making them public. Garrison had alleged on several occasions that Shaw was a CIA operative, but was never able to prove his contention. These same high Agency officials also often expressed the need to give help to Shaw and his defense team during Garrison's investigation. Marchetti also related that Shaw, David Ferrie, E. Howard Hunt, Frank Sturgis, Bernard Barker, and others were all working together in the CIA's Bay of Pigs planning operation. This information becomes very important when one considers the fact that Garrison and other JFK assassination researchers have long contended that President Kennedy was killed with the help of CIA operatives who were infuriated over the manner in which Kennedy handled the Bay of Pigs fiasco."[Jones, *Forgive My Grief, Volume IV*, pp. 173-174]

Robert Groden Interview continued…

Steve: One of the reasons why I didn't answer the phone when you first called today, I was in the middle of transcribing an interview that I conducted a few days ago with the last living relative who saw Roger Craig alive.

Robert: Oh my!

Steve: Her and her husband, who was Roger's older half-brother Donald, went to the house to pick up some items they left behind when they moved from the home to their own apartment. They had lived there with Roger and his father, but moved out a couple weeks earlier. So Kristel, Roger's dad, invited them to come by that day to pick up some belongings that they left behind. And they went over there around ten in the morning. They were there for about an hour and a half, having coffee with Roger and Kristel. She explained that Roger was in a great mood. Joking around, asking her, "Have you learned how to boil water yet, or have you learned how to burn it?"

Robert: Or did she lose the recipe (laughter)?

Steve: The way she explained it, she was the new kid on the block, and Roger was always pestering her, and playing pranks on her. Said he was a fun guy to be around. And even that day, when he supposedly killed himself, he was in a great mood, joking around with her. He knew she could cook, because she lived there for six weeks, but he was still joking with her. And he also had plans to go fishing with them in Oklahoma. And on that day, Roger told them that he had just gotten his fishing license, because he didn't want to get a ticket as long as his short arm. So, he was even joking about that. When I spoke to Roger Craig Jr., he told me that he saw his dad's driver's license shortly after he died, and he saw that it had just been renewed on his birthday, May 12, which was just three days before he was found dead. He had plans. His own son doesn't believe he killed himself. Roger Craig's sister-in-law, who knew him, lived with him, and saw him the day he was found dead, doesn't believe he killed himself. And neither do I. His father Kristel said he didn't believe it. He also said that the gun found in the house wasn't Roger's rifle, and that he didn't own a rifle at the time he died, and that he had never seen that gun in the house before. So, his own father, who probably knew him the best, didn't believe it.

Robert: Let me add this to your pile of information, which is quite impressive. Why would Roger agree to an interview with me, when I wasn't really that well known back then, and have me and my wife fly down 1,600 miles to do an interview, and then kill himself before it ever took place? Think about that one.

Steve: That's right. It makes no sense. It only makes sense in Bizarro World.

Robert: Yeah. Another thing, if his father was there, why would he do it so that his father would find the body? It doesn't make sense. I've told people all through the years, if anyone ever finds me as a result of a suicide, not to believe it. With four kids and seven grandchildren, I'm not about to take my own life.

Steve: Same here. Well, thank you for your time, Robert. If you have any final thoughts, or maybe something we haven't touched on, or if you'd like to expound on anything we have talked about, I'd like to give you the opportunity to do that right now if you'd like?

Robert: Well, all I can say, is that I never believed Roger killed himself. I've always felt very, very sad about it. And very sorry. But I do appreciate the fact that you're doing this.

Steve: Thanks, Robert.

"There have been many books written about the assassination. Some of the information was asked of me, which I gave freely, and will until they get someone good enough to silence me. I have not read many of the books written, as that day, November 22, 1963, has been burned in my mind as if with a branding iron."

-Roger Dean Craig

Phil Singer

Steve Cameron: Thanks for calling. As you know, I'm writing a book about Roger Craig. I got a message from Gary Fannin, and he said you wanted to get in touch with me. What was it that you wanted to talk about?

Phil Singer: Well, first of all, I assume you've seen the documentary that Mark Lane did on Roger Craig many years ago, right?

Steve: Yeah, I did. But before we go forward, could you please tell me a little about yourself, so the people reading can have a little more information to go on, before we get started?

Phil: My background in the Kennedy case, you mean?

Steve: Yeah.

Phil: Well, I'm from the Chicago area. Still live in the Chicago area. I was nine years old when Kennedy died. I'm 64 years old now. I've been following the Kennedy case since it happened. Meaning, reading the newspapers, collecting the magazines. Books started coming out in the '60s, by Harold Weisberg, Sylvia Meagher, Mark Lane, Josiah Thompson, and others. And back in 1975, as a 20-year-old college student, I met Mark Lane, who wrote *Rush to Judgment*. Probably one of the biggest and most important books on the case, certainly in the early days.

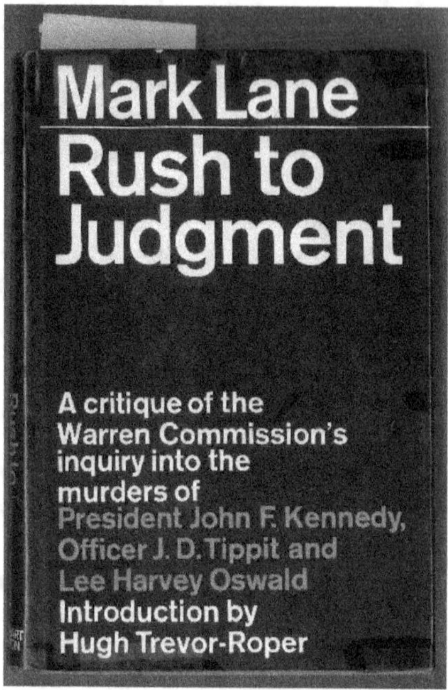

Photo courtesy of Phil Singer.

Phil: And so, I started working for him and his organization called "The Citizens Commission of Inquiry." And we were trying to get the Kennedy case reopened. This was back twelve, thirteen years after the assassination. And it seemed like a long time then. Obviously, it's many years ago now, but it was like, "Wow, Kennedy's been dead ten years, twelve years already, thirteen years. How come we can't see the files to get to the truth?" So, I was writing letters to senators and congressmen. I still have many return letters from them.

Author's note: After the interview, I asked Phil if he could provide me with copies of his return letters, so I could share them with the readers. The following are some of those letters, printed in chronological order:

MAJORITY WHIP
...TIONS COMMITTEE

...KING MEMBER
, EDUCATION, AND WELFARE
...BCOMMITTEE

...HINGTON OFFICE:
...AYBURN BUILDING
...02) 225-6201

DISTRICT OFFICE
1007 FIRST NATIONAL BANK
PEORIA, ILLINOIS 6
(309) 673-6358

COUNTIES:
BROWN   MASO
BUREAU   PEORI
CASS   SCHU
KNOX   STAR
TAZEWELL

Congress of the United States
House of Representatives
Washington, D.C. 20515

February 6, 1976

Mr. Philip M. Singer
Citizens Commission of Inquiry
  in Illinois
Knox College
Box 1445
Galesburg, Illinois 61401

Dear Mr. Singer:

Thank you for your letter of January 27 with regard to an investigation into the facts surrounding the assassination of President John F. Kennedy.

Representative Gonzalez of Texas has introduced H. Res. 204, which proposes the establishment of a Select Committee to investigate the assassinations of John F. Kennedy, Robert Kennedy, Martin Luther King, and the shooting of George Wallace.

This resolution has been referred to the House Committee on Rules. No action has been scheduled to date, nor is any future action contemplated as of this writing. I appreciate the very sincere concern which prompted your communication, and should I secure additional information in the matter, I will be pleased to advise you.

Sincerely,

Robert H. Michel
Member of Congress

RHM::sw

Ninety-Fourth Congress

U.S. House of Representatives
Committee on Rules
Washington, D.C. 20515

February 18, 1976

Mr. Phillip M. Singer
Knox College Box 1445
Galesburg, Ill.   61401

Dear Mr. Singer:

Chairman Madden appreciates your interest in legislation referred to the House Rules Committee which would create a special congressional committee to further investigate the assassination of former President Kennedy and others.

Congressman Downing and Congressman Gonzalez have introduced similar bills and a number of congressmen have cosponsored the measures.

Your correspondence will be kept here for further reference as the Rules Committee works with the House Leadership on this important issue.

Sincerely,

D. Gregory Nicosia
Chief Counsel

I. RAYBURN BUILDING
TON, D.C. 20515
(2) 225-5271

FOR
AG

PAUL FINDLEY
20TH DISTRICT, ILLINOIS

Congress of the United States
House of Representatives
Washington, D. C.

February 24, 1976

Mr. Phillip M. Singer
Knox College - Box 1445
Galesburg, Illinois   61401

Dear Mr. Singer:

As you will note from the attached, I have co-sponsored Congressman Downing's proposal to provide for the creation of a select committee to conduct an investigation and study of the death of President Kennedy.

You may be sure I will promote consideration of this resolution in every way possible.

Warm regards,

Paul Findley
Representative in Congress

HOUSE OF REPRESENTATIVES
LONGWORTH OFFICE BUILDING
WASHINGTON, D.C. 20515
(202) 225-5976

COMMITTEES:
EDUCATION AND LABOR
SCIENCE AND TECHNOLOGY

NEIL L. McGRATH
ADMINISTRATIVE ASSISTANT

TIM L. HALL
15TH DISTRICT, ILLINOIS

Congress of the United States
House of Representatives
Washington, D.C. 20515

DISTRICT:
1015 LASALLE
OTTAWA, ILLINOIS
(815) 43

507 N. T
DWIGHT, ILLIN
(815) 58

523 W. GA
AURORA, ILLI
(312) 89

July 30, 1976

Mr. Phillip H. Singer
Citizens Commission of Inquiry in Illinois
Knox College Box 1445
Galesburg, Illinois 61401

Dear Mr. Singer:

Thank you for your letter urging my support of H. Res. 204.
I appreciated receiving the benefit of your thinking.

As you know this measure, which has been referred to the
Rules Committee, calls for the establishment of a select
committee to conduct an investigation of the circumstances
surrounding the deaths of John F. Kennedy, Robert F.
Kennedy, and Martin Luther King, and the attempted assassination of George Wallace. You may be assured I will
keep your feelings in mind when the bill comes before the
full House of Representatives.

If I can be of assistance in other matters, please do
not hesitate to call upon me.

                              Sincerely yours,

                              Tim L. Hall

                              TIM L. HALL
                              Member of Congress

United States Senate
SELECT COMMITTEE ON INTELLIGENCE
WASHINGTON, D.C. 20510

August 2, 1976

Mr. Phillip M. Singer
8715 No. Harding
Skokie, Illinois   60076

Dear Mr. Singer:

Thank you for taking the time to share with me your thoughts on the investigation of the assassination of President John F. Kennedy. Before making any decision regarding further investigation of this tragic event, the members of the newly created Select Committee on Intelligence will want to study carefully the findings which have already been reported.

Enclosed is a copy of S. Res. 400, which established the Select Committee on Intelligence. In it, you will note, schedules and time limits are set for certain continuing responsibilities and special studies to be undertaken by the Select Committee. For this reason, a decision on reopening of the John F. Kennedy assassination investigation will have to take account of the requirement to complete the tasks mandated in its authorizing resolution.

With kind regards,

John,

Daniel K. Inouye
Chairman

Encl.

Interview continued...

Phil: We were trying to appeal to the government, that the Kennedy case had many unanswered questions, like today. So, eventually the case did get reopened, and that became The House Select Committee on Assassinations. I tried to get a job working on The House Select Committee on Assassinations, but they didn't hire me. Probably, because I worked for Mark Lane's organization, I suspect. But I've been working on the case in my own private way for many years. Interviewing a lot of people who've been involved in the case. From Secret Service members, to doctors at Parkland Hospital that tried to save Kennedy, to people that were in the autopsy room and at the morgue at the Bethesda Naval Hospital that night. And I still stay in touch with many of these witnesses that have a connection to the case. A few years ago, I put together a couple of events, where I brought together seven people that were at the Bethesda Naval Hospital the night of the autopsy. Brought them all together in the Chicago area, where we had a conference. A couple years ago, I put together an event where I reunited the J.F.K. Honor Guard guys, the original six pallbearers that carried his coffin for four days, from Friday, November 22nd, to the funeral at Arlington National Cemetery on Monday, November 25th, 1963. They hadn't seen each other since Kennedy's funeral. I brought them all together. They're from different branches of the military. We filmed and spoke at this reunion event. These guys were at Bethesda the night of the autopsy. They carried the coffin in. They carried the coffin out. There at the White House.

President John. F. Kennedy's flag-draped casket lies in repose in the East Room of the White House on November 23, 1963.

Phil: They carried the coffin into the Capital Building, where it lied in state at the Rotunda. To St. Matthew's Cathedral. And then to Arlington National Cemetery.

President Kennedy's funeral procession through the Capitol begins on November 24, 1963.

Honor Guard carrying the casket of President Kennedy up the steps of the Capitol Building.

President Kennedy's casket lay in state in the Capitol Rotunda.

The casket of President Kennedy is carried out of the Rotunda
by the Honor Guard on November 25, 1963.

Honor Guard prepares to fold American flag over John F. Kennedy's casket during his funeral ceremony at Arlington National Cemetery.

Jackie Kennedy walks away holding the flag under her arm after receiving it from the Honor Guard on November 25, 1963.

Phil: They folded the flag, which was presented to Jackie Kennedy. Then they were dismissed and went their separate ways for over fifty years. But I reunited them, because I discovered that the original six guys were still alive, and that they hadn't been in touch with each other since the day of the funeral.

The original six J.F.K. Honor Guard members together at their October 2016 reunion, held in Westmont, Illinois. From left to right are James Felder, Richard Gaudreau, Hubert Clark, Bud Barnum, Tim Cheek, and Doug Mayfield (on the computer screen via Skype).

Phil Singer conducts a recreation of the Honor Guard's 1963 flag-folding ceremony to commemorate their reunion.

J.F.K. Honor Guard members proudly holding up the American flag, after successfully performing the ceremony on their first attempt in over fifty years, since they first did it together during John F. Kennedy's funeral on November 25, 1963.
(Reunion photos courtesy of Phil Singer)

Phil: So, that's some of my background in the case.

Steve: What's a good way for the readers to find your information? Are you online? Do you have a website?

Phil: No, no. But if I stay healthy and live long enough, I'd like to get a book and a documentary out on some of the things I alluded to. There are things I guess people can find on the computer, if you Google my name, and then put in "J.F.K."

Steve: But you do have an online presence. I researched you a little bit, and saw some YouTube videos and things like that. Do you have a YouTube channel?

Phil: No. There are some things people have posted on YouTube. And if you Google stuff, there's some things about me. I'm in a lot of books actually.

Steve: Please, go ahead and name a few of them, or one or two, or as many as you want.

Phil: Well, I'm in James Tague's book *LBJ and the Kennedy Killing*. Robert Groden's book *Absolute Proof*. Doug Horne's book *Inside the Assassination Records Review Board*. William Law's book, that I wrote a couple chapters for, *In the Eye of History*. Jim Jenkins just came out with a book about the autopsy of President Kennedy, called *At the Cold Shoulder of History*. He was in the morgue that whole night. I'm listed in there a couple times. Hubert Clark has a book *Betrayal: A J.F.K. Honor Guard Speaks*. He was one of the Honor Guard guys. I'm listed in there about ten times. Judyth Vary Baker's book on Oswald.

Steve: *Me and Lee?*

Phil: Yep, *Me and Lee*. I'm mentioned in there. I've supported her work. Been kind of her bodyguard, her friend and take care of her when she comes to Chicago. Take her around everywhere, you know, kind of watch out for her.

Steve: Okay. Well, where would you like to take it from here, Phil?

Phil: Well, I mentioned James Tague's book earlier. He was a witness to the John F. Kennedy assassination. I knew him very well and he was a friend of mine. He passed away in February of 2014. Well, on November 22nd, 1963, he was working as a car salesman in Dallas. Jim took off work to take his girlfriend out to lunch, who he referred to as, "A cute little redhead." So, he was on his way to pick her up, and he was driving eastbound on Commerce, toward Dealey Plaza, from the other side of the triple underpass, and then got stuck in traffic where the streets of Dealey Plaza converge under the triple underpass. So, he was at the convergence end, where these three streets, Elm, Main, and Commerce, all come together. He had no idea that Kennedy's motorcade would be traveling through that part of town. So, he got out of the car and was kind of frustrated. Like I say, he was on a lunch date, to meet with his girlfriend. When he got out of his vehicle, he saw the motorcade traveling westbound on Main Street. And so, he says to himself, "Oh yeah, the president's in town, I forgot about that. I'm stuck here in traffic, so I guess I'll have to wait." He then looked up at the Hertz digital clock on top of the School Book Depository, and he told me it said, "12:29 p.m." And then the shooting sequence began, which he thought were firecrackers, and then something stung his cheek. And right after the motorcade drove past him and away from Dealey Plaza, he crossed the street, and started walking up toward the grassy knoll, toward that area where everyone was running. And then he ran into Deputy Sheriff Buddy Walthers, who said, "Hey man, what happened to you?" or words to that effect. And Jim Tague says, "What are you talking about?" And Buddy Walthers kind of points at him with his index finger and says, "Man, you got some blood on your cheek there." And Jim Tague took a couple fingers from his right hand and rubbed it on his right cheek, and sure enough there were a couple drops of blood on his fingertips. And then Buddy Walthers asks him, "Well, where were you standing?" And they walked over, and before they even got to Main Street, they saw an indentation about the size of a dime or a nickel in the curved portion of the curb. And it seemed to be a fresh mark. So, they looked at it and realized a bullet had struck there and either sprayed some metal, or concrete particles, up into Jim Tague's face, causing the stinging sensation and the drops of blood. Jim used to say he got "peppered." He liked using that word. But just to finish this story, after he reported what happened to Buddy Walthers, he was told, "Go to police headquarters and file a statement." But, instead of going to police headquarters, he's thinking, "I have this date with this cute little redhead." And of course, nobody had cellphones back in '63, so he drove over to where his girlfriend was working, and said to her, "You won't believe where I just was. I was in Dealey Plaza. The president got shot. And they want me to go over to police headquarters to make a statement." Then he left, and headed over to police headquarters. He knew where to go. And so, he's sitting down there, and being interviewed by detective Gus Rose. And by this time, who knows what time it was, it might have been 1:30 p.m. or maybe 2:30 p.m. And he's about to give his statement, and then there's this commotion outside the office where Jim Tague is being interviewed. So, Jim Tague says, "What's that all about?" And detective Gus Rose says, "That's the guy who was just arrested for shooting a policeman in Oak Cliff," and he leaves the room. Well, that guy was Lee Harvey Oswald. The detective who was interviewing Jim Tague never came back, because they were preoccupied now with the arrest of Oswald. Who at that point, had not been arrested yet for killing Kennedy, but had been arrested for shooting police officer J.D. Tippit. So, Jim Tague, after waiting a number of minutes, says to himself, "Well, I guess they're no longer interested in my story," so he got up and left. When he got home, he sat down and turned on the T.V. and watched the news coverage about Kennedy being killed, like everyone else. But after a while, he decided to grab a spiral notebook, and proceeded to write down all of his recollections from that day. And what he witnessed changed the Warren Report. Because now they had to account for a missed shot.

Warren Commission Exhibit No. 34: A section of the Main Street curb containing lead markings where a bullet hit. It was removed near the location where James Tague's face was wounded by concrete particles.

Phil: They were locked into Oswald firing three shots, and three shots only. That's based on him owning the Mannlicher-Carcano, an old-fashioned rifle, as I'm sure you know. And it could only be fired as fast as once every 2.3 seconds, which didn't account for aiming, according to Robert Frazier of the F.B.I. and his testimony. And so, they kind of got locked into a no-more-than-three-shot scenario. Originally, how the Warren Report was going to be written, was that the first shot hit Kennedy in the back. The second hit Connally. And the third hit Kennedy in the head. There was no accounting for the throat wound to Kennedy or the missed shot that hit the curb. And then once Jim Tague's story broke after he came forward, and after they interviewed him in '64, they basically said, "Okay, one shot hit Kennedy in the head. One shot hit this curb, and superficially wounded Jim Tague. Now we have to deal with the back wound and the throat wound to Kennedy, and five wounds to Connally." And that's when Arlen Specter sort of trumped up the single-bullet theory, that a bullet went through Kennedy's back, came out his throat, went into Connally's back, and came out his chest, went into one side of his wrist, came out the other side of his wrist, and ended up in his thigh. But didn't even stay there. It came out and was found on a stretcher and was virtually undeformed. And they call that the single-bullet theory, or "the magic-bullet" theory, as you know.

The Warren Commission's Arlen Specter demonstrates his implausible single-bullet theory on May 24, 1964.

Jim Tague (left) with Phil Singer.
(Photo courtesy of Phil Singer)

Phil: Jim Tague actually had a lot to do with the writing of the Warren Report after he came forward, saying he was wounded. And there was evidence that he was wounded. Buddy Walthers knew it and other people knew it too.

Steve: Was Jim present when they were examining the brain matter and blood that was next to the curb in the grass, and the bullet that was seen there next to it? It's in photographs.

Phil: Well, that's a different bullet. The one that hit the curb, that I'm talking about, was much further west, almost to the triple underpass. The one you're talking about, is by the concrete manhole cover, on the south side of Elm, and there seems to be all those pictures that you're talking about, of people bending over, and allegedly Bob Barrett of the F.B.I. picking up a bullet and putting it in his pocket. That was probably a hundred feet east of where Jim Tague was standing. So that appears to be another missed bullet. Then there's evidence that the windshield may have been penetrated. There's a lot of evidence of several missed shots. There are also several people that said a bullet hit the street near the limousine during the shooting sequence. Steve Ellis saw that, and a bunch of other people saw that.

Steve: It was Deputy Sheriff Buddy Walthers, who originally told people, including Roger Craig, that there was a spent bullet laying in the grass beside the blood and brain matter from Kennedy's head. Then a man, who identified himself as F.B.I. to Buddy, picked up the bullet and put it in his pocket. But Buddy Wathers later changed his story. Why, I don't know. Unfortunately, he's not around anymore to ask him why.

Author's note: On December 14, 1967, The Waco News-Tribune published an article concerning New Orleans District Attorney Jim Garrison's claim that photos taken near a manhole cover on the south side of Elm Street in Dealey Plaza, ten minutes after Kennedy was shot, show a federal agent pick up a bullet from the grass and walk away, while Deputy Sheriff E. R. Buddy Walthers stood by watching. In the article, Walthers denies that a bullet was found, and is quoted as saying, "If it was anything it was a piece of skull. Nothing significant." Regardless whether Walthers saw a man pick up a bullet or not, I would think it would be highly significant if Walthers allowed anyone to freely walk into the crime scene, then pick up a piece of the President's skull, and walk away with it without being questioned or identified. So, who was this man, and why was he allowed to enter the crime scene?

Deputy Sheriff Buddy Walthers points to himself in a photo taken soon after the assassination. [The Waco News-Tribune, Dec. 14, 1967]

Eric R. Tagg, author of *Brush with History: A Day in the Life of Deputy E. R. Buddy Walthers*, explains in his book that Buddy Walthers told several people that he found a bullet lying in the grass in Dealey Plaza after the President was shot:

"Buddy Walthers told his partner Alvin Maddox, Jr., Deputy Roger Craig, his wife Dorothy, Inspector Sawyer, and some reporters that a .45 caliber slug was found at that time… Walthers later denied to the Warren Commission that a bullet was found… an extra bullet would have destroyed both the Single Bullet Theory and the Lone Gunman Hypothesis, two necessary precepts to prove the government's case against Oswald… The significance of this piece of evidence to the case is staggering…" [Tagg, *Brush with History*, pp.10–11]

Tagg goes on to explain that:

"Newsman Richard Dudman also told of the missed shot in the December 21, 1963 issue of the New Republic, "On the day the President was shot, I happened to learn of a possible fifth. A group of police officers were examining the area at the side of the street where the President was hit and a police inspector told me they had just found another bullet in the grass." [Tagg, *Brush with History*, p. 11]

Two witnesses by the name of Wayne and Edna Hartman came forward to report that they saw gouged-out holes in the grass near the manhole cover minutes after the shooting had ended. Below are excerpts from their F.B.I. report that was written in August of 1964:

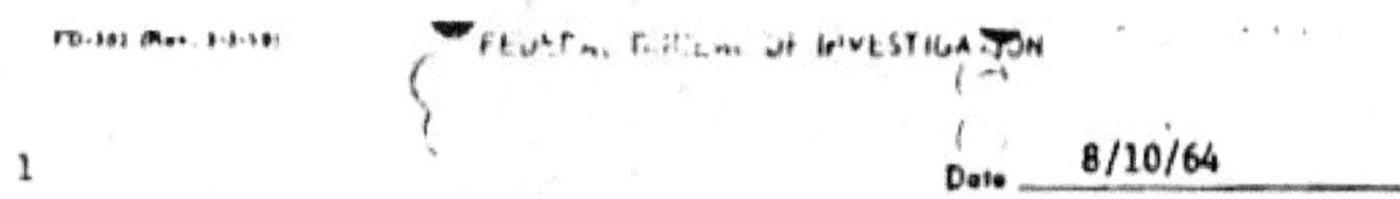

FD-302 (Rev. 1-3-58)

FEDERAL BUREAU OF INVESTIGATION

Date ___ 8/10/64 ___

1

WAYNE E. HARTMAN, accompanied by his wife, EDNA, was interviewed in the office of the Federal Bureau of Investigation. HARTMAN said he is self-employed as a manufacturer's representative calling on drugstores, department stores, and gift shops in various states throughout the country. He said he resides at 3217 Seaside, Irving, Texas.

HARTMAN said he had learned through a radio broadcast that the Federal Bureau of Investigation had been conducting additional investigation in the area of the triple underpass where President KENNEDY was assassinated and reportedly was looking for another bullet that might possibly have been fired at the time of the assassination. Upon hearing this broadcast, HARTMAN said he felt he should report the following information to the Federal Bureau of Investigation:

[…]

that someone had shot at the President. At this time, HARTMAN stated he noted a gouged out hole in the grass that was about one and one half inches in diameter. He stated this hole continued just beneath the roots of the grass for about 18 to 24 inches. He said the ground was not heaved up but was soft to the touch and could be depressed. HARTMAN said he was able to fit three fingers into the hole.

HARTMAN was exhibited photographs 7 and 8 of the photography exhibits appearing in the report of Special Agent ROBERT P. GEMBERLING dated November 30, 1963. HARTMAN stated he and his wife were standing about five feet south of the curb in the area where the culvert or manhole cover is located. He said this gouged out hole was in line with the general area of the Texas School Book Depository Building. He

[...]

HARTMAN advised that on Sunday, November 24, 1963, he and his wife returned to the area where they had observed the gouged out hole on November 22, 1963. He said the grass was trampled down by people and they could not locate the hole.

HARTMAN stated he did not know if this incident had any significance but thought he should bring it to the attention of the Federal Bureau of Investigation.

[...]

Mrs. HARTMAN advised while they were talking to the above police officer and young boy she and her husband noticed a gouged out hole in the grass. She said the hole was about one and one half inches in diameter and went right under the roots of the grass for a distance of about 18 to 24 inches. She said she was able to determine this by softly pressing on the grass above the hole and in this manner determined the length of the hole. She said a bystander had informed that he believed some shooting had come from the general

[...]

Mrs. HARTMAN advised that she and her husband returned to this area on Sunday, November 24, 1963, and attempted to locate the gouged out hole they had observed on November 22, 1963. She stated the grass was all trampled down and she and her husband could not locate the hole.

Mrs. HARTMAN was exhibited photographs 7 and 8 of the photography exhibits in Dallas report of SA ROBERT P. GEMBERLING dated November 30, 1963. She stated she and her husband were standing about five feet south of the curb in the general vicinity of the culvert or manhole cover.

On September 18, 1964, the F.B.I. created a follow-up report stating that Special Agents Nat A. Pinkston and Robert M. Barrett conducted a search of the area using a metal detector, where the Hartman's said they saw gouged-out holes in the grass near the manhole cover on November 22, 1963. However, the agents reported that they did not find any bullet fragments or any other evidence during their search:

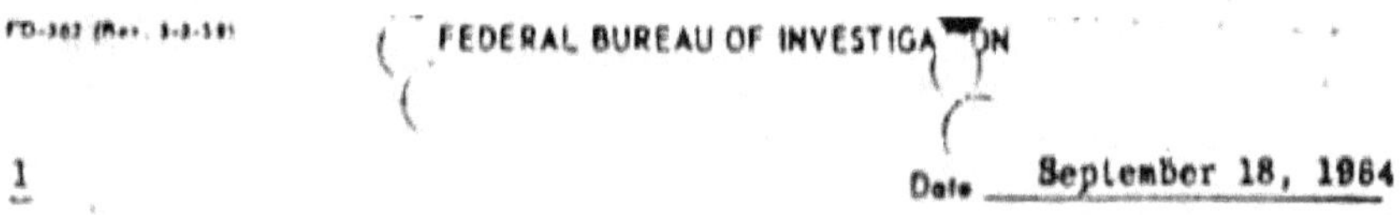

FD-302 (Rev. 1-2-59)

(FEDERAL BUREAU OF INVESTIGATION

1

Date ___September 18, 1964___

     With the use of a Detectron, Model 27, metal detector, Special Agents NAT A. PINKSTON and ROBERT M. BARRETT searched a three hundred square foot area, which area was located at the culvert on the South side of Elm Street in Dealey Plaza. This area was located based on a description of a gouged-out hole in the grass as furnished by Mr. and Mrs. WAYNE K. HARTMAN of Irving, Texas, on August 6, 1964. This gouged-out hole had been observed by the HARTMANs on November 22, 1963, subsequent to the assassination of President JOHN F. KENNEDY. The HARTMANs had pinpointed the area where they had observed this gouged-out hole from Photographs Seven and Eight from the photography exhibits appearing in the report of Special Agent ROBERT P. GEMBERLING dated November 30, 1963. The area searched was a half-circle area, using the culvert as the center. Found through the use of the metal detector were one bottle cap and one aluminum plug, measuring one inch long and one-half inch wide. No fragments or other evidence was found in the area observed.

Why would the F.B.I. wait over eight months to search this area with a metal detector, after numerous reports had already surfaced within days, hours, and even minutes after the assassination that a bullet had hit a manhole cover, and the grass located a few feet away from it on the south side of Elm Street? Was it because a bullet, or bullets had already been recovered from this area on November 22, 1963? If so, was this evidence withheld from the official record because it contradicted the F.B.I.'s report released on December 9, 1963, stating that only three shots were fired, from a rifle that could not be fired less than every 2.3 seconds? According to the official record, only three shells were recovered from the presumed murder weapon, a .65 Italian Mannlicher-Carcano.

The timing of the entire shooting sequence was determined by the F.B.I. and the Warren Commission after analyzing film footage of the assassination that Abraham Zapruder captured, using an 8 mm Bell & Howell Zoomatic camera. Their analysis determined that Zapruder's camera recorded a minimum of forty-two frames every 2.3 seconds.

Abraham Zapruder's movie camera, an 8 mm Bell & Howell Zoomatic Director Series Model 414 PD.

So apparently, in order to account for the seven bullet wounds to President Kennedy and Governor Connally, and at least one missed shot that hit the curb on Main Street near the triple underpass where Jim Tague was standing, the Warren Commission was forced to come up with the single-bullet-theory to account for the timing discrepancies found in Abraham Zapruder's film of the assassination.

In February of 1983, an interview with the Hartman's was published in Gary Mack's newsletter, "Coverups!" The Hartman's allege that the F.B.I. wasn't very interested in what they had to say, and that the agents who took their report falsified their statements to make it appear as if the gouged-out hole was in line with the school book depository. The Hartman's also clarify that they saw two separate gouges that were eighteen to twenty-four inches long, and not only one gouge as the F.B.I. had entered into their original report taken on August 6, 1964, and that the gouges were running almost parallel to each other, and were aligned in the direction of the grassy knoll, not the school book depository:

COVERUPS!

Number 7　　　　　Gary Mack, Editor & Publisher　　　　　February, 1983

(...)

Mr. and Mrs. Wayne Hartman visited the Dallas FBI office on August 6, 1964, to report their sighting of the disarrayed turf minutes after the assassination. They said they saw "two separate gouges, more or less running parallel," in the grass near the manhole about midway between where Tague was standing and the Texas School Book Depository from where Oswald allegedly fired the shots. The gouges, however, were not in line with the shots fired from the depository building, Mrs. Hartman said, but were aligned in the direction of the grassy knoll across the street and to the right front of the limousine.

"The FBI didn't seem very interested in us," Mrs. Hartman recalled last year. "They said they felt they had all the information, that they knew everything that had happened and they really didn't need our information. They talked with us a minute and then said, 'Well, we know what that [gouges] was; that was bone from Kennedy's body [skull] where it had split off.'. . . .My husband and I thought we had done all we could do; but, still and all, it sounds kind of fishy. I have never heard of a bone—have you? —that would do that."

The FBI report of the Hartmans' interview incorrectly stated that the couple found only one gouge in the grass, 18 to 24 inches long. Mrs. Hartman recalled she had pressed down along the top of each furrow to see how far they extended, and each "went much farther than that." The report also falsely quoted Hartman as saying the gouge "was in line with the general area of the Texas School Book Depository Building." This, in fact, contradicts the bureau's own explanation that a piece of Kennedy's skull struck the grass and caused the gouge. The bone couldn't have flown from the limousine and landed in the direction of the depository building unless it turned 90 degrees in midair.

(...)

Excerpts from Gary Mack's, "Coverups!" [Feb. 1983, Number 7, p. 5]

While researching the story about a bullet, or bullets found in the grass near the manhole cover on the south side of Elm Street, I watched a documentary that was produced in the early 1990s, that Phil Singer sent me after our interview called *On the Trail of the Mystery F.B.I. Man.* In this documentary, producer and historian Mark Oakes investigates what may have occurred, by interviewing several people, including Edna Hartman, who tells Oakes in a videotaped interview, that the F.B.I. did in fact falsify her and her husband's report from August 6, 1964, by making it appear that they only saw one gouge in the grass, and that it was in line with the school book depository.

Oakes also interviewed a woman named Dorothy, who was the widow of Buddy Walthers. She corroborates that her husband told her that an

F.B.I. man picked up a bullet that was lying in the grass next to the manhole cover —the same area where the Hartman's said they saw two gouged-out holes in the turf, approximately eighteen to twenty-four inches in length, running in an almost parallel direction, and were aligned with the grassy knoll on the opposite side of Elm Street.

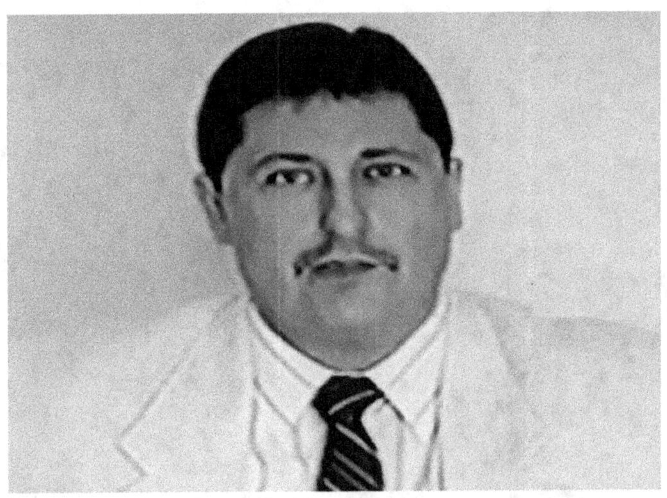

Image of researcher and historian Mark Oakes from his documentary, *On the Trail of the Mystery F.B.I. Man.*

Below are some excerpts from the documentary:

"I'm Mark Oakes. Thank you for joining me…. As you are aware, there was an investigation immediately after the assassination… A Dallas Patrolman, J. W. Foster, made his way to the south side of Elm Street, where he would later tell the Warren Commission, "To see if I could find where any of the shots hit…. I found where one shot had hit the turf there at that location, that caught the manhole cover right at the corner." In 1991, I interviewed J. W. Foster, and he confirmed his Warren Commission testimony in a videotaped interview.

Mark Oakes: You saw where a shot hit the turf on the south side of Elm Street?

J. W. Foster: Yes, Sir.

Oakes: And you said the shot had caught the manhole cover?

Foster: It caught the grate of the manhole cover, yes Sir.

Image of former Dallas Patrolman J. W. Foster during a videotaped interview with Mark Oakes in 1991, as seen in the documentary *On the Trail of the Mystery F.B.I. Man.*

Excerpts continued:

Foster was joined by Deputy E. R. Buddy Walthers, and Walthers began to inspect the area. They were joined by another man… And there were two photographers who took a series of photographs of this investigation by the names of (Jim) Murray and (William) Allen. Let's take a look at these photographs."

(Images from *On the Trail of the Mystery F.B.I. Man*)

Excerpts continued:

These are photographs of the investigation just minutes after the assassination. The mystery man bends down to pick up something, and regardless of what it was, we have not seen any report of what was recovered. What clues do we have to identify the mystery man? One clue was published in Police Chief Jesse Curry's *Assassination Files*. On page 46, Chief Curry wrote, "An

F.B.I. agent, Deputy Sheriff Walthers, and a Dallas police officer inspect the area for bullet fragments."

Also presented in the documentary is an interview with Buddy's former partner, Dallas Deputy Sheriff Alvin Maddox, who tells Oakes that a bullet was picked up from that area. When Oakes showed Maddox photos of the scene near the manhole cover in Dealey Plaza with Buddy Walthers, and of another man who appears to pick something up and walk away, Maddox immediately points to the man in the photo and says the following:

"This man right here in an F.B.I. agent, I'll promise you that! At the time, Buddy said he was. Buddy knew him. Buddy Walthers knew who he was."

Images from the documentary *On the Trail of the Mystery F.B.I. Man*. Mark Oakes (on the left) shows J.F.K. assassination evidence photos to former Dallas Deputy Sheriff Alvin Maddox (right) who then tells Oakes that the man in the photos was an F.B.I. agent.

Image from *On the Trail of the Mystery F.B.I. Man*, showing a newspaper article published on November 23, 1963, by the Fort Worth Star Telegraph. Underneath the photo, the caption reads, "ASSASSIN'S BULLET – One of the rifle bullets fired by the murderer of President Kennedy lies in the grass across Elm St."

Dallas Police Lt. J. C. Day of the crime lab estimated the distance from the sixth-floor corner window the slayer used to the spot where one of the bullets was recovered at 100 yards. He added that it could be more. Another Dallas policeman estimated the distance at 125 yards.

Another image from the documentary shows an article published on November 24, 1963 by the Dallas Times Herold, reporting that a bullet was recovered in Dealey Plaza.

In October of 1992, Mark Oakes also interviewed a man by the name of Robert Gemberling, who was a Supervisor for the F.B.I. when President Kennedy was killed. During the interview, Oakes asks Gemberling if he recognizes the man in the photographs, who Buddy Walthers said was an F.B.I. agent. Gemberling then makes the following statement to Oakes while looking at the photos:

> "I know Bob Barrett very well. Of all the agents who worked on the case, it resembles Bob Barrett.

Former F.B.I. Supervisor Robert Gemberling during his October 1992 on-camera interview, presented in Mark Oakes's documentary *On the Trail of the Mystery F.B.I. Man.*

However, approximately twenty days after the interview, Robert Gemberling sent Mark Oakes a letter retracting his statements about Robert M. Barrett resembling the man in the photos. Then, during a Dallas J.F.K. Symposium in 1993, a disgruntled Gemberling confronted Oakes for attaching his name and the statements he made about former F.B.I. Special Agent Robert Barrett to his documentary, which Oakes was able to capture in an audio recording. The following are excerpts from that recording presented in the documentary:

> **Robert Gemberling:** What grabs my ass is that you conned me!

Mark Oakes: No, I didn't.

Gemberling: I did you a damn favor, and you went and commercialized it!

Oakes: Because my interest was to find out who the man was.

Gemberling: So was mine. I made some inquiries into it. I don't know who it was. But I know it's not Bob Barrett.

Oakes: Chief Curry said it was an F.B.I. agent.

Gemberling: Well, Chief Curry isn't alive to defend himself.

Oakes: It's in his book. He wrote a book. I'll show it to you.

Gemberling: So what! Does that make it true?

Whether Robert Gemberling ever knew if the man he saw in the photographs was Robert Barrett is confusing, due to his contradictory statements that he made to Mark Oakes in the early 1990s. However, what's not confusing is the fact that Robert Barrett was indeed in Dallas working as a Special Agent for the F.B.I. on November 22, 1963. And it has been firmly established through documentation, that he was also in Dealey Plaza shortly after the President was assassinated. Barrett confirmed this in a sworn statement that he made on October 18, 1967 in connection with his investigation of film footage that was recorded by Patsy Paschall, which captured moments during the assassination, and some of the aftermath following it, including Barrett's presence in Dealey Plaza shortly after the shooting occurred:

> "I, Robert M. Barrett, am employed as a Special Agent of the Federal Bureau of Investigation and have been so employed since April 14, 1952.
>
> [...]
>
> I also recall reviewing a movie film which depicts a scene in Dealey Plaza some 30 minutes after the assassination. I am sure of this time because this film depicts myself, in one sequence,

from the rear crossing Houston Street, and I arrived at this particular area at about 1:00 p.m. on November 22, 1963.

[…]

I wish to state that I had no copy made of the film which depicts myself crossing Houston Street. I have no knowledge of any copy of this film ever being made. The film which contained a sequence showing me in the Dealey Plaza area was the same film which was subsequently returned.

I swear that the above statements are true to the best of my belief.

ROBERT M. BARRETT

Special Agent

Federal Bureau of Investigation"

The photos in question near the manhole cover were taken at approximately 12:40 p.m., according to the Hertz clock seen in the photographs located on top of the Texas School Book Depository. Barrett's admission that he appeared in Patsy Paschall's film at about 1 p.m. would put him in Dealey Plaza close to the time that the photographs near the manhole cover were taken.

Furthermore, Special Agent Robert Barrett documented in his own F.B.I. report from November 22, 1963, that he was also present at the crime scene where Dallas Police Officer J. D. Tippit was found shot to death in the Dallas suburb of Oak Cliff, and while there, at about 2 p.m. he heard a report over a police radio saying there was a possible sighting of Tippit's killer at the Texas Theater, which was located about a half-mile away. Barrett then states in his report that he went over to that theater and participated in the search, and the arrest of Lee Harvey Oswald.

Decades after the assassination, Barrett claimed that a wallet was found at the Tippit murder scene while he was there investigating it, and that it contained identification for both Oswald, and Alek Hidell (the name allegedly used by Oswald to purchase the thirteen-dollar Mannlicher-Carcano from Klein's mail-order catalog in March of 1963). However, no wallet belonging to Oswald was ever entered into evidence as being found at that scene.

As a proponent of Oswald's guilt, Barrett has insisted publicly that a wallet was found at the Tippit murder scene, and that it was a "slam-dunk" for the case against Oswald being the killer of Officer Tippit. He's also called Dallas police detective Paul Bentley's story "Hogwash," about him finding the wallet in Oswald's back pocket after he frisked him inside of a police car, shortly after Oswald was arrested at the Texas Theater.

In November of 2013, Barrett was interviewed by WFAA-TV about the wallet:

> "As I walked up, I happened to not knowingly step in a puddle of blood, which was Tippit's blood," retired FBI Special Agent Bob Barrett recalled. "I thought, 'Oh God, what have I done?'"

> [...]

> After arriving at 10th and Patton in North Oak Cliff, Barrett said, he recognized a Dallas police captain thumbing through a billfold.

> "He said, 'Bob, you know all the crooks in town, all the hoodlums, etc. You ever heard of a Lee Harvey Oswald?' I said, 'No, I never have.' He said 'How about an Alec Hiddell?' I said, 'No. I never have heard of him either,'" Barrett explained. "Why would they be asking me questions about Oswald and Hiddell if it wasn't in that wallet?"

> [...]

> "They said they took the wallet out of his pocket in the car? That's so much hogwash," Barrett said. "That wallet was in [Captain] Westbrook's hand." [Excerpts from WFAA-TV, November 20, 2013]

More detailed information pertaining to Oswald's wallet can be read in John J. Johnson's journal, "Dealey Plaza Echo," Volume 6, Issue 2: The Mystery of the Wallets. [pp. 42-49]

Mark Oakes also presented an interview with Robert Barrett over the phone in his documentary, to ask him if he was in fact the man seen in the photographs taken in Dealey Plaza next to the manhole cover:

"In June of 1992, I called Mr. Barrett. I told him that I collected autographs from witnesses and police, which is true. So, I asked Mr. Barrett if he would autograph some photos that I thought I had of him. And I sent them in the mail. And within seven days, I got the photos back, unsigned, and my original letter that I sent Mr. Barrett, with this note attached to it:

Image from *On the Trail of the Mystery F.B.I. Man.*

The note reads, "Mark, this is a photo of me – sorry. Yours truly, Bob Barrett." Totally confused on how a man of his background could make a mistake like that, I called Mr. Barrett to ask him about the note, and this was his reply:

Mark Oakes: Hi, Mr. Barrett?

Robert Barrett: Yeah.

Oakes: Hi, this is Mark Oakes. How are you?

Barrett: Fine.

Oakes: I wanted to thank you for sending that back so quick. I was just confused about your note. It says, "This is a photo of me."

Barrett: I should have said, "it's not." It's not a photograph of me.

Oakes: Oh, it's not a photograph of you?

Barrett: No.

Oakes: Oh, I see. Do you know by any chance who?

Barrett: I haven't the slightest idea. I've never seen that photograph before.

Oakes concludes his documentary with:

> "…Will we ever hear a report about this investigation? And what happened to the disappearing evidence? We will keep trying until we find the answers."

It can be argued that Mark Oakes was not able to definitively prove whether or not the man in the photographs was Special Agent Robert Barrett. And it could also be argued that Deputy Walthers made up the entire story about an F.B.I. agent who picked up a bullet from the grass, and walked away. However, in my opinion, it would be very difficult to argue that there isn't strong evidence of a cover-up by the Warren Commission, and the F.B.I. about what happened near the manhole cover in Dealey Plaza on the south side of Elm Street. And according to the Hartman's, Robert Barrett participated in that cover-up by falsifying their statements about what they actually witnessed in Dealey Plaza, in their report that was taken by him and another F.B.I. agent on August 6, 1964:

the grassy area that separates Main and Elm Streets about midway
between Houston Street and the triple underpass. HARTMAN advised he
and his wife, out of curiosity, proceeded down to the location where

on   8/6/64   at   Dallas, Texas   File #   DL 100-10461

A. RAYMOND SWITZER and
by Special Agent   ROBERT M. BARRETT:vm   Date dictated   8/7/64

This document contains neither recommendations nor conclusions of the FBI. It is the property of the FBI and is loaned to your agency; it and its contents are not to be distributed outside your agency.

Excerpt from the Hartman's 1964 F.B.I. report, showing that Robert Barrett was one of the agents responsible for taking their statements.

The Hartman's have emphatically said numerous times, through interviews with Mark Oakes and others, that the report taken by F.B.I. agents on August 6, 1964, was falsified in such a way that made their statements appear to support the official narrative – that three shots, and three shots only, were fired from a lone assassin's rifle, who was located on the sixth-floor of the Texas School Book Depository.

The Hartman's aren't the only witnesses who've come forward to say their statements were tampered with by government officials. Several have, including former Dallas Deputy Sheriff Roger Craig.

If we are to believe these eyewitnesses, then why would officials purposely falsify their statements? The most obvious reason to me, is because their statements contradicted the official narrative that was being created to frame Lee Harvey Oswald as being the only person responsible for the assassination of President John F. Kennedy.

Phil Singer interview continued...

Phil: Well, as I'm sure you know, Buddy Walthers died under some strange circumstances himself.

Steve: Yeah, I think he was possibly set up. He was shot in the chest and killed in a motel room on January 10th, 1969, while trying to arrest an escaped prisoner named James Walter Cherry, just a few weeks before

Jim Garrison's trial of Clay Shaw, scheduled to begin in February of that same year. Garrison tried to get Buddy to testify at Shaw's trial, but due to his timely death, he wasn't able to.

Deputy Is Killed In Motel Shootout

DALLAS, Tex. (AP) — A couple described as "known characters" by Sheriff Bill Decker were charged with murder late Friday in the slaying of one of the sheriff's deputies and wounding of a second.

The shooting erupted at an East Dallas motel when the sheriff's officers arrived their on a routine check.

Charged with murder were James Walter Cherry, 41, and Twyna Lovell Blankenship, 26. Justice of the Peace Bill Richburg declined to set bond for either. They also were charged with assault to murder, and sheriff's deputies said other charges were pending.

Sheriff Decker said both Cherry and Miss Blankenship had been residents of Dallas County for many years and that both had previous police records. A third person, Carl Ray Thacker,

26, who was arrested when police nabbed the woman, was charged with illegal possession of narcotics. No bond was set immediately.

Serious Condition

Cherry, shot three times, was listed in serious condition at Parkland Hospital. The Blankenship woman, not hit in the quick fire, was held in the Dallas County Jail.

The dead officer was identified as Eddie Ray (Buddy) Walthers, 38, who died shortly after arriving at the hospital. His partner, Al Maddox, 38, was shot once in the foot and clubbed over the head with a blunt instrument. His condition was undetermined late Friday. He underwent emergency treatment at the hospital.

Checked In

A receptionist at the Eastern Hills Motel told officers the shootout took place shortly af-

ter the two investigators arrived at the office inquiring about a couple who had just checked into the motel.

The receptionist, said the couple checked in under names believed to be aliases.

She said, "It was quite and all of a sudden it sounded like fireworks."

The receptionist told authorities the man and the woman did not come to the motel originally in a car of their own. Another couple driving a black car dropped them off at Eastern Hills Friday morning, she said, and then they checked in.

Officers said the couple fled the motel in a car believed to be stolen.

The couple escaped during the shootout with the woman wearing only a nightgown.

Associated Press news article from January 1969 about the murder of Dallas Deputy Sheriff Eddie Raymond (Buddy) Walthers.

Phil: Well, as with Roger Craig, Buddy Walthers was involved with a variety of very important things. But I don't think Buddy Walthers had the courage, or the integrity that Roger Craig appears to have had.

Steve: Roger Craig's 1971 manuscript *When They Kill A President* has an entire section about Buddy Walthers. In it, Craig describes his personal experiences working with him and his reputation as a not-so-law-abiding officer of the law. He also details Buddy's alleged dirty dealings with underworld crime figures throughout the Dallas area. Now, I'd like to ask you something that's unrelated to Buddy Walthers. Before we started recording this interview, you asked me if I've spoken to Gary Shaw about Roger Craig. Can you please tell me a little more about Gary?

Phil: Well, Gary Shaw is a Texan, and is a very good, diligent, intelligent, longtime J.F.K. assassination researcher. And he knew a lot of people in this case from the sixties, to the seventies, and worked with Penn Jones, and many other people, for many, many years. And I'm going to contact him for you, if it's okay?

Steve: Yeah, absolutely. I would love to talk to him about Penn Jones. I'd also like to talk to him about a story that Robert Groden told me. He said that he had a scheduled face-to-face interview with Roger that was supposed to take place in Dallas, just days after his death, and that he and his wife had flown down to Dallas for that interview. But when they got off the plane, they were met by Penn Jones, Larry Harris and Gary Shaw, who gave Robert and his wife the bad news, that Roger had just died. So, Robert never got the chance to interview him in person. Robert was working for Congressman Thomas Downing of Virginia, who was in the process of working on legislation to try to get the J.F.K. assassination case reopened. Anyway, let's go back to Gary. So, he knew Roger, is that correct?

Phil: Yeah, he knew him. Gary Shaw wrote a phenomenal book on the case, called *Cover-up*. I believe it came out in '76. There's quite a lot of stuff in there about Roger Craig. And Gary Shaw had interviewed Roger Craig, and told his story, of what Roger saw and heard that day in Dealey Plaza.

Steve: Well, I would love that. If you could arrange that, I would love to talk to Gary. Maybe he could fill in some blanks about Roger's life, and his death. That would be fantastic.

Phil: As soon as I get off the phone, I'll call him. We're on good terms. We have a good relationship. So, I think if I say, "I'd like you to do me a favor, I think you ought to call this guy," I think he will give you a call. I think someone told me you were in Ohio.

Steve: No, no. Not Ohio. I'm originally from the Detroit area. But I moved to Los Angeles in 2000, and that's where I live now.

Phil: Oh, okay. Well, when I get off the phone with you, I'll give him a call.

Steve: Thanks a lot, Phil. I really appreciate that. Before we get off the phone, is there anything else you'd like to talk about? Any closing words?

Phil: Well, I just wish you luck on your project. Because Roger Craig is a person that a lot of people need to know more about. At least to me, he seemed like a brave and heroic guy. Like Abraham Bolden, that you may, or may not know of, who was also compelled to say, "Hey, this is what I saw, this is what I heard," and not back down.

Steve: Yeah, I'm friends with Abraham on Facebook, and somewhat familiar with his case. He was the first African-American Secret Service agent that Kennedy hired, wasn't he?

Phil: Yeah. That's pretty much it. If you want to hear it, I'll tell you the story really quick.

Steve: Yeah, please. Go ahead.

Phil: Alright. So, Kennedy wins the election as we all know, over Nixon in 1960. But he doesn't get inaugurated and sworn in, until January of '61. And Abraham Bolden, at that time, was working for the Secret Service in Chicago. They have branches all over. And being a division of the Treasury Department, they would primarily handle things like counterfeiting and extortion, and other kinds of cases. And of course, if a president came to town, then they had double-duty of protection. Well, Kennedy had a trip in the spring to come to Chicago, just a couple months after he became president. Bolden, like I said, was working for the local Secret Service, and was told, "You're going to McCormick Place to provide extra security for President Kennedy," where Kennedy had a scheduled speaking engagement at this big venue. So, they assigned Abraham Bolden, this young African-American Secret Service agent, to go over to McCormick Place. Of course, they used the term "Negro" back then. They said, "You have to guard the basement washroom." And Bolden's thinking, "Aw man, I want to be on the main floor, I want to see Kennedy and hear him give his talk. Maybe get to shake his hand." But they assign him the basement washroom. Well, he goes down there, makes sure no one's hiding in the washroom, and there's nothing concealed in there. And so, he's standing guard at the door to the washroom in the basement. And then he hears all these footsteps and commotion, and he sees all these feet and legs coming down the stairs. And sure enough, there's Mayor Daley, and I think Senator Everett Dirksen, and then there's President Kennedy. Well, they just got in from the airport, and they wanted to use the washroom before they got started with the, you know, festivities. Well, Abraham Bolden is standing at the bottom of the stairs, in front of the washroom. Here he is, a young African-American Secret Service agent. This is the spring of '61. And Kennedy stops in front of him and says, "Hello, how are you?" And Bolden says, "Doing fine, Mr. President." The president shakes his hand, and asks him, "Are you with the Police Department or the Secret Service?" And Bolden says, "I work for the Secret Service, sir." And Kennedy asks him, "Do you know if there's ever been a negro on the White House detail of the Secret Service?" And Bolden answers, "Well, I don't know for sure, but I don't think so." So, Kennedy asks, "Well, how would you like to be the first one?" And Bolden says, "Well, yes sir, Mr. President, I would." So, Kennedy says, "Then I'll get the paperwork ready for your transfer. Thank you." And Bolden couldn't believe it, you know? He's there in the basement, thinking that he's never gonna see the president. And the next thing he knows, he's shaking hands with him, and having a one-on-one conversation with him, and is asked if he'd like to be the first negro on the White House Secret Service detail. He just couldn't believe it. So, Abraham goes home that night, and he says to his wife, "Guess who I met today?" And she asks, "Who?" And he says, "President Kennedy!" And she says, "Aw, you're full of shit." She didn't believe him and said he was full of shit (laughter). So, he says, "No, no, he wants me to come to Washington." Then a month or two later, the paperwork goes through, and he's transferred to Washington, and he's the first negro, or African-American, on the White House detail of the Secret Service. Everyone else is white. Most of them are southerners. Almost all of them are racist. And it didn't go well. It did not go well at all for him. And I can go into those stories, if you'd like to hear them.

Secret Service Adds Negro to JFK Guard

WASHINGTON (AP) — For the first time, a Negro is one of the Secret Service agents guarding the President.

The agent, Abraham Bolden, is on a 30-day temporary assignment to the White House detail. If he does all right, he could be assigned there permanently.

Michael Torina, chief inspector of the Secret Service, said Bolden was routinely transferred from Chicago and "we aren't making anything of it or providing any biographical matter, as is the same for any other agent."

June 16, 1961: Associated Press reports on Abraham Bolden's transfer to President Kennedy's White House Secret Service detail.

Steve: Well, I think I know the story about Abraham being very critical of the Secret Service detail in Dallas. Didn't he come forward with information about Secret Service agents going to bars, I think the night before, and were hungover the next day? And then the next thing you know… what was the case against him?

Phil: They said he was trying to sell government documents and they put him in prison, for a number of years. I think it was to shut him up, and it was to send a very clear warning to anybody, especially Secret Service people, and also people like Roger Craig who caught wind of it. Like, "You better keep your mouth shut!" That's what I suspect. He's still alive. I'm very good friends with him. He's not in the best of health. He's 84 years old. But he tried coming forward to the Warren Commission in the spring of '64, to tell them some things he knew.

Steve: Can you briefly go over some of the things he knew, and what he was trying to bring to the commission?

Phil: Yeah? Do you want to hear them?

Steve: Yeah, go ahead.

Phil: A number of these agents weren't happy that Kennedy hired a black man to be a part of the White House Secret Service team. He was the first. And they were resentful. They didn't like blacks. They didn't like him. And they didn't like Kennedy for hiring him. And several of these agents would say out loud in front of him, "Kennedy is a nigger lover." Which not only knocked Kennedy, but also knocked Bolden. And they would say that where Bolden could hear it. At one point there was a noose that was hung above Bolden's desk, which was a huge symbol, especially back in '61, of southern lynchings by white people of black people. Then on one day, he's guarding the hallway of the White House, and Kennedy peeps his head out of the door to the Oval Office, and he says, "Mr. Bolden, come here, I want to introduce you to a couple of people." So, Bolden walks over, and goes into the Oval Office, and Kennedy introduces him, "This is Mr. Bolden from Chicago. He's new on the Secret Service. This is my brother Bobby, the Attorney General." And there's a couple other people. I think Senator Hubert Humphrey is there. And Kennedy says, "This is the Jackie Robinson of the Secret Service." Well, to a young black man at that time, to be compared to Jackie Robinson, there's nothing that could make you feel more proud, you know? So, after that, Bolden goes back to his position in the hallway, and his superior comes up to him later and asks, "What was that all about earlier?" And Bolden asks, "What are you talking about?" And then his superior says, "Well, you left your position in the hallway." And Bolden says, "Oh yeah, the president asked me to come into the Oval Office." And his superior says, "You're not allowed to leave your position; Why did you leave your position? You're supposed to be guarding the president." And Bolden says, "I was with the president, he's the one who told me to come into the Oval Office." Well, his superior was messing with him.

Abraham Bolden (far right) stands at his post, while serving on President Kennedy's White House Secret Service detail.

Phil: Then one day, they're off-duty, and they're at a hotel, in this lounge, all these Secret Service guys, and they're sitting back, drinking beers, but they were technically off-duty. And his superior, named Harvey Henderson says, "Bolden, I need to tell you something." And Abraham Bolden says, "Harvey, what's that?" Harvey Henderson looks at him, he's got a beer in his hand, and he says, "I'm gonna tell you once, and I want you to listen good, you understand me?" And Bolden says, "Yeah okay Harvey, what do you have to tell me?" And this is Bolden's superior in the Secret Service. Harvey Henderson goes on to say, "You're a nigger. You were born a nigger. And you're gonna die a nigger. So, you might as well start acting like a nigger. Do you understand me?" This was his superior. Well, he couldn't go to his superior with this. So, he went over him, and went to the head of the Secret Service, a man by the name of U. E. Baughman. And Baughman tells Bolden, "You're just being thin-skinned, he doesn't really mean that. Don't let it bother you." So, it just got to be enough is enough, and Abraham decided to go back to Chicago. Now a couple of times, these agents said right in front of Bolden, "If someone shoots at the president, I'm not gonna take a bullet for him, because he's a nigger lover." Now, when Kennedy was shot on November 22nd, 1963, Abraham Bolden was not in Dallas. He was in Chicago. He had transferred back, like I said, and he was in Chicago, but he knew there was some stuff up. Primarily he knew, because three weeks earlier there was an aborted attempt on Kennedy's life in Chicago, when he was going to attend a football game at Soldier Field. And the Secret Service in Chicago caught wind of this, and it never happened of course, because Kennedy's trip to Chicago was immediately canceled. This whole thing was covered up. Then Kennedy dies three weeks later after this aborted attempt on November 2nd, 1963, because the Secret Service in Chicago dismantled it before it ever happened. Well, three weeks later Kennedy's killed in Dallas and Bolden is just shaking his head. He knew these guys drank on the job. And sure enough, that did come out later, that a lot of these guys were out late-night drinking at clubs, didn't get sleep, were tired, and didn't react well. So, Bolden happened to be in Washington in the spring of '64, and he tried to contact J. Lee Rankin, who was the General Counsel of the Warren Commission. So, he came forward to tell him what he knew, that there was an attempt in Chicago on November 2nd, twenty days before Kennedy actually died. And that he knew these guys, that they drank on the job, that they said they weren't gonna take a bullet for Kennedy. Blah, blah, blah. Well, they were listening in on his phone call. They arrested him immediately. They flew him back to Chicago. Charged him with trying to sell government documents. And put him in jail for a number of years. Ended his career. Put him on all kinds of psychotropic drugs, where he was being held in Springfield, Missouri.

Suspended Agent Charges Drinking By Kennedy Guards

Accuser Facing Allegations Of Soliciting Pay-Off

CHICAGO, May 21 (AP)—A Secret Service agent, accused of soliciting a $50,000 pay-off, charged yesterday that the Government framed him because he planned to reveal the "over-all general laxity" of agents guarding President Kennedy.

Abraham Bolden, 29, said yesterday that agents guarding President Kennedy drank heavily before and after tours of duty at Washington and Hyannis Port, Mass. He also said they often reported half-drunk for duty or missed their assignments completely.

A federal attorney scoffed at Mr. Bolden's accusations.

Mr. Bolden was suspended Tuesday after he was charged with attempting to sell a top-secret government file to a

—Associated Press Wirephoto
ABRAHAM BOLDEN
Secret Service agent

Associated Press article, May 21, 1964.

Secret Service Agent Gets 6 Years In Jail

CHICAGO (AP) — U.S. Atty. Edward V. Hanrahan has hailed the conviction of Secret Service Agent Abraham Bolden as clearing the integrity of the U.S. Secret Service.

Bolden, the first Negro ever assigned to guard a U.S. president, was convicted and sentenced to six years in prison Wednesday of trying to sell government evidence in a counterfeiting case for $50,000.

He had charged that the government framed him because he planned to tell the Warren Commission about what Bolden contended was laxity and drunkenness among secret service agents assigned to guard President Kennedy in 1961.

Bolden was not on the White House detail in November 1963 when President Kennedy was assassinated in Dallas. He offered to testify before the Warren Commission, however, that agents were engaged in excessive girl-chasing, and turned up bleary-eyed for duty guarding the President in Hyannis Port and Washington.

The commission did not hear him.

Secret Service," Hanrahan told newsmen.

He said it was to Bolden's credit that he "apologized for the charges he made against the Secret Service and the government in general."

Bolden, 29, made his apology in a tearful plea for mercy after his conviction was announced and before sentencing in U.S. District Court by Judge Joseph Sam Perry.

Bolden wiped tears from his eyes as he stood before Judge Perry.

Judge Perry then sentenced Bolden to 6 years. He could have sentenced him to 25 years in prison and fined him $15,000 plus three times the amount of the $50,000 payment sought, a total of $165,000.

It was the second trial for Bolden, with the first ending in a hung jury.

He was convicted on three counts of attempted sale of Secret Service documents, obstruction of justice and conspiracy. He was found guilty of trying to sell a government file on May 12 to Joseph Spagnoli, alleged head of a counterfeiting ring.

Associated Press article, August 13, 1964.

Steve: Sorry to interrupt you, but just for the people reading this, you got this straight from Abraham? Is that correct?

Phil: Got it straight from Abraham a number of times. And it's in his book, called *The Echo From Dealey Plaza*. Came out in 2008. But he told me the stories repeatedly, because we became good friends, and still are good friends. He was always consistent in what he said. And I believe him. You know, like Roger Craig. You can believe him or not believe him. But I believe Roger Craig and I believe Abraham Bolden.

Abraham Bolden in 2014.
(Photo courtesy of Phil Singer)

Steve: I'm in that same camp too. I haven't spent nearly as much time as you have on Abraham's story, and I don't know him personally. I've never had a conversation with the man in my life. But he did wish me a happy birthday on my Facebook page a couple of weeks ago, which was really nice.

Phil: Oh, really? Good.

Steve: He has a pretty large following on Facebook. Many people do admire him. And I'm definitely one of them.

Phil: Good.

Steve: Yeah. And from what I read about his situation, it definitely looked like a set-up to keep him quiet, and like you said earlier, for others who may have wanted to come forward with information to keep them quiet too.

Phil: Yeah. Some people like Roger Craig were still brave. But other people, like Buddy Walthers, got the hint.

Steve: Well, thank you very much for sharing that story about Abraham, Phil. Some of that stuff I've never heard before, and it's good to know. And I really appreciate this interview. And I think the readers will too.

Phil: You're welcome. I'll go ahead and give Gary a call right now, and hopefully he'll be in touch with you.

Steve: Okay, that would be great. Thanks, Phil.

"I have been financially ruined. My reputation has suffered. And I've been left totally disabled. But until they silence me, I will continue to tell it like it was."

-Roger Dean Craig

J. Gary Shaw

Steve Cameron: Hi Gary. You caught me by surprise this morning. A happy surprise. I've been wanting to interview you for a long time, and waiting for other people to get you in touch with me. How did that come about? Who contacted you?

J. Gary Shaw: Phil did. He called me two days ago.

Steve: Phil Singer?

Gary: He said that I really needed to talk to you. He had talked to me in the past, quite a few times, about Roger. Because he knew of the relationship, I had with him, and with Penn. So, I decided well, maybe I can help. The story is important. The truth and the lies that were told about Roger. Both are important. I got to know him fairly well. He wasn't a close confidant or friend, but I knew him well enough. I was impressed with his intelligence, his street smarts as a policeman, as an officer of the law. I think he was intelligent in every aspect. And articulate for the most part. And so, I enjoyed my relationship with him.

Steve: Before we go further, if it's ok, can you please tell me about your background? Where you're from? And how did you become involved in the J.F.K. assassination case?

Gary: Ok, it's a rather lengthy story. I'll give it to you as briefly as possible.

Steve: Thank you.

Gary: As a senior in high school, we formed a doo-wop group. We were singing, and got acquainted with a local rockabilly singer named Johnny Carroll. And did some records with him, and did some performances.

1957 photo of The Matadors, with Shaw on the far right.
(Courtesy of J. Gary Shaw)

Johnny Carroll
(Courtesy of Dragon Street Records)

Gary: In fact, in late 1956 or early 1957, we actually performed at the Texas Theater in Dallas. And it was there where I first met, Jack Ruby. He came to the performance. The agent who was handling Johnny Carroll was a man named J. G. Tiger [real name Jack Goldman]. If you looked in Jack Ruby's phonebook, you'd find his name in there. They were close buddies. But he's the one who had gotten the show together. And Jack had come over there. And he came backstage after we performed with Carrol, and wanted us to join the AGVA, which is the artists guild there in Dallas. He wanted us to come over to the Ed McLemore arena in Dallas, where a group of AGVA folks were meeting, and do a little performance for them. And we did. So, that's how I became acquainted with Jack Ruby. From there, until about '61 or '62, I was in and out of Dallas a lot. Cleburne is where I live. And we're about an hour's drive from Dallas.

Jack Ruby shortly after being arrested for killing Lee Harvey Oswald.

Steve: Let's back up there for a second. What was your first impression of Jack Ruby when you first met him?

Gary: A Yankee (laughter).

Steve: A Yankee? Oh yeah, from Chicago.

Gary: Yeah. He was a fast-talking Yankee (laughter). Very friendly. And so was J. G. Tiger. Later we went to Ruby's club quite often. It was a nightclub. And we had gone there quite often. Up until about 1962, I guess. And he would come and sit at our table on occasion. I didn't "know" him, but I "knew" him.

Steve: You knew his reputation?

Gary: Yeah. Somewhat. My first thought when he was introduced, I thought, "That's a good mafia name" because the scuttlebutt was, "Watch out for him, he's mafia." I thought of Legs Diamond, who was an old mafia guy, well known in the '30s and '40s, and I thought, "What a good name for a mafia guy, Jack Ruby."

Steve: This encounter with Jack Ruby, how long before November 22, 1963?

Gary: I was eighteen, probably, so it was about seven years. At that time, just a little item of interest, there were three clubs like his, that were within a block of each other in downtown Dallas. The Colony Club right next door to The Carousel Club. And right around the corner was The Theater Lounge. All of them had girls, and dancing, and that sort of thing. They staggered their shows, where you could actually go to one, and then go to the other, and go to the other. You could get through three and a half hours of entertainment when you went to Dallas. So, we did that on occasion. And that's how I got to know Ruby. And when he shot Oswald, I thought, "Hey, there's something wrong here." And I began to get my hands on every newspaper I could. Life Magazine. Time. Save them, and read them. But it was not until about '66, somewhere along in there, that I became acquainted with Penn Jones. Penn Jones was a small-town weekly newspaper owner, and editor. He was writing stories about the Kennedy assassination, and he had put out a book called *Forgive My Grief*. And I read that, and I was more or less hooked. I went and met with him. And at that time, he was selling entire sets of the Warren Commission's Report, as well as critical books on the subject. So, I bought everything, including two sets of the 26 volumes of *The Warren Report*. And I began to pour through that. I began to visit with Penn frequently. He would call when he was gonna give a talk, and I would carry his projector, and whatever else. That was my initiation into the thing. When Garrison announced that he was reopening the investigation down in New Orleans, it was an exciting thing for us. I had decided at about that time, I should try to write. I wrote several articles for Penn's paper, books, and newsletter. I read enough of the 26 volumes, that I was convinced beyond any shadow of a doubt, that we didn't have the truth. That's how I got started. That's it in a nutshell.

Members of the Warren Commission meet with President Johnson in the Cabinet Room of the White House, to present their final report on their investigation of former President Kennedy's assassination. Left to right: John McCloy, J. Lee Rankin, Senator Richard Russell, Congressman Gerald Ford, Chief Justice Earl Warren, President Lyndon Johnson, Former Director of the C.I.A. Allen Dulles, Senator John Sherman Cooper, and Congressman Hale Boggs.

Gary: Oh, and the book that really, really turned me on was Mark Lane's book. I was a member of the Book of the Month Club, and it came up, and I bought it for I think two bucks at the time (laughter). And so, I got the hardcopy version of *Rush to Judgment*. And then I knew. I *thought* there was something wrong, but then I *knew* something was wrong. And that was my initiation into the critical community.

Steve: When you met Penn Jones, during your first encounter, what was your impression of him?

Gary: My first impression was: "Here is a great guy! He's my height, he's got a ready laugh, and he's tough as a boot!" And here he was in the shadow of Dallas, writing articles that condemned the official version of what happened over there. And he wasn't pulling any punches at all. And I liked him immediately. I walked in when I first met him, and he came up with a big smile on his face. I told him why I was there. And by the time I bought everything he had, he said, "You're really serious, aren't ya?" And I said, "Yes I am!" So that's how I met him.

Steve: He took you under his wing?

Gary: He really did. He took me under his wing.

Steve: This is leading up to my first question about Roger. Can you recall the first time you ever heard Roger Craig's name?

Gary: Yeah. Not exactly of course. He was in Penn's *Forgive My Grief,* and Mark Lane had written about him, so I knew a little bit about him. But it wasn't until after Garrison opened his investigation, that I think Penn brought him, for the first time, over to my office in Cleburne.

Steve: Garrison, or Roger?

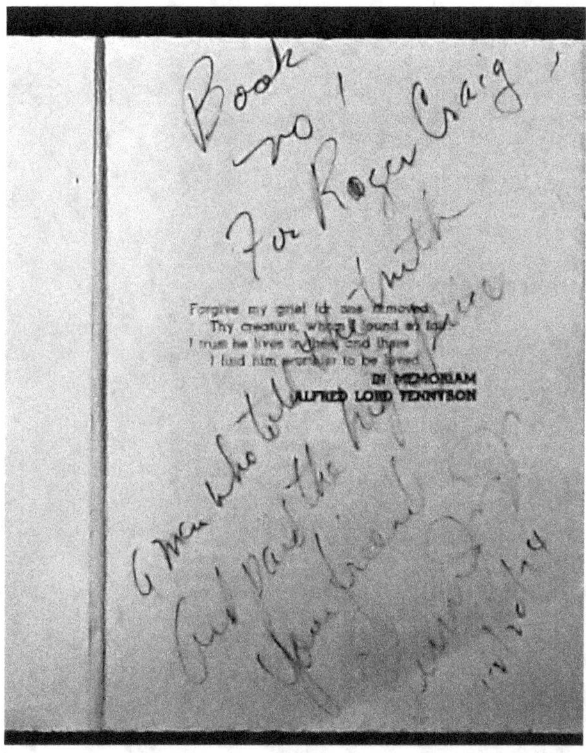

Signed copy of Penn Jones' book *Forgive My Greif, Volume IV* (1974), given to Roger Craig five months before his death.
(Photo courtesy of Roger Craig Jr.)

Gary: Penn brought Roger over. And I liked him immediately. Here was a tall, good looking guy, you know? Intelligent. Articulate. That's the first time I met him. Penn had kind of taken him under his wing. Penn was trying to help Garrison at that time.

Steve: Have you read Roger's manuscript *When They Kill A President?*

Gary: Yes, but a long time ago.

Steve: He documents the first time that he met Penn. It was right after he was shot at the first time. He had just returned from New Orleans, after Jim Garrison had arranged a trip for him to come there, so that he could interview him for his upcoming trial against Clay Shaw. So, Roger called Garrison to let him know what just happened, that he had been shot at. Garrison told him, "I'll send somebody over!" And he got a knock on his door, I think the next day, and it was Penn. And I believe that was the first time that Penn Jones and Roger Craig met each other, at least in person.

Gary: It was some time after that, that Penn brought him over and introduced him to me, as I recall.

Steve: Did you guys have private conversations about Roger when he wasn't around?

Gary: I'm sure we did. Yeah. What they were about, I don't recall. I believed Roger's testimony, reading it out of the volumes.

Steve: What year would that have been, if you can recall, what year did you first meet Roger face to face?

Gary: I would think it was '67 or '68.

Steve: But it was leading up to Garrison's trial, correct?

Gary: Yeah, that's right

Steve: So, you met Roger. You had conversations with Roger. Many of the things that Roger talked about, were explosive to the official version of what happened. Is there anything that stands out in your mind? A key piece of information that Roger had?

Gary: Yeah, I thought it was explosive. Here was a guy, that saw Lee Harvey Oswald doing something, that they denied he did. He wasn't in

The School Book Depository right after the shots. He didn't get on a bus. He got in a car. That was devastating to their official conclusion. And boy, he never backed off of it. It wasn't long after that, that Richard Randolph Carr came to Penn, and when I decided to write *Cover-up*. I interviewed Roger in Penn's living room, probably in '70 or '71. And then not long after that, I interviewed Richard Carr. And he basically tells a story that coincides with Roger's story.

Steve: About the Rambler?

Gary: Yeah, about the Rambler. And not long after, I interviewed Marvin Robinson. Do you know that name?

Steve: Yes. How many were there? Was it three corroborating stories of a man getting into a station wagon?

Gary: I think last count I had was four. Michael Kurtz out of Louisiana wrote a book, and he had another person. I think another lady. I don't remember her name, but he had a lady that said the same thing. So, actually there's about five, including Roger.

Author's note: Upon further research, I found a total of eight witnesses who corroborate Roger Craig's testimony about the Rambler station wagon.

Author, Michael L. Kurtz, identifies Helen Forrest as the woman J. Gary Shaw mentioned in our interview, who witnessed a man identical to Lee Harvey Oswald get into the passenger side of a Rambler station wagon in his book *Crime of the Century* [pp. 132, 189]. Forrest is quoted as saying, "If it wasn't Oswald, it was his identical twin." Kurtz also names James Pennington as an additional witness who saw a man identical to Lee Harvey Oswald run from the School Book Depository and get into a Rambler station wagon [p. 189].

Author, James Douglass, also identifies the witnesses who corroborate Roger Craig's testimony in his book *J.F.K. and the Unspeakable*. Douglass writes:

> "After Oswald mentioned Ruth Paine's station wagon, he said, "Now everyone will know who I am." At this point Fritz ushered Craig out of his office. It was too late — for the

government and for Craig who had seen and heard too much. What Roger Craig would testify to in the years ahead would be corroborated by a parade of other witnesses: Ed Hoffman, Carolyn Walther, James Worrell, Richard Carr, Helen Forrest, James Pennington, Marvin Robinson and Roy Cooper. The Rambler was the getaway car." [Douglass, *J.F.K. and the Unspeakable*, p. 274]

Furthermore, writer Richard Charnin defends Roger Craig, by blasting the Warren Commission's official version of Oswald's movements. In his 2014 article, "J.F.K. Explosive Testimony: Roger Craig, Will Fritz and Oswald," Charnin writes:

> "In choosing to dismiss Craig's testimony, the WC relied on the tortured testimony of:
>
> – Cab driver Whaley, whose manifest showed he picked up Oswald at 12:30. He failed to identify him in the lineup and his description of Oswald's clothing was full of contradictory statements.
>
> – Bus driver McWatters could not identify Oswald.
>
> – Bus passenger Mary Bledsoe, who McWatters did not recall seeing on the bus. Her testimony was disjointed and unintelligible. She was Oswald's former landlady – a perfect witness." [richardcharnin.wordpress.com]

Interview Continued…

Steve: Did the Warren Commission interview Marvin Robinson? Isn't he in their report?

Gary: No. But I interviewed Marvin Robinson. He was scheduled to testify to the Warren Commission as a Key Person. Roger was a Key Person. The commission staff marked them as "KP," meaning Key Person. They scheduled Marvin Robinson, because they had an F.B.I.

report of what he saw, and they had him scheduled on the same day as Roger, to give his testimony to the commission. But Robinson was in the Navel Reserve, and he had one of those excursions they always do with the reservists, where he had to go to sea for a week. So, he called them, and they said, "We can postpone yours." Well, they never called him back. Because after they heard Roger, they didn't want any corroborating evidence. So, they ignored Marvin. He was really resentful of that. He sent me all of the letters that the commission wrote to him, the copies of them, and so forth.

Author's note: The following documents were found in the National Archives, under the name "Robinson, Marvin C."

JLR: JAB: jhm
25Mar64

KP
Robinson, Marvin C.

MAR 26 1964

AIR MAIL

Mr. Marvin C. Robinson
5120 South Marsalis Avenue
Dallas, Texas

Dear Mr. Robinson:

On November 29, 1963, this Commission was established and authorized to investigate and report on all the circumstances surrounding the assassination of President Kennedy and the killing of the alleged assassin, Lee Harvey Oswald. Joseph A. Ball and David W. Belin, attorneys on the staff of the Commission, desire to take your deposition in Dallas on Wednesday, April 1, 1964, at 2:00 p.m., in the office of the United States Attorney, United States Post Office Building. Will you please telephone the United States Attorney's office on receipt of this letter and advise whether or not you can be present at that time and place? The telephone number is Riverside 8-6961.

For your information, I am enclosing copies of Executive Order No. 11130 creating this Commission, S. J. Res. 137, and the Rules of Procedure of this Commission for the questioning of witnesses by members of the Commission staff.

Sincerely,

J. Lee Rankin
General Counsel

Letter to Marvin Robinson from the Warren Commission to schedule his deposition for April 1, 1964.

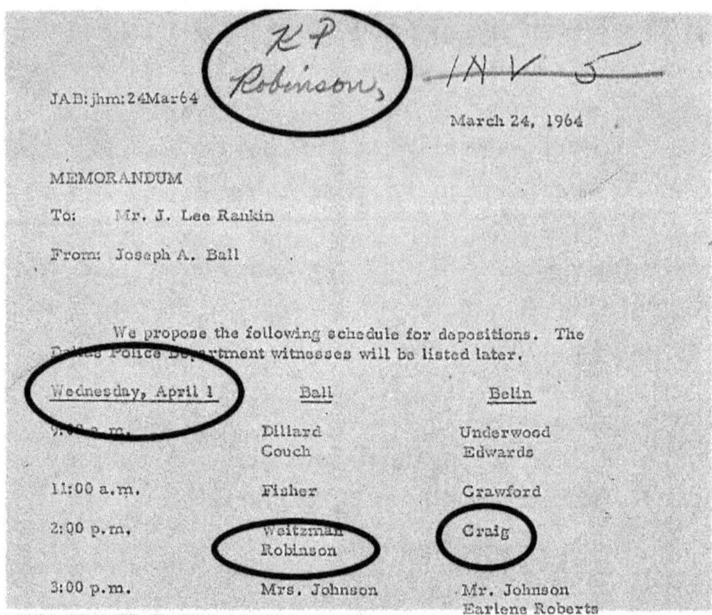

Marvin Robinson and Roger Craig were scheduled on the same day, April 1, 1964, to give depositions to the Warren Commission.

Other individuals and Organizations
Involved of Interviewed

Robinson, Marvin C.

FEDERAL BUREAU OF INVESTIGATION

1-302 (Rev. 1-3-59)

Date November 23, 1963

NOV 30 1963

MARVIN C. ROBINSON, 5120 South Marsalis Avenue, telephone number FRanklin 4-5834, advised that approximately between 12:30 and 1:00 p.m. on the afternoon of November 22, 1963, while traveling west on Elm Street he crossed the intersection of Elm and Houston Streets shortly after the assassination of President KENNEDY. ROBINSON stated that after he had crossed Houston Street and was in front of the Texas School Book Depository building a light colored Nash stationwagon suddenly appeared before him. He stated this vehicle stopped and a white male came down the grass covered incline between the building and the street and entered the stationwagon after which it drove away in the direction of the Oak Cliff section of Dallas. ROBINSON stated he does not recall the license number on the stationwagon or whether or not it bore a Texas license plate.

Marvin Robinson's F.B.I. report from the day after the assassination, that describes his sighting of a man running from the School Book Depository, who was then picked up by a light-colored Nash station wagon, before driving away from Dealey Plaza.

Interview Continued...

Steve: For the readers, can you explain what Roger reported, and what the people who corroborate his story reported?

Gary: Yeah. As briefly as possible, I'll tell you. Sheriff Decker had told his deputies to stand out in front of the Sherriff's Department. The entrance was located at the corner of Main and Houston Street. And that they were not to take part in the security of the motorcade. Roger was standing out there when he heard the shots. And of course, like any officer, he ran toward where the shots came from. As he ran down there, people were telling him a bullet hit the ground, or something like that, so he was looking around for that. As he did so, he heard a whistle. He looked up, and there was a young man coming down the knoll, from the school book depository area. He saw a light-colored Rambler station wagon, with a luggage rack on top, pull over and let this young man get in the station wagon. And then they leave out of Dealey Plaza. And later that day, he was asked by Captain Fritz to come down to the Dallas Police Department, after they brought Oswald in, to see if he was the same man Roger had seen. Well, when he sees Oswald inside Captain Fritz's office, he tells Fritz that it was the same man he saw running down the hill from the depository, and get into a car. And it shook Oswald to the core. And he gets upset and says something like, "Don't bring that up! That station wagon belongs to Mrs. Paine! Don't try to drag her into this!" And then Oswald says, "Now everyone is gonna know who I am." What that meant to Roger, is that he acted like he had blown his cover. And that's basically the story in a nutshell.

Steve: And "Mrs. Paine" is Ruth Paine?

Gary: Best friends with Marina Oswald, who Marina was living with at the time.

Steve: And if I'm not mistaken, it was Ruth Paine who helped Oswald get the job at the Texas School Book Depository?

Gary: That's what we're told.

Steve: Do we know where Ruth Paine was when the assassination occurred?

Gary: Well, she was home when the officers came to her house, not long after Oswald was arrested. I believe she said something like, "Come on in. I've been expecting you." I'm assuming she was in the area, or possibly at home. I don't remember reading in her testimony that she was at home, or somewhere else.

Steve: I thought I read that they confiscated some filing cabinets from her home?

Gary: They did.

Steve: Do we know the contents of those filing Cabinets?

Gary: No, we don't know the contents of them.

Author's note: Deputy Sheriff Buddy Walther's documented his confiscation of the file cabinets from Ruth Paine's home in his typed report from November 22, 1963, stating that they contained names and activities of Cuban sympathizers:

COUNTY OF DALLAS
SHERIFF'S DEPARTMENT

SUPPLEMENTARY INVESTIGATION REPORT

Name of Complainant   Serial No.

    Page 3 - continued - Deputy Buddy Walthers

Offense

[...]

Will Fritz' office. We arrived at location and met Detectives Rose and Adamcik from the Homicide division of the Dallas Police Department. Upon getting to this residence, we were met by a Mrs. Michael Payne and upon showing our credentials and advising her who we were, she stated, "It's about the President being shot. We've been expecting it. Come on in".

[...]

Upon searching this house we found stacks of hand-bills concerning "Cuba for Freedom" advertising, seeking publicity and support for Cuba. Also found was a set of metal file cabinets containing records that appeared to be names and activities of Cuban sympathizers. All of this evidence was confiscated and turned over to Captain Fritz of the Dallas Police Department and Secret Service Officers at the City Hall.

However, during Wather's July 23, 1964 testimony to the Warren Commission, he denied seeing any records inside the file cabinets containing names and activities of Cuban sympathizers:

> Mr. WALTHERS. ...we found some little metal file cabinets---I don't know what kind you would call them---they would carry an 8 by 10 folder, all right, but with a single handle on top of it and the handle moves.
>
> Mr. LIEBELER. About how many of them would you think there were?
>
> Mr. WALTHERS. There were six or seven, I believe, and I put them all in the trunk of my car...
> Mr. LIEBELER. What was in these file cabinets?

Mr. WALTHERS. We didn't go through them at the scene. I do remember a letterhead--I can't describe it--I know we opened one of them and we seen what it was, that it was a lot of personal letters and stuff and a letterhead that this Paine fellow had told us about...

Mr. LIEBELER. I have been advised that some story has developed that at some point that when you went out there you found seven file cabinets full of cards that had the names on them of pro-Castro sympathizers or something of that kind, but you don't remember seeing any of them?

Mr. WALTHERS. Well, that could have been one, but I didn't see it.

Mr. LIEBELER. There certainly weren't any seven file cabinets with the stuff you got out there or anything like that?

Mr. WALTHERS. I picked up all of these file cabinets and what all of them contained, I don't know myself to this day.

Interview Continued...

Steve: Let's go back for a second, to when Roger saw Oswald in Captain Fritz's office. When Oswald said, "That's Mrs. Paine's station wagon! Leave her out of this!" — what do you think he meant by that? I'm asking, because she did own a station wagon, but it was a 1955 Chevy BelAir station wagon, and not a Rambler. So that's a little confusing to me, as I'm sure it probably is to others, who've studied this area of research.

Gary: Well, I don't think Ruth Paine's station wagon had anything to do with it. That was a perception that Oswald had, and his connection with Ruth Paine. Not in the assassination necessarily. But in the relationship that they had with some other shenanigans that may have been going on in Dallas at that time.

Steve: Right. I think that's where a lot of the confusion lies for people.

Author's note: Lee Harvey Oswald was known to have used Ruth Paine's car in the past. According to his barber, Clifton Shasteen, he occasionally saw Oswald drive a 1955 Chevy station wagon to his shop to get haircuts. Below are excerpts from his testimony to the Warren Commission on April 1, 1964:

Mr. JENNER. I understand that in the course of your looking at television on the 22d of November 1963, there occurred to you upon seeing some of the people shown on the screen that you had rendered some tonsorial services to Lee Harvey Oswald?

Mr. SHASTEEN. ...when I saw his picture I remembered him coming in the shop...All three of the barbers in there have cut his hair, but I cut it more ...I cut his hair three or four times...

Mr. JENNER. And did you recognize any of the persons who were accompanying him?

Mr. SHASTEEN. No; I wouldn't say I did because most of the time---they headed--they got out of the car and we saw their backs, and I would see him and I just knew it was him...

Mr. JENNER. So, you're not in a position, I take it, then, to say that you have a distinct recollection that Mrs. Paine accompanied them at anytime?

Mr. SHASTEEN. Well, now, that part of it I would have to take for granted because they were in his car. Now, she, I understand through one of the men who questioned me out at the shop, said he never did drive her car. Again, I'm going to disagree because I know that he did. He drove it up there and got a haircut.

Mr. JENNER. You have a distinct recollection that on occasions when this man came into your shop for a haircut, he drove an automobile up to your shop?

Mr. SHASTEEN. He drove that there 1955, I think it's a 1955, I'm sure it's a 1955 Chevrolet station wagon. It's either blue and white or green and white it's two-toned--I know that. Now, why I say--why I take it for granted that Mrs. Paine was with him when he come to the grocery store I do remember he wasn't driving when they would come to the grocery store, there would be a lady driving and I'm assuming that that was Mrs. Paine....

Mr. JENNER. Were there any occasions when you have a recollection as to his being accompanied by more than one person?

Mr. SHASTEEN. Yes; that's what I said--I saw him and two ladies get out and go in the store.

Mr. JENNER. On how many occasions did you see that?

Mr. SHASTEEN. Well, I was trying to think of that coming over here and I know of twice and one of the times that I'm saying.... whenever I saw him come with somebody else in the car he wasn't driving, but occasionally he drove himself up there to get a haircut...

Four months before Clifton Shasteen testified to the Warren Commission, he reported to the F.B.I. in December of 1963, that he saw Oswald driving Ruth Paine's station wagon to his barber shop to get haircuts in the months leading up to the assassination:

Mr. CLIFFORD M. SHASTEEN, 2214 Fairfax, (BL 3-6181), Irving, Texas, operator of Clifford's Barber Shop, 1321 South Story, Irving, Texas, advised that since the assassination and the appearance of LEE HARVEY OSWALD on television, he had identified OSWALD as an individual who had been appearing at his barber shop for purposes of obtaining a haircut for the past two or three months, usually on a Friday evening or on Staurday morning early.

[...]

SHASTEEN stated that at times OSWALD came to the shop apparently on foot. Occasionally, however, he would drive to the shop, driving a car which SHASTEEN had identified as belonging to Mrs. PAINE, a station wagon which he had seen parked in the PAINE's driveway.

On occasions, upon leaving the barber shop, SHASTEEN said that he had seen OSWALD cross the street to enter Hutch's Grocery Store.

[...]

        On several occasions, SHASTEEN said that OSWALD came
to the shop in the company of a fourteen-year-old boy, whom he
described as a white male, short hair, not a flat top, dark brown
in color. He described him as a little bit freckled with brown
eyes and stated he usually wore blue jeans. On one occasion
when this boy came into the shop for a haircut alone, not accompanied by OSWALD, he had made some statements which had astounded
SHASTEEN, and it was for this reason that he had asked him his
age and he was told that the boy was fourteen. SHASTEEN stated

[...]

DL 100-10461
BDO:cv
1

        The following investigation was conducted by
SA BARDWELL D. ODUM at Irving, Texas, on December 16,
1963, in an effort to identify a fourteen year old boy
reportedly present with OSWALD on one occasion at
Clifford's Barber Shop, Irving, Texas.

However, in the same F.B.I. Report, it goes on to explain that Ruth
Paine denied knowing who the fourteen-year-old boy was, and she also
denied ever allowing Lee Harvey Oswald to drive her station wagon by
himself:

        Mrs. RUTH PAINE, 2515 West Fifth, Irving, Texas,
advised that she has no child even as old as school age
and knows of no boy of about fourteen with whom OSWALD
was ever associated in the neighborhood. She further repeated

DL 100-10461
BDO:cv
2

that she had never allowed OSWALD to take her car by himself
anywhere.

Who was this fourteen-year-old boy that Oswald was seen
driving around town with, in Ruth Paine's vehicle? And why did Ruth
Paine tell

F.B.I. investigators that she didn't let Oswald drive her station wagon by himself?

And upon further research, I discovered that someone else who was very closely linked to the J.F.K. assassination case, actually did own a Rambler station wagon. His name was none other than Clay LaVerne Shaw – the same Clay LaVerne Shaw that Jim Garrison had arrested and put on trial in 1969 for participating in a conspiracy to assassinate President Kennedy.

In a letter dated, March 24, 1964, automobile insurance agent T.G. Womack Jr., wrote to his client Clay L. Shaw of New Orleans about Shaw's plans to transfer the title of his 1962 Rambler station wagon into his father's name. The date "March 24, 1964" also happened to be just one week before Roger Craig and Marvin Robinson were scheduled to give their testimony to the Warren Commission about seeing Lee Harvey Oswald being picked up by another man driving a Rambler station wagon minutes after the assassination, and then speed away from the Texas School Book Depository, and Dealey Plaza:

WOMACK INSURANCE AGENCY

222 W. THOMAS STREET
HAMMOND, LOUISIANA

March 24, 1964

Mr. Clay L. Shaw
1313 Dauphine Street
New Orleans, Louisiana

RE: Marquette No. 105628

Dear Clay:

Your dad was in my office this morning and returned the above
policy covering liability on the 1962 Rambler Station Wagon.
I agreed to hold up cancellation of this policy until I had
word from you that you had arranged for coverage with your New
Orleans agent. Just for your records the automobile is described
as being a 1962 Rambler Ambassador M#H171787.(4-Dr. Sta. Wagon).

If you plan to go ahead with your plans to transfer title of this
automobile to your dad's name (which I believe is a good idea),
it will be necessary to complete the forms required by the Department of Revenue. I checked with Hammond Motors this morning while
your dad was in my office and they advise that it could best be
done by your coming to Hammond. As you know, they are holding the
title to this vehicle and it would be very simple for you to sign
the original title they are holding and then apply for a Certificate
of Title in the name of G. L. Shaw. Up to this writing I have not
had a request from my company to cancel the physical damage coverage,
but if you want your agent in New Orleans to go ahead and issue this
coverage for your dad, let me know and I will cancel the Physical
Damage policy.

Be sure to drop me a note when your agent has issued the liability
coverage so we can process cancellation of our policy. Enjoyed
seeing you last Sunday. I appreciate your's and your dad's confidence
in my and am sorry that there was no other way to work out this
insurance problem.

Sincerely,

T. G. Womack, Jr.

MARQUETTE CASUALTY COMPANY

NEW ORLEANS 12, LOUISIANA

A Multiple Line Insurance Company

Worth noting, the letter is also dated one week before Clifton Shasteen
was scheduled to give his testimony on the exact same day as Roger

Craig and Marvin Robinson, to tell the commission about previous statements he made to the F.B.I. about seeing Oswald driving a station wagon to his barber shop in the months leading up to the assassination of President Kennedy.

Journalist James Phelan with Clay Shaw (right).

Interview Continued…

Steve: Of all the conversations you had with Roger, was he absolutely convinced that it was Oswald that got into the Rambler?

Gary: Oh, beyond a shadow of a doubt. As soon as he saw the guy in Fritz's office. Remember, law enforcement are trained to do that sort of thing. To be really conscious of what somebody looks like. How they're dressed. How tall they are. All of these things. He told me that he remembered him, "precisely." Kind of blew Roger away.

Steve: There was a jewel thief that he identified, I think his name was Harry Day?

Gary: Yeah, I remember reading that. And I'm not surprised. You know he was officer of the year for the sheriff's department.

Steve: Yeah. Can you tell me a little bit about that?

Gary: Well, all I can tell you, is I got a copy of his certificate.

Steve: You do?

Gary: Yes, sir.

Steve: I'm friends with his granddaughter, Nita Edwards. And she's been trying to find a copy of that. Is there a way you could email that to me?

Gary: I can take a photograph of it, and send it to you that way?

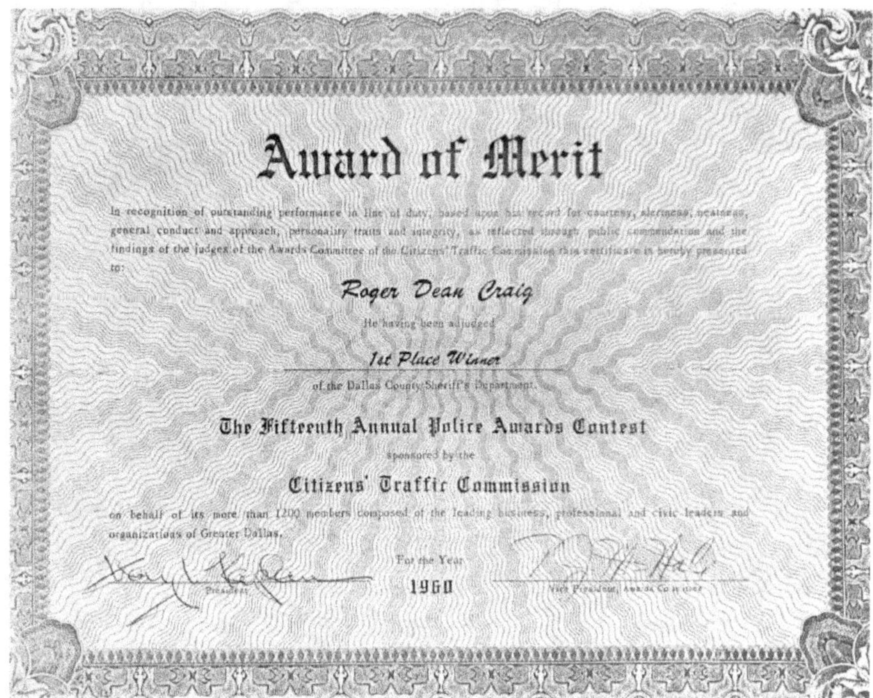

Roger Craig's 1960 Award Certificate for Officer of the Year.
(Courtesy of J. Gary Shaw)

Steve: Thank you. And that way I can send it to Nita. I think she would really appreciate it. When I first started this project, I was reaching out to people, and she was the first person to get me in touch with her father, Roger Craig Jr. She never knew her grandfather. She had always heard these bad things about him, so she was really happy to get involved with this project, to learn more about who he really was.

Gary: I believe I met her at Chris Gallop's luncheon. And she hugged me. And I was delighted to meet her.

Nita Edwards and J. Gary Shaw, attending Chris Gallop's November 2018 J.F.K. Luncheon in Mansfield, TX.
(Photo courtesy of J. Gary Shaw)

Gary: I also have a copy of his private investigator's license. I don't know whether you knew he became a private investigator or not.

Steve: Yeah, I know he had several jobs. He was a judge at one point. He did manual labor. Anything he could to support his family.

Gary: Yeah.

Roger Craig's 1972 Private Investigator License.
(Courtesy of J. Gary Shaw)

Steve: So, to pick up where we left off, his identification of the jewel thief showed that he had a keen eye. Once it was known who Lee Harvey Oswald was, Roger was one hundred percent positive it was the same person he saw get into the Rambler station wagon?

Gary: Yeah. Let me tell you something. You may have caught this, but if you didn't, it should be part of your book. Roger, in 1967 he did an interview in New Orleans with Jim Garrison, Bill Boxley, and Mark Lane. This was on October 25, 1967. It was one of the first interviews that he gave to the New Orleans people. In it he says this, and I've never seen anybody else come up with this, but it just tells me how smart the guy was. Roger said, "The effect of the announcement that Tippit had been killed was to immediately switch the entire investigation from one which sought the President's assailant to a search for Tippit's murderer. If the assassins were aware that a police officer's death might bring about such a response — if the Dallas Police Department's response was predictable — the role played by the murder of Tippit as part of an escape scheme by the assassins must be evaluated." What he's saying is, "If the people who killed Kennedy knew that the Dallas police would immediately turn their efforts toward finding the killer of a policeman, rather than the killer of the president, why wouldn't they shoot a policeman? They just shot a president!" That played right into their hands to get Oswald at the theater. Because they went to the theater supposedly not to capture the President's assassin, but to capture the killer of a policeman.

Author's note: According to Deputy Sheriff Roger Craig, when he first heard that Dallas Police Officer J. D. Tippit had been shot, he looked at his watch, and the time was 1:06 p.m., approximately thirty-five minutes after the assassination of President Kennedy. However, the Warren Commission puts the time of the shooting at 1:15 p.m., giving Oswald several more minutes to travel the 2.6 mile distance from the Texas School Book Depository, to where Tippit was shot in Oak Cliff, and made it appear that Oswald had enough time to commit the murder.

Dallas Police Officer J. D. Tippit.

FROM: MARK LANE

RE: Interview with ROGER CRAIG, October 25, 1967,
        Fontainebleau Hotel, New Orleans, Louisiana

PRESENT: ROGER CRAIG, JIM GARRISON, BILL BOXLEY, MARK LANE

[...]

missing. CRAIG said that the effect of the announcement that
TIPPIT had been killed was to immediately switch the entire
investigation from one which sought the President's assailant
to a search for TIPPIT's murderer. If the assassins were aware
that a police officer's death might bring about such a response --
if the Dallas Police Department's response was predictable --
the role played by the murder of TIPPIT as part of an escape
scheme by the assassins must be evaluated. Even now the Dallas
Police Department betrays a sensitivity to questions about TIPPIT'
death not present when one explores the facts surrounding the
assassination. TIPPIT had been involved with a car-hop at Billy's
Drive In on South Lamar.

Excerpt from Mark Lane's notes of an October 1967 interview with
Roger Craig, about the murder of Dallas Police Officer J. D. Tippit.

Interview continued...

Steve: Let's go back to Ruth Paine for a moment. I thought I read somewhere that Ruth Paine's family had some connections to the C.I.A.

Gary: That's possible. They're a suspicious couple, to have befriended Oswald and Marina for no other reason than they felt sorry for them. That whole thing is a convoluted mess. Too deep for me to even try to figure it out.

Steve: I'd like to talk a little more about some of the things Roger saw on the day of the assassination. He said that after he saw the man get into the Rambler station wagon and speed away from Dealey Plaza, that it had been determined by the Dallas Police Department that the shots came from the southeast corner of the Texas School Book Depository.

Gary: Gerald Hill, one of the Dallas police detectives, he stuck his head out of the Oswald window and waved his hat, and said, "This is where it is!"

Steve: And when Roger arrives on the sixth-floor, he begins looking for evidence. And before photographs were taken of the spent cartridges laying on the floor of the so-called sniper's nest, he said that he saw three of them lined up, side by side?

Gary: Yeah, almost side by side.

Steve: And in the photographs that we have, they're scattered.

Gary: Yeah. They're scattered. It wasn't very good planning for whoever was planting evidence to lay them side by side. If you've ever shot a rifle, bolt action, they land randomly.

Warren Commission Exhibit 510, showing three spent shells.
(Arrows added by Steve Cameron)

Steve: So, there was somebody up there messing around with the evidence. I'm trying to envision this, how somebody that was involved, or maybe it was by accident. Maybe somebody kicked them because they were on the ground and didn't see them, and that's why they scattered. Whatever the reason. And then Roger said everyone began searching for a weapon. And he was walking about eight feet behind Officer Eugene Boone, when Boone found a rifle located near the north west corner of the sixth-floor between some boxes. Is that correct?

Gary: Yeah, I think that's right.

Steve: Can you explain how the weapon was determined to be a Mauser?

Gary: Well, Roger heard Seymour Weitzman say it was a Mauser. Weitzman had been in the business of selling arms at one time. So, he was not a stranger to firearms. And he was the one who identified it as a Mauser.

Steve: And that was Deputy Constable Seymour Weitzman, correct?

Gary: Yeah. Roger heard him say that.

Steve: Well, according to Roger he said he saw the stamp on the barrel. He said it read, "7.65 Mauser."

Gary: Yeah, I think he said that, and maybe there was another rifle up there. But the rifle I see them taking out of the boxes is a Mannlicher-Carcano, it isn't a Mauser. I know guns, too. I've collected them, and shot them all my life. That's what we do in Texas, you know (laughter).

Steve: Yeah. Robert Groden, he's also convinced that they found more than one rifle up there. The identification of the Mauser by Seymour Weitzman, he actually signed a sworn affidavit the next day, saying it was a 7.65 Mauser rifle. And Officer Eugene Boone, who found the rifle, also put in his report that it was a 7.65 Mauser.

Gary: I don't know how that could be an error, you know?

Steve: That's a huge error, if it is.

Gary: It is. And I think Seymour saw that. It's just not the one they have in films and the photographs, because I know exactly what that one is.

Steve: I think Lieutenant Day was in charge of taking the rifle down from the School Book Depository and over to the police station for further analysis. There're photos of Day walking from the School Book Depository with one of the rifles, whether it was a Mauser, or an Italian made Mannlicher-Carcano, that rifle had side sling mounts on it.

Gary: I've heard that.

Lieutenant John Carl Day of the Dallas Police Department's Crime Lab is photographed escorting a rifle with side sling mounts (circled) from the Texas School Book Depository to Police headquarters.

Steve: Yeah, in the photos, the front of the rifle has a side sling mount, and the back of the rifle also has a side sling mount.

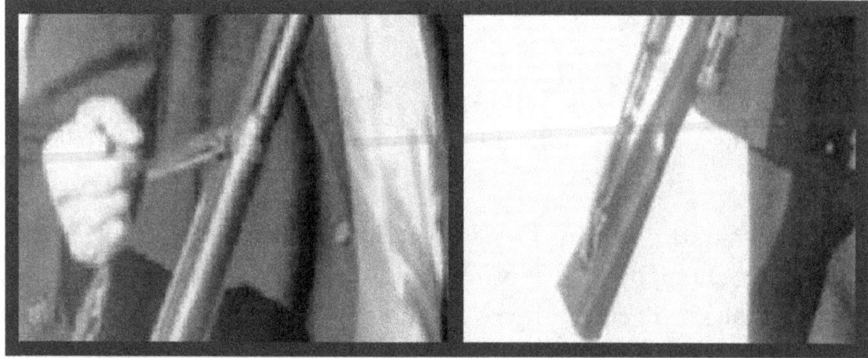

Gary: Right.

Steve: But in the famous backyard photos from *Life Magazine* supposedly showing Lee Harvey Oswald holding the rifle up, that rifle has bottom sling mounts on it.

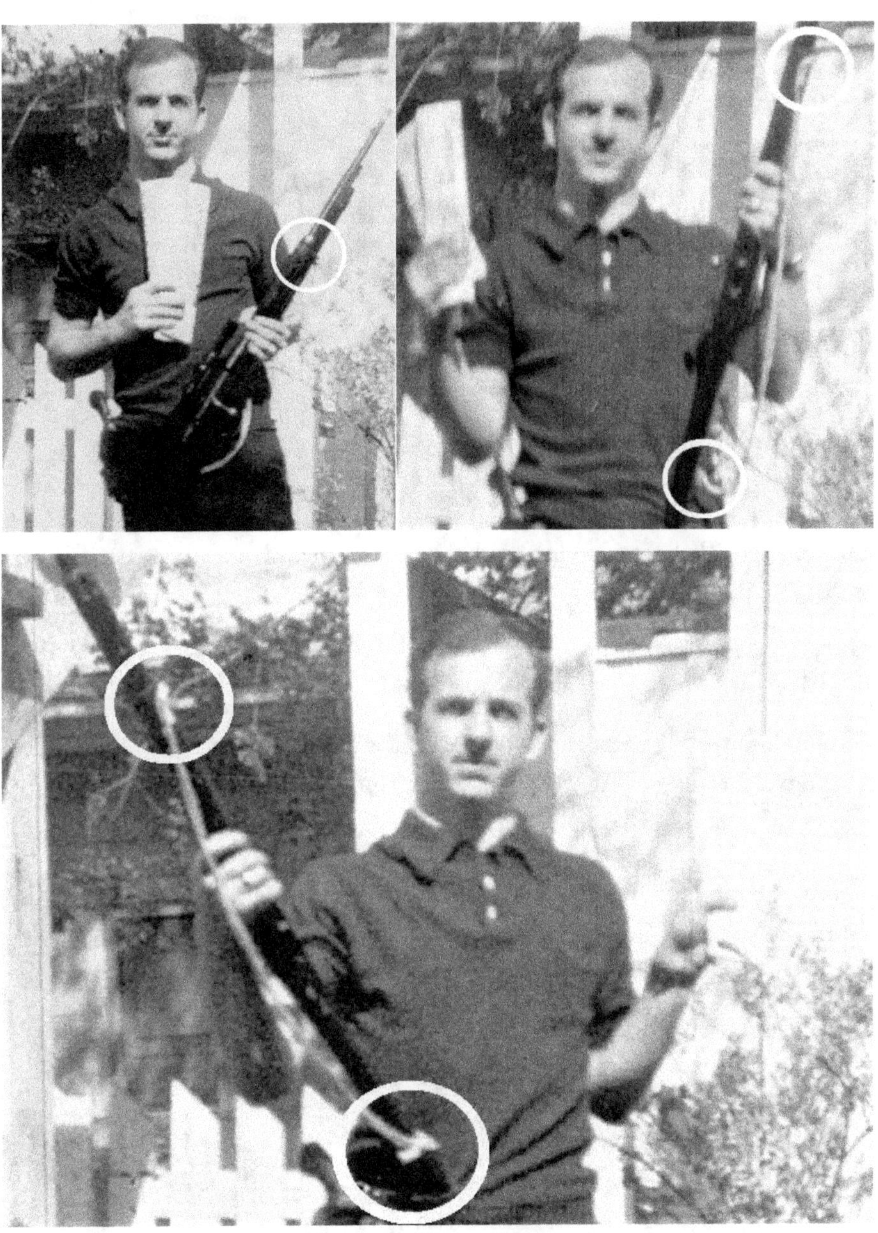

(Circles added by Steve Cameron)

Steve: And the Klein's catalog that he supposedly bought it from, the ad also shows that the rifle had bottom sling mounts. To me it just looks like a completely different rifle coming out of that building compared to the one Oswald's supposed to be holding in the backyard.

Advertisement from Klein's Sporting Goods catalog selling an Italian Mannlicher-Carcano with bottom sling mounts.
(Circles added by Steve Cameron)

Steve: Also, Robert Groden told me that there was another rifle found on the roof.

Gary: That was reported, yes. I printed that in my book *Cover-up* back in 1976.

Steve: The way Robert put it was, "We have the magic bullet, and we also have the magic rifle," because that one just disappeared.

Gary: Yeah.

Steve: Okay, let's switch gears a little. After Roger's testimony in Jim Garrison's trial of Clay Shaw, how many times did you come into contact with Roger?

Gary: Boy, that would be hard to say. Enough to see him on a downhill slide.

Steve: Can you tell me a little bit about that?

Gary: Just his entire attitude. His demeanor I guess you could say. The more I was around him, the more I saw. He seemed to lose weight, and get thin in the face. You could tell that things in his life weren't good. And they weren't going good for him. I'll tell you a quick story. Penn was trying to help him, both financially and physically. I think Penn helped him get that job in Midlothian, Texas as a county judge. Anyway, one of my good friends here in Cleburne, Texas had a dairy. And in a dairy, your milk cows have calves in order to produce milk. And you sell the little calves off as fast as you can. So, my buddy wanted a set of the 26 volumes of *The Warren Report*. So, I said, "You can buy one from Jones, let's go over there." When we got there, Penn said, "Well, if you got some calves, I'll trade you a set for a calf, and then I can give it to Roger so he can make him some money." So, he did. He made that little transaction. That's how down on his luck Roger was at that particular time.

Steve: Do you remember that last time that you saw Roger?

Gary: I think the last time I saw him would have been in the early '70s. I think it was when he was living in Midlothian. He drove over to Cleburne for some business, and he stopped in the office. We had some coffee and chatted. And I think that was the last time I ever saw him.

Steve: Okay. I just have a couple more questions. When I interviewed Robert Groden, he told me a story about how he was trying to build a case with Congressman Thomas Downing of Virginia to reopen the J.F.K. assassination case, and that he travelled to Texas to interview Roger Craig. I think it was Penn Jones who told Robert that he should interview Roger. And so, he flew to Dallas in May of 1975 to meet with him for a scheduled interview. He was also down there for some other things, but he said that the big excitement was to meet with Roger and interview him. And after he landed at the airport, he was greeted by Penn Jones, Larry Harris, and yourself.

Gary: Yes.

Pictured left to right: J. Gary Shaw, Penn Jones Jr., and Larry Harris.
(Photo courtesy of Chris Gallop)

Steve: Can you please tell me a little about that day? How it all came together. What transpired right before, and right after Roger's death?

Gary: I had met Robert in '73, when he first showed the Zapruder film to a group of us in Washington. This would have been in November of 1973. And two years later he was on *Good Night America,* with Geraldo Rivera. Do you know about that?

Steve: Yes.

Gary: Okay. He went on there and showed the film nationally. It caused quite a stir. And when he came to Dallas to interview Roger, it was Penn Jones and I, and Larry Harris who met him at Love Field, where we informed him that we had just learned that Roger had committed suicide, and that Roger was at the funeral home over there in Mesquite, a suburb of Dallas. And so, we went to the funeral home where Roger was resting. We met Molly at that time as I recall. I don't remember meeting Roger Jr., or if he was around.

Steve: Yeah, Roger Jr. was there that day. He actually had to go down to the morgue to identify his dad. He said that he read the autopsy report, and his dad had ligature marks around his wrists, and had bruising on his knees. Apparently when they found him, he was in his boxer shorts with nothing else on, and face-down in the middle of the room, and there was a rifle laying long ways on the bed. And from all the interviews that I've conducted with people, all the information that I've gathered, I do believe he was murdered, and did not commit suicide.

Gary: I don't doubt that he was murdered. But even if he committed suicide, I blame it on "them," if you understand what I mean?

Steve: Yeah, absolutely.

Gary: "They" killed him. Whether "they" fired the bullet or not.

Steve: Yeah. The conversation that I had with Roger's sister-in-law Dennie Wood, she actually saw Roger on the day that he died. She and her husband Donald who was Roger's older half-brother, went over to the house to pick up some belongings that their father Kristel had waiting for them to take to their new apartment. When they arrived, they saw both Kristel and Roger. And they all had coffee together. They were all laughing and joking. Roger was in a cheery mood. They had plans to go fishing up in Oklahoma a few days from that day. Roger had recently renewed his driver's license, because his birthday was on May 12, just three days before he died. And he had also just gotten a fishing license for the planned fishing trip. They were discussing that with him, and Roger told them, "I just got my fishing license, because I don't want to get a ticket as long as my short arm." So, he was joking around, and in a good mood. When they saw him he was fully clothed. Didn't seem suicidal at all. He was even joking around with Dennie about her cooking. He asked her, "Have you learned how to boil water yet, or have you just learned how to burn it?" So, the mood was "Cheery" in her words. And later that day, Kristel came over to their apartment and gave them the news, and told them what happened. Dennie said that Kristel didn't believe Roger took his own life, and that the rifle that was found on the bed wasn't Roger's gun, and that he had never seen that gun in the house before that day. And for as long as Dennie knew Kristel after that, he was absolutely convinced that Roger was murdered. He was out in the yard working on his lawnmower at the time. He said the last time he saw Roger right before he went to go in the backyard to work on the lawnmower, that Roger was dressed, and sitting on the couch watching TV. And about a half an hour or so later, Kristel came back into the house, and that's when he found Roger, laying face-down in the middle of his bedroom. Another thing about Kristel, he was hard of hearing. He had some issues with his hearing that stemmed back to when he was in World War II. Kristel said he never heard a gunshot. Dennie explained to me that they had lived across the street from an armory. So, they were always doing training drills over there. Shooting, etc. And anyone who heard a gunshot would have probably just thought it was training drills, and not reported the gunshot. And I found on Google Maps the area of that house. It's very secluded. Not a lot of witnesses around, put it that way. I think he had one neighbor next to him, and that was it. And that neighbor was at work when it happened, according to Dennie.

Home where Roger Craig died.
(Courtesy of Google Maps, Street View)

Steve: So, there was all this effort being organized to reopen the case on a government level. And many other people were silenced around the same timeframe, leading up to the House Select Committee on Assassinations. So, I do believe Roger was silenced too, so he couldn't be a part of that.

Gary: Yeah. You look at it, and you see three periods of deaths. You have a spurt of them right after the assassination. You have a spurt when Garrison opens his investigation down there in New Orleans. And then you have another spurt when the House Select Committee was being formed. So that's a very valid point, that Roger died at that time. Do you know if Roger Jr. ever got a copy of the autopsy?

Steve: There is a copy of it online. And Roger had the original copy. I think he said that they were different than what he saw. But in the online version, you can see all the damage to him. The injuries that he sustained over the years, from all the attempts on his life. He was really banged up.

Gary: Was there ever an inquest held?

Steve: No. I asked Roger Jr. if prints had ever been taken off that rifle, or…

Gary: No investigation?

Steve: No investigation at all. Just wrapped it right up really quick. There was a newspaper article written about it. They did mention in there that he had attempts on his life previously. When you got the news about it, who gave you the news?

Gary: Penn called me.

Steve: And how did Penn describe it?

Gary: That he was dead. Penn definitely thought it was murder. Another one of those strange deaths. He didn't believe Roger would commit suicide. We both decided, whether he killed himself or not, "they" killed him.

Steve: Right. With Robert coming down to interview him. And his plans to go fishing. Yeah, it just doesn't add up.

Gary: It just doesn't make sense. It never did. But that's what we're left with.

Steve: Robert told me that he's always had in the back of his mind a great sadness, that maybe his going down there to interview Roger may have had something to do with what happened to him. And Robert also said that Roger would have definitely been called before the House Select Committee. He had already given testimony to the Warren Commission, and Garrison's trial. And he definitely would have been called as a witness.

Gary: Oh definitely. Definitely, no doubt about it.

Steve: Well, Gary, I'd like to give you this opportunity to add anything we left out, or if you'd like to have any closing words about Roger, or the case in general?

Gary: Well, I admired him. I admired his tenacity. His courage. Not everybody would have been able to stand up for as long as he did. But forces came against him while he was trying to help solve the case. He was definitely a proponent of conspiracy, that Oswald didn't act alone, if he acted at all. And I admire him for standing up, as he did. He's one of the heroes in the Kennedy case.

Steve: Yeah, he sure was. And we don't want his story to be forgotten.

Gary: No, we don't. And I'm glad you're doing this.

Steve: Thank you, Gary. And thanks for doing this interview. Is there a way for people to find your work on the internet? Do you have a website?

Gary: No, I don't. I pretty well put this aside for a good many years. After I wrote with doctor Crenshaw *Conspiracy of Silence*, that came out in 1992, I put this aside for twenty-five years. I didn't quit researching, but I quit writing and doing the legwork, for a considerable length of time. Do you know the story about doctor Crenshaw?

Steve: No, I don't.

Gary: Okay. Well, we wrote a book. Came out in '92. Right after the Oliver Stone movie *JFK* came out. This was Crenshaw's story. He worked on Kennedy, and Connally, and Oswald for that weekend. He was at Parkland Hospital, a surgeon. And he's in the Warren Commission Report. They bring up his name. But he never was called to testify or anything. But he decided he needed to write what he knew. So, we got together this book. And it went directly to the number one spot on The New York Times bestseller list for paperbacks.

"All I could see there was mangled, bloody tissue. From the damage I saw, there was no doubt in my mind that the bullet had entered his head through the front." —Dr. Charles Crenshaw.

Gary: And the next thing you know – and you talk about an attack – the next thing we know, the New York Times has a story out saying he's a liar. And then the American Medical Association (AMA), and the Journal of the American Medical Association (JAMA) does a big press conference on television, in front of the seal of the American Medical Association calling him a liar. And they call me a liar. Bad news. The book immediately dropped off the list. But we sued, and got a substantial amount. But it took another three or four years before we got a conclusion out of it. They really burnt me out.

Steve: Is there a book besides that one, that people can still get, like *Cover-up?*

Gary: *Cover-up* may one of these days go back into print. There's work being done for that. And *Trauma Room One* by doctor Charles Crenshaw, and J. Gary Shaw, can still be bought. It's still in print.

Steve: Is that on Amazon?

Gary: Yeah, it's on Amazon. And you can still buy a copy of *Cover-up*, but they're higher than a cat's back (laughter). You can buy one for around three hundred dollars, on up to about three thousand, which I think is ridiculous. But that's the way things go with the collectors out there.

Steve: Well, thank you, Gary.

Gary: You're welcome, Steve. If there's anything I can help you with, you've got my number now. I don't know if this will help your story about Roger, but all I can say is that I really admired the guy.

(Photo courtesy of Ruthann Starkey-Shipley)

ACKNOWLEDGMENTS

Most of the content within this book came from official government records, and interviews, that I conducted between February 14, 2017 and November 11, 2019. I would like to thank members of Roger Craig's family, for trusting me with the great privilege, and responsibility of bringing his story out from the shadows, and into the light of day for the world to see. Without their help, this book never would have been possible. I would also like to especially thank his granddaughter Nita Edwards, who helped me from day one of this journey. Without her contributions to this work, this book never would have been written. I would also like to explicitly thank Kathleen McGuire, Phil Singer, David T. Ratcliffe, Dennie Darnell Wood, J. Gary Shaw, Robert Groden, Janet Boschock Groden, Peter Hymans, Judyth Vary Baker, Vince Palamara, Cathy Montgomery-Shepard, Chris Gallop, Ruthann Starkey-Shipley, Scott Edwards, Gary Fannin, Donald Jeffries, Michael Silver, Tom Lipscomb, David Wood, and Ernie Wood. Thank you for sacrificing your time, and supporting my efforts during this process, to help me shine the brightest light that I possibly could onto Roger's story. And finally, thank you to everyone whose names are not printed within these pages who reached out to me, to send well wishes, feedback, research information, and encouragement, which I so dearly appreciate. Thank you for trying to help me write the most comprehensive work that I could, about one of America's greatest unsung heroes, Roger Dean Craig.

"I believe in my country. I have done nothing but tell the truth, and I will continue to do so."

-Roger Dean Craig

WHEN THEY KILL A PRESIDENT

BY

R̲OGER D̲EAN C̲RAIG

I

Our president John Kennedy went down to Dallas town

Where the hired assassins waited and there they shot him down

Because he dreamed of peace and plenty and he talked it 'round

His dream goes marching on

The Dallas County Court House at 505 Main Street was indeed a unique place to come to hear what was WRONG with John F. Kennedy and his policies as President of these United States.

This building housed the elite troops of the Dallas County Sheriff's Department (of which I was one), who, with blind obedience, followed the orders of their Great White Father: Bill Decker, Sheriff of Dallas County.

From these elite troops came the most bitter verbal attacks on President Kennedy. They spoke very strongly against his policies concerning the Bay of Pigs incident and the Cuban Missile crisis. They seemed to resent very much the fact that President Kennedy was a Catholic. I do not know why this was such a critical issue with many of the deputies but they did seem to hold this against President Kennedy.

The concession stand in the lobby of the court house was the best place to get into a discussion concerning the President. The old man who ran the stand evidenced a particular hatred for President Kennedy. He seemed to go out of his way to drag anyone who came by his stand into a discussion about the President. His name is J. C. Kiser.

He was a little man with a short mustache and glasses that he wore right on the end of his nose. He was a particularly good friend of Sheriff Decker, and he held the concession in the lobby for many years. Like

Decker, he was unopposed when his lease came up for renewal. It was common knowledge that Bill Decker made it possible for him to remain there as long as he wished. This sick little man not only had a deep hatred for John F. Kennedy, he also hated the black people, even those who spent their money at his stand. He would often curse them as they walked away after making a purchase from him. He flatly refused to make telephone change for them even though he would be simultaneously making change for a white person.

This little man was a typical example of the atmosphere that lingered in this building that housed law and order in Dallas County.

Many of the deputies had a dislike for the President—some more so than others. However, there were those who would not degrade themselves by taking verbal punches at our President. One of these was Hiram Ingram. Although devoted to Bill Decker, he was also a good friend of mine. We often discussed the political debates that took place in the lobby. Hiram had a great dislike for this sick little man who seemed to lead the attack on the President. He also had little respect for the deputies, attorneys and court house employees who tolerated or even agreed with this philosophy of attacking John F. Kennedy.

Hiram Ingram was a small man—in stature. He was always ready with a friendly smile and greeting. He began his association with the County during the Bonnie and Clyde era—when he was an ambulance driver and inside employee at a local funeral home. In fact, Hiram prepared Bonnie and Clyde for burial after they were brought back to Dallas from the ambush in Louisiana.

Hiram and I were very close—one of those friendships which develops when some people first meet. I had known Hiram for about four years at the time of the assassination. He was working in the Civil Division and shortly after November 22, 1963 he had a heart attack. When he returned to work Decker put him on the Bond Desk, where I would later be and work closely with Hiram. I worked the day shift one month and the evening shift the following month. Hiram worked only evenings. So every other month we worked together. This gave us time to talk and discuss the events in Dallas and even the Sheriff's Office itself. The Department was not well organized.

To clear some of the bonds and bondsmen we would have to call Decker at home—no matter what time of the day or night—for his approval or any decision. This applied only to certain bondsmen. Decker had his chosen few who were not questioned. Hiram was a very dependable employee and should not have had to clear the minor decisions with our Great White Father, Bill Decker.

As the months passed and Hiram and I worked together we built a mutual respect for each other. When Decker fired me on July 4, 1967 Hiram was infuriated but, like any employee of Decker's, he couldn't say anything in my defense for fear of having his employment cut short or his reputation ruined. One of Decker's favorite past times was ruining reputations.

Our friendship did not end with my termination. We continued to talk from time to time and Hiram was very helpful when Penn Jones wanted information concerning records at the Sheriff's office. However, in March of 1968 Hiram explained to me that information was getting more difficult to get for some reason. Fortunately, by this time I had already supplied Penn Jones and Bill Boxley (investigator for Jim Garrison) with much information from Hiram.

About two weeks later, near the end of March 1968, I heard that Hiram had fallen at home and broken his hip and was in the hospital. I went to see my good buddy to cheer him up and received the shock of my life. Hiram was under oxygen and could not have any visitors. Three days later he was dead—of cancer. He had been working just prior to the fall. I think that we owe a debt of gratitude to this great man who, in his own quiet way, helped us all so much.

Thus . . . we have the atmosphere that was to greet the President of the United States upon his arrival in Dallas. However, things were to get even worse before he arrived.

The battle ground had been picked and the UNwelcome mat was out for President Kennedy. Unknown to most of us, the rest of the plan was being completed. The patsy had been chosen and placed in the building across from the court house—where he could not deny his presence after it was all over. This was done with the apparent approval and certainly with the knowledge of our co-workers, the F.B.I., since they later admitted that they knew Lee Harvey Oswald was employed at the School Book Depository Building located on the corner of Elm Street and Houston Street across from the Sheriff's Office.

The security had been arranged by the Secret Service and the Dallas Police—our boys in blue. The final touch was put on by Sheriff James Eric (Bill) Decker. On the morning of November 22, 1963, the patrolmen in the districts which make up the Dallas County Sheriff's Patrol Division were left in the field, ignorant of what was going on in the downtown area, which was just as well. Decker was not going to LET them do anything anyway.

About 10:30 a.m. November 22, 1963, Bill Decker called into his office what I will refer to as his street people—plain-clothes men, detectives and warrant men, myself included—and told us that President Kennedy was coming to Dallas and that the motorcade would come down Main Street. He then advised us that we were to stand out in front of the building, 505 Main Street and represent the Sheriff's Office. We were to take no part whatsoever in the security of that motorcade. (Why, James Eric?) So . . . the stage had been set, all the pawns were in place, the security had been withdrawn from that one vulnerable location. Come John F. Kennedy, come to Elm and Houston Streets in Dallas, Texas and take your place in history!

The time was 12:15 p.m. I was standing in front of the court house at 505 Main Street. Deputy Sheriff Jim Ramsey was standing behind me. We were waiting for the President of the United States. I had a feeling of pride that I was going to be not more than four feet from the President but deep inside something kept gnawing at me. I said to Jim Ramsey, "He's late." Jim's reply stunned me. He said, "Maybe somebody will shoot the son of a bitch." Then I realized the crowd was hostile. The men about me felt that they were forced to acknowledge his presence. Although he was the President, they were making statements like, "Why does he have to come to Dallas?"

Something else was bothering me . . . being a trained officer, I always looked for anything which might be amiss about any situation with which I was confronted. Suddenly I knew what was wrong. There were no officers guarding the intersections or controlling the crowd. My mind flashed back to the meeting in Decker's office that morning, then back to the lack of security in this area.

Suddenly the motorcade approached and President Kennedy was smiling and waving and for a moment I relaxed and fell into the happy mood the President was displaying. The car turned the corner onto Houston Street. I was still looking at the rest of the people in the party. I was soon to be shocked back into reality. The President had passed and was turning west on Elm Street . . . as if there were no people, no cars, the only thing in my world at that moment was a rifle shot! I bolted toward Houston Street. I was fifteen steps from the corner—before I reached it two more shots had been fired. Telling myself that it wasn't true and at the same time knowing that it was, I continued to run. I ran across Houston Street and beside the pond, which is on the west side of Houston. I pushed a man out of my way and he fell into the pond. I ran down the grass between Main and Elm. People were lying all over the ground. I thought, "My God, they've killed a woman and child," who were lying beside the gutter on the South side of Elm Street. I checked them and they were alright. I saw a Dallas Police Officer run up the grassy knoll and go behind the picket fence near the railroad yards. I followed and behind the fence was complete confusion and hysteria.

I began to question people when I noticed a woman in her early thirties attempting to drive out of the parking lot. She was in a brown 1962 or 1963 Chevrolet. I stopped her, identified myself and placed her under arrest. She told me that she had to leave and I said, "Lady, you're not going anywhere." I turned her over to Deputy Sheriff C. I. (Lummy) Lewis and told him the circumstances of the arrest. Officer Lewis told me that he would take her to Sheriff Decker and take care of her car.

The parking lot behind the picket fence was of little importance to most of the investigators at the scene except that the shots were thought to have come from there.

Let us examine this parking lot. It was leased by Deputy Sheriff B. D. Gossett. He in turn rented parking space by the month to the deputies who worked in the court house, except for official vehicles. I rented one of these spaces from Gossett when I was a dispatcher working days or evenings. I paid Gossett $3.00 per month and was given a key to the lot. An interesting point is that the lot had an iron bar across the only entrance and exit (which were the same). The bar had a chain and lock on it. The only people having access to it were deputies with keys. Point: how did the woman gain access and, what is more important, who was she and why did she have to leave?

This was to be the beginning of the never-ending cover up. Had I known then what I know now, I would have personally questioned the woman and impounded and searched her car. I had no way of knowing that an officer, with whom I had worked for four years, was capable of losing a thirty-year-old woman and a three-thousand-pound automobile. To this day Officer Lewis does not know who she was, where she came from or what happened to her. Strange!

Meanwhile, back at the parking lot, I continued to help the Dallas Officers restore order. When things were somewhat calmer, I began to question the people who were standing at the top of the grassy knoll, asking if anyone had seen anything strange or unusual before or during the President's fatal turn onto Elm Street.

Several people indicated to me that they thought the shots came from the area of the grassy knoll or behind the picket fence. My next reliable witness came forward in the form of Mr. Arnold Rowland. Mr. Rowland and his wife were standing at the top of the grassy knoll on the north side of Elm Street. Arnold Rowland began telling me his account of what he saw before the assassination. He said approximately fifteen minutes before President Kennedy arrived, he was looking around and something caught his eye. It was a white man standing by the 6th floor window of the Texas School Book Depository Building in the southeast corner, holding a rifle equipped with a telescopic sight and in the southwest corner of the sixth floor was a colored male pacing back and forth. Needless to say, I was astounded by his statement. I asked Mr. Rowland why he had not reported this incident before and he told me that he thought they were secret service agents—an obvious conclusion for a layman. Rowland continued. He told me that he looked back at the sixth floor a few minutes later and the man with the rifle was gone so he dismissed it from his mind.

I was writing all this down in my notebook and when I finished, I advised Mr. and Mrs. Rowland that I would have to detain them for a statement. I had started toward the Sheriff's Office with them when lo and behold I was approached by Officer C. L. (Lummy) Lewis, who asked me "What ya got"—a favorite expression of most investigators with Bill Decker. I explained the situation to him and told him of Rowland's account. Being the Good Samaritan he was, Officer Lewis offered to take the Rowlands off my hands and get their statements. This worked out a little better than my first arrest. The Warren Commission decided not to accept Arnold Rowland's story but at least they did not lose them. Hang in there, Lummy!

The time was approximately 12:40 p.m. I had just turned the Rowlands over to Lummy Lewis when I met E. R. (Buddy) Walthers, a small man with a very arrogant manner. He was, without a doubt, Decker's favorite pupil. He wore dark-rimmed glasses and a small-brimmed hat because effecting them meant that he would resemble Bill Decker. Walthers had worked for the Yellow Cab Company of Dallas before coming to the Sheriff's Office, about a year before I began working there. His termination from the cab company was the result of several shortages of money. He came to the Sheriff's Department as a patrolman but because of his close connection with Justice of the Peace Bill Richburg—one of Decker's closest allies—Buddy soon was promoted to detective. He had absolutely no ability as a law enforcement officer. However, he was fast climbing the ladder of success by lying to Decker and squealing on his fellow officers.

Walthers' ambition was to become Sheriff of Dallas County and he would do anything or anybody to reach that goal. It was very clear Buddy enjoyed more job security with Decker than anyone else did. Decker carried him for years by breaking a case for him or taking a case which had been broken by another officer and putting Walthers' name on the arrest sheet. Soon after he was promoted to detective, he became intimate with such people as W. O. Bankston, the flamboyant Oldsmobile dealer in Dallas who furnished Decker with a new Fire Engine Red Olds every year and who was arrested several times for Driving while Intoxicated but never served any jail time.

Buddy's acquaintances also included several independent oil operators throughout Texas, several anti-Castro Cubans and many underworld characters—especially women! He was frequently crashing parties which were given by wealthy friends of Decker's—of course while he was on duty. He often became drunk and belligerent at these parties and at one point, when asked to leave, he threatened to pull his gun on the host. This information can be verified by Billy Courson, who was Buddy's partner at that time.

Walthers hit the big time when, in 1961, two Federal Narcotics Agents came to Decker's office with charges that Buddy was growing marijuana in the back yard of his home at 2527 Boyd Street in the Oak Cliff section of Dallas. This could be considered conduct unbecoming to a police officer—but not for Buddy! After a secret meeting between the Federal Agents, Decker and Buddy, the matter was dropped and—needless to say—covered up, thus enabling Buddy to continue his career as Decker's Representative of Law and Order in Dallas County.

However, the Dallas Police began receiving complaints that Buddy was shaking down underworld characters for loot taken in several burglaries and selling the stuff himself. After several reports the Dallas Police began to investigate and, finally, obtained a search warrant for Buddy's home. Their BIG mistake was securing the warrant from Judge Richburg—which was bad enough—but Buddy's wife also worked for Richburg and this made matters worse. Strangely enough, they did not find anything. However, a few weeks later they were a little more careful and made a surprise visit to Buddy's home, where they, indeed, recovered such things as toasters, clothing and various items—just as their informers had said. It would seem they had him this time, wouldn't it? But not so. Buddy explained that he had recovered the merchandise from where it had been hidden and had not had time to make a report on them and turn them in to the Property Room! The Dallas Police didn't buy this story but the pressure was again brought to bear by our Protector, Bill Decker, and the Dallas Police were left out in the cold— no charges filed! They were certainly furious but what could they do? If WE as citizens cannot fight the Establishment, how can the Establishment fight the Establishment?

It was clear in my mind, and if the people with whom I worked could talk, I am sure they would agree that Buddy had a powerful hold on Decker. I base this on the fact that Buddy's popularity with Decker greatly increased after the assassination. Buddy was a chronic liar—he was always telling Decker things he thought were happening in the County which he was checking on. Things which he was not doing. He also told Decker that he was in the theater when Oswald was captured and that he, in fact, helped the Dallas Police. This was completely untrue. Buddy never entered the Texas Theater—his partner, Bill Courson, did.

Buddy also told Decker about a family of anti-Castro Cubans living in the Oak Cliff area and said that he was watching them. This part may have been true because we received the same information from the Dallas Police Intelligence Division. But one day Buddy made a visit to the house in Oak Cliff and when the Police and Sheriff's Deputies went to question them a few days later, they were gone. Did Buddy warn them? After all, he was very, very close to Jack Ruby. In fact, every time Buddy was in trouble with one of Jack Ruby's employees—especially Nancy Perrin Rich—Decker would send Buddy to straighten things out and put Nancy in her place—with the help of Judge Richburg. Touching Jack Ruby was a no-no!

There were many other things which made Buddy suspect as a not-so-law abiding lawman, such as the swimming pool he built in his back yard (on his salary?). The concrete was furnished by a local contractor free of charge. Buddy used many pills he carried in the trunk of his unmarked squad car for trading with certain underworld characters—pills for information. I learned from what I consider a reliable source that these pills had been confiscated (although no reports were made nor the pills turned in). Most of those involved in this exchange were women. It would seem that Buddy Walthers could not be terminated from the Sheriff's Department, no matter what.

One incident in 1966 which would have resulted in the firing of any other deputy occurred when Buddy was sent to Nevada to transfer a suspect wanted in Dallas. It seemed Buddy was given a certain amount of travel money which he lost at the gambling table in Las Vegas. Broke and in trouble, Buddy called none other than W. O. Bankston, who wired him enough money to bring his prisoner back to Dallas. Many times I wondered who was REALLY Sheriff but Buddy was about to reach the end of his rope.

In late 1968, when the Clay Shaw trial was being prepared, there was talk of bringing Buddy to New Orleans to testify. Well, that was a blow to the power which ruled Dallas. They could not have this half-wit on the witness stand. When the word reached Dallas, Decker was working on a double-murder which occurred in his county and had a lead on the suspect in January of 1969. The Shaw trial was scheduled for February and Decker sent Buddy and his partner, Alvin Maddox (who was about as efficient as a nutty professor), to a motel on Samuell Boulevard in Dallas to question a Walter Cherry about the killings. Cherry was an escaped convict and a suspect in the double-murder. Decker sent them to talk to Cherry without a warrant. When they entered the room at the motel Buddy was shot dead and Maddox wounded in the FOOT. Coincidence? Maybe! At any rate Buddy had been silenced. One more point for Dallas!

Back to November 22, 1963. As I have earlier stated, the time was approximately 12:40 p.m. when I ran into Buddy Walthers. The traffic was very heavy as Patrolman Baker (assigned to Elm and Houston Streets) had left his post, allowing the traffic to travel west on Elm Street. As we were scanning the curb, I heard a shrill whistle coming from the north side of Elm Street. I turned and saw a white male in his twenties running down the grassy knoll from the direction of the Texas School Book Depository Building. A light green Rambler station wagon was coming slowly west on Elm Street. The driver of the station wagon was a husky looking Latin, with dark wavy hair, wearing a tan wind breaker type jacket. He was looking up at the man running toward him. He pulled over to the north curb and picked up the man coming down the hill. I tried to cross Elm Street to stop them and find out who they were. The traffic was too heavy and I was unable to reach them. They drove away going west on Elm Street.

In addition to noting that these two men were in an obvious hurry, I realized they were the only ones not running TO the scene. Everyone else was running to see whatever might be seen. The suspect, as I will refer to him, who ran down the grassy knoll was wearing faded blue trousers and a long-sleeved work shirt made of some type of grainy material. This will become very important to me later on and very embarrassing to the authorities (F.B.I., Dallas Police and Warren Commission). I thought the incident concerning the two men and the Rambler Station Wagon important enough to bring it to the attention of the authorities at the command post at Elm and Houston.

I ran to the front of the Texas School Book Depository where I asked for anyone involved in the investigation. There was a man standing on the steps of the Book Depository Building and he turned to me and said, "I'm with the Secret Service." This man was about 40 years old, sandy-haired with a distinct cleft in his chin. He was well-dressed in a gray business suit. I was naive enough at the time to believe that the only people there were actually officers—after all, this was the command post. I gave him the information. He showed little interest in the persons leaving. However, he seemed extremely interested in the description of the Rambler. This was the only part of my statement which he wrote down in his little pad he was holding. Point: Mrs. Ruth Paine, the woman Marina Oswald lived with in Irving, Texas, owned a Rambler station wagon, at that time, of this same color.

II

From the book depository and of course that grassy knoll

And the Dal Tex building's shooter fulfilled his deadly role

The noon day sun was witness as they took their awful toll

His dream goes marching on

I learned nothing of this "Secret Service Agent's" identity until December 22, 1967 while we were living in New Orleans. The television was on as I came home from work one night and there on the screen was a picture of this man. I did not know what it was all about until my wife told me that Jim Garrison had charged him with being a part of the assassination plot. I called Jim Garrison then and told him that this was the man I had seen in Dallas on November 22, 1963. Jim then sent one of his investigators to see me with a better picture which I identified. I then learned that this man's name was Edgar Eugene Bradley. It was a relief to me to know his name for I had been bothered by the fact that I had failed to get his name when he had told me he was a Secret Service Agent and I had given him my information. On the night of the assassination when I had come home and discussed the day with my wife I had, of course, told her of this encounter and my failure to get his name.

As I finished talking with the Agent, I was confronted by the High Priest of Dallas County Politics, Field Marshal Bill Decker. Decker had, apparently, been standing directly behind me and had overheard what I was saying. He called me aside and informed me that the suspect had already left the scene. (How did you know, James Eric? You had just arrived.) Decker then told me to help them (the police) search the Book Depository Building. Decker turned toward his office across the street, then suddenly stopped, looked at me and said "Somebody better take charge of this investigation." Then he continued walking slowly toward his office, indicating that it was not going to be him.

When I entered the Book Depository Building, I was joined by Deputy Sheriffs Eugene Boone and Luke Mooney. We went up the stairs directly to the sixth floor. The room was very dark and a thick layer of dust seemed to cover everything. We went to the south side of the building, since this was the street side and seemed the most logical place to start.

Luke Mooney and I reached the southeast corner at the same time. We immediately found three rifle cartridges laying in such a way that they looked as though they had been carefully and deliberately placed there—in plain sight on the floor to the right of the southeast corner window. Mooney and I examined the cartridges very carefully and remarked how close together they were. The three of them were no more than one inch apart and all were facing in the same direction, a feat very difficult to achieve with a bolt action rifle—or any rifle for that matter. One cartridge drew our particular attention. It was crimped on the end which would have held the slug. It had not been stepped on but merely crimped over on one small portion of the rim. The rest of that end was perfectly round.

Laying on the floor to the left of the same window was a small brown paper lunch bag containing some well cleaned chicken bones. I called across the room and summoned the Dallas Police I.D. man, Lt. Day. When he arrived with his camera Mooney and I left the window and started our search of the rest of the sixth floor.

We were told by Dallas Police to look for a rifle—something I had already concluded might be there since the cartridges found were, apparently, from a rifle. I was nearing the northwest corner of the sixth floor when Deputy Eugene Boone called out, "here it is." I was about eight feet from Boone, who was standing next to a stack of cardboard boxes. The boxes were stacked so that there was no opening between them except at the top. Looking over the top and down the opening I saw a rifle with a telescopic sight laying on the floor with the bolt facing upward. At this time Boone and I were joined by Lt. Day of the Dallas Police Department and Dallas Homicide Captain, Will Fritz. The rifle was retrieved by Lt. Day, who activated the bolt, ejecting one live round of ammunition which fell to the floor.

Lt. Day inspected the rifle briefly, then handed it to Capt. Fritz who had a puzzled look on his face. Seymour Weitzman, a deputy constable, was standing beside me at the time. Weitzman was an expert on weapons. He had been in the sporting goods business for many years and was familiar with all domestic and foreign weapons. Capt. Fritz asked if anyone knew what kind of rifle it was. Weitzman asked to see it. After a close examination (much longer than Fritz or Day's examination) Weitzman declared that it was a 7.65 German Mauser. Fritz agreed with him. Apparently, someone at the Dallas Police Department also loses things but, at least, they are more conscientious. They did replace it— even if the replacement was made in a different country. (See Warren Report for Italian Mannlicher-Carcano 6.5 Caliber).

At that exact moment an unknown Dallas police officer came running up the stairs and advised Capt. Fritz that a Dallas policeman had been shot in the Oak Cliff area. I instinctively looked at my watch. The time was 1:06 p.m. A token force of uniformed officers was left to keep the sixth floor secure and Fritz, Day, Boone, Mooney, Weitzman and I left the building.

On my way back to the Sheriff's Office I was nearly run down several times by Dallas Police cars racing to the scene of the shooting of a fellow officer. There were more police units at the J. D. Tippit shooting than there were at President John F. Kennedy's assassination.

Tippit had been instructed to patrol the Oak Cliff area along with Dallas Police Unit #87 at 12:45 p.m. by the dispatcher. Unit #87 immediately left Oak Cliff and went to the triple underpass, leaving Tippit alone. Why? At 12:54 p.m., J. D. Tippit, Dallas Police Unit #78, gave his location as Lancaster Blvd., and Eighth St., some ten blocks from the place where he was to be killed. The Dallas dispatcher called Tippit at 1:04 p.m. and received no answer. He continued to call three times and there was still no reply. Comparing this time with the time I received news of the shooting of the police officer at 1:06 p.m., it is fair to assume Tippit was dead or being killed between 1:04 and 1:06 p.m. This is also corroborated by the eye witnesses at the Tippit killing, who said he was shot between 1:05 and 1:08 p.m.

According to Officer Baker, Dallas Police, he talked to Oswald at 12:35 p.m. in the lunch room of the Texas School Book Depository. This would give Oswald 30 minutes or less to finish his coke, leave the building, walk four blocks east on Elm Street, catch a bus and ride it back west in heavy traffic for two blocks, get off the bus and walk two more blocks west and turn south on Lamar Street, walk four blocks and have a conversation with a cab driver and a woman over the use of Whaley's (the cab driver) cab, get into the cab and ride to 500 North Beckley Street, get out and walk to 1026 North Beckley where his (Oswald's) room was located, pick up something (?); and if that is not enough, Earlene Roberts, the housekeeper where Oswald lived, testified that at 1:05 p.m. Oswald was waiting for a bus in front of his rooming house and finally, to make him the fastest man on Earth, he walked to East Tenth Street and Patton Street, several blocks away and killed J. D. Tippit between 1:05 and 1:08 p.m. If he had not been arrested when he was, it is my belief that Earl Warren and his Commission would have had Lee Harvey Oswald eating dinner in Havana!

I was convinced on November 22, 1963, and I am still sure, that the man entering the Rambler station wagon was Lee Harvey Oswald. After entering the Rambler, Oswald and his companion would only have had to drive six blocks west on Elm Street and they would have been on Beckley Avenue and a straight shot to Oswald's rooming house. The Warren Commission could not accept this even though it might have given Oswald time to kill Tippit for having two men involved would have made it a conspiracy!

As to Lee Harvey Oswald shooting J. D. Tippit, let us examine the evidence: Dallas Police Unit #221 (Summers-refer-police radio log) stated on the police radio that he had an "eye ball" witness to the shooting. The suspect was a white male about twenty-seven, five feet, eleven inches, black wavy hair, fair complexioned, (not Oswald) wearing an Eisenhower-type jacket of light color, dark trousers, and a white shirt, apparently armed with a .32 caliber, dark-finish automatic pistol which he had in his right hand. (The jacket strongly resembles that worn by the driver of the station wagon).

Dallas Police Unit #550 Car 2 was driven to the scene of the Tippit murder by Sgt. Gerald Hill. He was accompanied by Bud Owens, Dallas Police Department, and William F. Alexander, Assistant D.A. for Dallas. Unit #550 Car 2 reported over the police radio that the shells at the scene indicated that the suspect was armed with a 38 caliber automatic. 38 automatic shells and 38 revolver shells are distinctly different. (Oswald allegedly had a 38 revolver in his possession when arrested?)

After much confusion in the Oak Cliff area the Dallas Police were finally directed to the Texas Theater where the suspect was reported to be. Several squads arrived at the theater and quickly surrounded it. At the back door was none other than William F. Alexander, Assistant D.A., and several Dallas Police officers with guns drawn. While Dallas Police Officer McDonald and others entered the theater and turned on the lights and the suspect was pointed out to them, they started searching people several rows in front of Oswald, giving him a chance to run if he wanted to—right into the blazing guns of waiting officers!

This man had to be stopped. He was the most dangerous criminal in the history of the world. Here was a man who was able to go from one location to another with the swiftness of Superman, to change his physical characteristics at will and who pumped four automatic slugs into a police officer with a revolver—indeed a master criminal!

Well, back to the facts? Oswald was captured by Officer McDonald, who was out cold from one blow from the suspect and woke up to find he had arrested the suspect! (Nice going, Mac).

Later that afternoon I received word of the suspect's arrest and the fact that he was suspected of being involved in the President's death. I immediately thought of the man running down the grassy knoll. I made a telephone call to Capt. Will Fritz and gave him the description of the man I had seen and Fritz said, "that sounds like the suspect we have. Can you come up and take a look at him?"

I arrived at Capt. Fritz office shortly after 4:30 p.m. I was met by Agent Bookhout from the F.B.I., who took my name and place of employment. The door to Capt. Fritz' personal office was open and the blinds on the windows were closed, so that one had to look through the doorway in order to see into the room. I looked through the open door at the request of Capt. Fritz and identified the man who I saw running down the grassy knoll and enter the Rambler station wagon—and it WAS Lee Harvey Oswald.

Fritz and I entered his private office together. He told Oswald, "This man (pointing to me) saw you leave." At which time the suspect replied, "I told you people I did." Fritz, apparently trying to console Oswald, said, "Take it easy, son—we're just trying to find out what happened." Fritz then said, "What about the car?" Oswald replied, leaning forward on Fritz' desk, "That station wagon belongs to Mrs. Paine—don't try to drag her into this." Sitting back in his chair, Oswald said very disgustedly and very low, "Everybody will know who I am now."

At this time Capt. Fritz ushered me from his office, thanking me. I walked away saddened but relieved that it was the end of the day and I could go home, where I could try—at least for a little while—to put the tragedy and the day's events out of my mind. I was soon to find out that my troubles had only begun—for I had seen and heard too much that fateful day.

Saturday, November 23, 1963, I spent the day at home talking to my wife, Molly, about Friday's events and playing with Deanna and Terry, not knowing that the very next day would bring another tragic event which would affect not only my job but my entire future.

Like many other Americans, I was watching television on Sunday morning, November 24, 1963 when Jack Ruby shot Lee Harvey Oswald. I would like to clear up one thing at this point concerning Ruby's access to the basement of the city jail. The Warren Commission concluded that Dallas Police Officer R. E. Vaughn, through negligence, let Jack Ruby into the basement. What they did not say is that Officer Vaughn was questioned extensively after the shooting and even submitted to a polygraph test, which he passed, showing that he did not let Jack Ruby go down the Main Street Ramp of the city jail. I have known Officer Vaughn for many years and feel that he is honest, conscientious and one of the finest people I have ever known. I feel that he was unjustly accused. However, bombing Vaughn was the easiest way out for Earl Warren's Commission.

III

The industrial and military complex can't survive

Without their little horror wars they artfully contrive

If they push us to the big one then we won't come out alive

His dream goes marching on

Things were fairly normal for me for the next few months, with the exception of curious persons who popped into the Sheriff's Office from time to time to ask me questions about the assassination.

On the first anniversary of the assassination a team of newsmen from NBC New York came to Dallas. They wanted to do a documentary on the assassination and they contacted Jim Kerr of the Dallas Times Herald who told them of me.

Jim approached me and said that the NBC people were interested in what I had to say and would I talk to them? Jim Kerr indicated to me that he had it all set up. However, because I knew how Bill Decker felt about anyone in his Department talking about this particular event, I told him I would have to get Decker's permission. NBC had been calling me since October 1964 asking to talk to me but I would not commit myself.

When they arrived during the week of November 22, I went to Decker to ask permission to do the story. Decker promptly sat me down in the private office, closed the door and sat there looking at me for several minutes. It was difficult to tell if Decker was looking at you—with that glass eye of his—but at the same time you had the uneasy feeling that he was looking straight through you. Decker began to talk with that even, never-rising voice which commanded attention and gave you the feeling that it was dangerous to interrupt or even question him.

Decker told me to tell these people (Jim Kerr and NBC) that I was a Deputy Sheriff—not an actor—and for me to keep my mouth shut. He then went on to say, "Tell them you didn't see or hear anything." He then went back to the papers on his desk and I knew he was through—and so was I. I relayed the message to Jim Kerr, who was very disappointed—and even mad, but he, like me, knew that he must not challenge Decker's law.

From that day forward Bill Decker began to watch my every move. People in the office who, before this, very seldom spoke to me, began to hang around watching my every move and listening to everything I said. Among these were Rosemary Allen, E. R. (Buddy) Walthers, Allen Sweatt and Bob Morgan—Decker's four top stoolies.

Combine the foregoing with the run-in I had with Dave Belin, junior counsel for the Warren Commission, who questioned me in April of 1964, and who changed my testimony fourteen times when he sent it to Washington, and you will have some idea of the pressures brought to bear.

David Belin told me who he was as I entered the interrogation room (April 1964). He had me sit at the head of a long table. To my left was a female with a pencil and pen. Belin sat to my right. Between the girl and Belin was a tape recorder, which was turned off. Belin instructed the girl not to take notes until he (Belin) said to do so. He then told me that the investigation was being conducted to determine the truth as the evidence indicates. Well, I could take that several ways but I said nothing. Then Belin said, "For instance, I will ask you where you were at a certain time. This will establish your physical location." It was at this point that I began to feel that I was being led into something but still I said nothing. Then Belin said, "I will ask you about what you thought you heard or saw in regard." Well, this was too much. I interrupted him and said, "Counselor, just ask me the questions and if I can answer them, I will." This seemed to irritate Belin and he told the girl to start taking notes with the next question.

At this point Belin turned the recorder on. The first questions were typical. Where were you born? Where did you go to school? When Belin would get to certain questions, he would turn off the recorder and stop the girl from writing. The he would ask me, for example, "Did you see anything unusual when you were behind the picket fence?" I said, "Yes" and he said, "Fine, just a minute." He would then tell the girl to start writing with the next question and would again start the recorder. What was the next question? "Mr. Craig, did you go into the Texas School Book Depository?" It was clear to me that he wanted only to record part of the interrogation, as this happened many times.

I finally managed to get in at least most of what I had seen and heard by ignoring his advanced questions and giving a step-by-step picture, which further seemed to irritate him.

At the end of our session Belin dismissed me but when I started to leave the room, he called me back. At this time, I identified the clothing worn by the suspect (the 26 volumes refer to a box of clothing—not boxes. There were two boxes.)

After I identified the clothing, Belin went over the complete testimony again. He then asked, "Do you want to follow or waive your signature or sign now?" Since there was nothing but a tape recording and a stenographer's note book, there was obviously nothing to sign. All other testimony which I have read (a considerable amount) included an explanation that the person could waive his signature then or his statement would be typed and he would be notified when it was ready for signature. Belin did not say this to me.

He said an odd thing when I left. It is the only time that he said it, and I have never read anything similar in any testimony. "Be SURE, when you get back to the office, to thank Sheriff Decker for his cooperation." I know of no one else he questioned who he asked to thank a supervisor, chief, etc.

I first saw my testimony in January of 1968 when I looked at the 26 volumes which belonged to Penn Jones. My alleged statement was included. The following are some of the changes in my testimony:

- Arnold Rowland told me that he saw two men on the sixth floor of the Texas School Book Depository 15 minutes before the President arrived: one was a Negro, who was pacing back and forth by the southwest window. The other was a white man in the southeast corner, with a rifle equipped with a scope, and that a few minutes later he looked back and only the white man was there. In the Warren Commission: Both were white, both were pacing in front of the southwest corner and when Rowland looked back, both were gone;

- I said the Rambler station wagon was light green. The Warren Commission: Changed to a white station wagon;

- I said the driver of the Station Wagon had on a tan jacket. The Warren Commission: A white jacket;

- I said the license plates on the Rambler were not the same color as Texas plates. The Warren Commission: Omitted the not— omitted but one word, an important one, so that it appeared that the license plates were the same color as Texas plates;

- I said that I got a good look at the driver of the Rambler. The Warren Commission: I did not get a good look at the Rambler. (In Captain Fritz's office) I had said that Fritz had said to Oswald, "This man saw you leave" (indicating me). Oswald said, "I told you people I did." Fritz then said, "Now take it easy, son, we're just trying to find out what happened", and then (to Oswald), "What about the car?" to which Oswald replied, "That station wagon belongs to Mrs. Paine. Don't try to drag her into this." Fritz said car—station wagon was not mentioned by anyone but Oswald. (I had told Fritz over the telephone that I saw a man get into a station wagon, before I went to the Dallas Police Department and I had also described the man. This is when Fritz asked me to come there.) Oswald then said, "Everybody will know who I am now;" the Warren Commission: Stated that the last statement by Oswald was made in a dramatic tone. This was not so. The Warren Commission also printed, "NOW everybody will know who I am", transposing the now. Oswald's tone and attitude was one of disappointment. If someone were attempting to conceal his identity as Deputy and he was found out, exposed—his cover blown, his reaction would be dismay and disappointment. This was Oswald's tone and attitude—disappointment at being exposed!

Shortly after the Kerr and Belin incidents, the Sheriff took me out of the field and assigned me to the Bond Desk. This meant that I was sitting directly in line with Decker's office door, where he could watch me. It made me feel a little like a goldfish in a bowl!

While I was on the Bond Desk, I noticed Eva Grant (Jack Ruby's sister) was making daily visits to Decker's office. During this time Eva and I came to be on good terms. It was convenient for her to speak to me when she came in because of the position of my desk—close to the door leading into the Sheriff's Department. As time went on Eva Grant would stop me in the hall every time I went for a cup of coffee or took a break. Decker became very concerned over this and it was not long before I realized that ever time Eva and I talked we were joined by someone. In addition to this, Buddy Walthers would be standing close by and listening (This is another example of his talents as a peace officer—that he would make himself so conspicuous). First, he would stand and listen, and then head into Decker's office.

After a few days of this and armed with information from this so- called detective—who couldn't track an elephant through the snow with a nose bleed—Decker called me into his office and pointed to a chair without saying a word. Well, knowing he wasn't giving me the chair or asking me to look it over, I sat down. After a long silence he finally said, "What about it?" This was Decker's way of telling you he knew it (whatever it was) and he wanted you to "confess." I felt sure Eva Grant was going to be the subject of conversation but I was determined to make him start the interrogation—after all he wanted the answers and, apparently, Buddy had not heard as much as he thought he had.

Finally, he gave in and said, "You've been talking to Eva Grant." I said, "Yes sir." Decker then said, "What about?" I replied, "She is concerned about Jack's depressed state of mind and worried about the fact that he looks ill." Decker said, "That's none of your business." I replied with the only thing that Decker would accept—I said, "No sir." Apparently sure that he had convinced me once again that there was no law except Decker's law, he pointed to the door and I left. He was a man of few words!

The next day Eva and I had another talk. She was getting more and more concerned about Jack's health. She had been to see Decker several times trying to secure medical help for her brother. By this time the rumor was all through the Sheriff's office that Jack was, indeed, ill. Most of this information came from the deputies assigned to guard him. The deputies were Walter Neighbors, James R. Keene, Jess Stevenson, Jr., and others. Finally, Decker permitted a doctor to see Jack, a psychiatrist, who said Jack Ruby had a cold!

A few weeks passed, during which time I received some telephone calls concerning the assassination and my testimony. These calls came from various people from different parts of the country who were, apparently, just interested. These calls somehow were reported to Bill Decker. Not having a reason to fire me, he did the next best thing, he had a monitoring unit connected to the telephone system so that he could periodically check any telephone calls.

I will not go into the events leading to Jack Ruby's death. Much has already been written about this but I would like to say that Jack Ruby made several statements to guards, jail supervisors and assistant D.A.'s in which he said "they are going to kill me." These statements became a private joke among these people and they discussed them freely in the hall of the court house. When the Sheriff from Wichita Falls, Texas came to observe the prisoner he was about to take charge of, due to Ruby's change of venue, he refused to accept the prisoner on the grounds that Ruby was very ill. Then, and only then, did Decker send Ruby to Parkland Hospital where he died a few short days later (some cold!).

I was not too concerned about the minor attention I was receiving from Decker regarding the assassination and its aftermath until August 7, 1966. At 2:30 a.m, I was approached by Hardy M. Parkerson, an attorney from New Orleans, La. Mr. Parkerson was interested in the assassination and the Jack Ruby trial. I was working late nights on the Bond Desk when he came to the Sheriff's office. He asked me several questions relating to these tragic events and I answered him as honestly as I could and he thanked me and left.

However, on October 1, 1966 Mr. Parkerson wrote to me advising me that I was receiving more publicity than I might be aware of. He mentioned in his letter that he had picked up a book on a New Orleans newsstand. The book was entitled, The Second Oswald by Richard H. Popkin and my report had been mentioned in the book. This disturbed me as I knew my popularity with Decker was fading anyway.

On October 18 I received another letter from Mr. Parkerson. It seemed that he had come across another book on a New Orleans newsstand which mentioned my name. This one was Inquest by Edward J. Epstein. Then I began to worry a bit. Of course, other names were mentioned also in these books, but I was concerned because of my employer's attitude and the fact that I was in definite conflict with the Warren Commission in my testimony.

In February of 1967 the lid blew off. District Attorney Jim Garrison announced publicly his probe into the John F. Kennedy Assassination. It wasn't long—in fact, a matter of hours—until Decker walked up to me and asked, "Have you been talking to Jim Garrison?" I told him that I had not, which was the truth. Decker then said, "Somebody sure as hell has." That was the beginning of the end of my career as a law officer and my future in Dallas County.

As more and more books critical of the Warren Commission began to hit the newsstands throughout the country and I received calls and visitors asking questions my future with the Sheriff's Office became very shaky. Finally, on July 4, 1967 Bill Decker called me into his office and told me to check out. Knowing there was no grievance board and that Decker was the supreme ruler of his domain, I left the Sheriff's Office for good.

I was saddened by the loss of eight years in a job that I had given my ALL to. But I was soon to find out that this was only the down payment on the price that I was to pay for the truth! I immediately began looking for work and found that the Commerce Bail Bond Company was just opening an office and needed someone to help in the office as Les Hancock, the owner, was just starting out.

Mr. Hancock and I had a long talk and he agreed that I would be an asset to the business because he knew nothing about it and I was familiar with bonds and most of the people at the Sheriff's Office as well as those wishing to make bond. Les and I seemed to get along very well. I posted most of the bonds and kept track of our clients. Posting the first few bonds with the county went slowly—although the money was in escrow, Decker wanted to personally approve all bonds posted by me. I did not mind this delaying tactic because all it involved was a little extra time for me. The bonding business was going very well—within two months we were making money.

I kept up as much as possible on Jim Garrison's probe and decided to write him and tell him what I knew—if it would help him. Jim Garrison answered my letter and asked me to call him, at which time he made arrangements for my trip to New Orleans.

Les Hancock tried to persuade me not to go, saying I shouldn't get involved (a little late). I arrived in New Orleans in late October and was picked up at the airport by Bill Boxley, one of Jim's investigators, and four men who didn't work for Jim. Boxley took me to a motel where I was to meet Jim and the other four men followed—apparently, they were not invited. Most of my talks with Jim were at his office while my "tails" (apparently government agents) searched my room. I must apologize to them for not bringing what they could "use."

I had several meetings with Jim Garrison. He showed me numerous pictures taken in Dealey Plaza on November 22, 1963. Among them was a picture of a Latin male. I recognized him as being the same man I had seen driving the Rambler station wagon in which I had seen Oswald leave the Book Depository area. I was surprised and I asked Jim who the man was. Jim did not know but he did say this man was arrested in Dealey Plaza immediately after the assassination but was released by Dallas Police because he could not speak English! This was, to me, highly unusual. In my experience as a police officer I had never known of a person (or prisoner) being released because of a language barrier. Interpreters were, of course, always available.

We also discussed the 45 caliber slug found on the south side of Elm Street, in the grass, by E. R. (Buddy) Walthers. Buddy had indeed found such a slug. He and I discussed it the evening of November 22, 1963. Buddy also gave a statement to the Dallas Press confirming this find (found among bits of brain matter). However, he later denied finding it—after Decker had a long talk with him and subsequent to newsmen questioning the Sheriff about the evidence.

Jim Garrison also had a picture of an unidentified man picking up this 45 slug and Buddy is also in that photograph. I asked Buddy about this many times—after his denial—but he never made any comment.

Jim also asked me about the arrests made in Dealey Plaza that day. I told him I knew of twelve arrests, one in particular made by R. E. Vaughn of the Dallas Police Department. The man Vaughn arrested was coming from the Dal-Tex Building across from the Texas School Book Depository. The only thing which Vaughn knew about him was that he was an independent oil operator from Houston, Texas. The prisoner was taken from Vaughn by Dallas Police detectives and that was the last that he saw or heard of the suspect.

Incidentally, there are no records of any arrests, either by the Dallas Police Department or the Sheriff's Office, made in Dealey Plaza on November 22, 1963. Very strange! Any and all arrests made during my eight years as an officer were recorded. It may not have been entered as a record with the Identification Bureau but a report was always typed and a permanent record kept—if only in our case files. A report on any questioning shows a reason for your action and protects you against false arrest. I am saying that there is absolutely no record in the case files or any place else.

Upon returning to Dallas from my first contact with Jim Garrison, I was picked up by another "tail." I was followed constantly after that. My wife could not even go to the grocery store without being followed. Sometimes they would go so far as to pull up next to her and make sure she saw them talking on their two-way radios. They would also park across from my house and sit for hours making sure I knew they were there.

On the morning of November 1, 1967, I received a call from a friend of mine. He owned a night club at Carroll and Columbia Streets in Dallas. Bill said that he wanted to see me and would I meet him in front of the club. Bill had called me many times when I was a deputy as he was frequently in financial trouble and I would have the citation issued for him held up until he was in a position to accept them. Some people in Dallas did receive Special Treatment in the matter of citations. Bill was not one of these but I did this for him because I knew that by holding it up a day or so I could save his credit rating—and the creditor would be paid without having a Judgment entered. We were friends and it was a natural—and practical thing to do.

When Bill called me on November 1st, he said he wanted to talk to me about money he owed the Bonding Company where I worked—for getting one of his employees out of jail on traffic tickets. He had asked that I meet him at 9:00 a.m. At about 8:30 a.m. "me and my shadows" started for the club, arriving at approximately 9:00 a.m.

When I parked in front of Bill's club "my shadows" began one of the sweetest set-ups I had ever seen. One car, a tan Pontiac, parked one block in front of my car, racing me, and the other, a white Chevrolet with a small antenna protruding from the roof, kept circling the block again and again, never stopping. There were two men in the Chevrolet. I couldn't get a good look at the driver but the other man was in his early thirties. He had dark hair, was nice looking and wore a black-and-white checked sport coat.

Bill had never been late before for an appointment with me but he was this time. When it was nearing 10:15 I began to worry that those poor bastards would get dizzy from driving around and around—and might hit someone.

Finally, at 10:15 a.m. Bill arrived and we went to the Waffle House across the street for coffee. There, as big as life, sitting on a stool was the man in the sport jacket—from the white Chevrolet. Well . . . we sat down and had coffee. We talked about how each of us was doing—just shot the bull—and Bill never did bring up the subject which he had said he wanted to discuss with me!

When we finished, we started to leave and the man in the sport coat jumped up and beat us out of the door. We paid our checks and walked out the door and my shadow was nowhere in sight—believe me, I looked. We crossed the parking lot and stopped at the traffic light, as it was red against us. For some reason I stepped down off the curb before the light changed. As I did, Bill fell flat on the sidewalk. I was about to find out why. At that very instant a shot rang out behind me and the hair just above my left ear parted. I felt a pressure and sharp pain on the left side of my head. I bolted for my car leaving Bill lying on the ground. I heard him say, "You son of a bitch" and I jumped into my car and drove home as fast as possible. When I arrived home, I told my wife what this good friend had done for me. I pondered the idea of moving my family to some safe place.

A curious note: my friend (?) Bill was deeply in debt and about to lose his business at the time of the shooting. However, about a month later he was completely out of debt, his business was doing great and he had invested in two other businesses which were doing very well. (Payment was, apparently, not withheld just because the trigger man missed.) I decided to get in touch with Jim Garrison. I tried all day and finally reached him around ten that evening. After I told him what had happened, he said someone would be at my home within the hour.

At approximately 11 p.m. someone knocked on the door and I opened it with my left hand, holding my 45 automatic in my right hand. Standing there was a small but well-built man in his late forties or early fifties. He said, "My name is Penn Jones. Jim Garrison called me." My hand tightened on the 45 when my wife, Molly, took hold of me and said, "I've seen him on T.V. He is Penn Jones." With that I relaxed and he remained Penn Jones!

Penn Jones listened to my story and then began making telephone calls to newsmen and wire services that he had contact with, explaining to me that the best protection for me was open coverage on the incident. After a long talk with Penn Jones I found that I had a great deal of respect and admiration for this man. Although small in stature, I felt he would fight the devil himself to find the truth about the assassination.

The next day, November 2, 1967, when I went to work at Commerce Bail Bonds, I was approached by two reporters and a photographer from Channel 8 in Dallas. They had picked the story up on the news wire and wanted a personal interview. After the interview my boss, Les Hancock, called me into his office and told me he didn't think that I should have done the interview (giving no specific reason).

The next few days Les' attitude was very cold and he would barely speak to me. Then, on the 7th of November he called me into his office once again. This time he told me the business wasn't doing well and he would have to let me go because he was closing the office. Of course, I knew better than this—after all I had access to all the records and I knew the business was making money. A few days later I found out Les merely moved to another location and his business continued as usual.

However, this knowledge did not help me for I was back pounding the pavement looking for work. In the meantime, I had been in contact with Jim Garrison. He informed me that there was an opening at Volkswagen International in New Orleans and that I might try there. By this time my health had begun to be affected. I had undergone a serious stomach operation in August of 1963 and I suffer from chronic bronchitis and emphysema (not to mention Dallas County Battle Fatigue).

My family and I made the trip to New Orleans, where I was interviewed by Willard Robertson, the owner of the company. Mr. Robertson told me he was looking for a Personnel Manager and because of my background of dealing with the public he hired me. After a long trip back to Dallas where we gathered up our meager belongings we moved to New Orleans and I felt good—I was working again!

We had been there but a few days when all of our neighbors and half the people where I was working knew who I was. This was due to the newspaper and television coverage of Jim Garrison's probe into the assassination. Again came the never-ending questions, which I did not mind because outside of Dallas people were sincerely interested and I certainly did not mind doing what I could to clear up any doubts they had. The people at the office treated me very well.

Unfortunately, after about a month I realized that I was not doing anything but going in to the office and coming home—nothing in between. Although I appreciated Jim Garrison recommending me for the job, I knew by this time that he had done this because he was concerned about my safety and wanted me out of Dallas. Because this company did not really need a Personnel Manager and I couldn't take the money for a job I was not doing, I submitted my resignation to Mr. Robertson and my family and I returned to Dallas.

We arrived back in Dallas on a cold and snowy seventh of January, 1968, and moved in with Molly's parents as we had very little money and nowhere to stay. The next few days I spent looking for work. I tried every ad and every lead I could find. The people who interviewed me always seemed interested but like all companies, they wanted to check out my references. When I failed to receive any results from my efforts, I called some of the places where I had placed applications to see what was wrong. I always received the same answer, "the position had been filled." Finally, I decided something was wrong and I suspected one employment reference, Bill Decker. I had a friend write Decker asking for an employment reference—he never received an answer!

My next move was to have someone call Decker and ask for a reference and this took some doing. Writing him was one thing but talking to him on the telephone was another. He would bait you on the telephone and, before you knew it, he knew who you were and whether you were legitimate or not.

Many people in Dallas liked Decker for the favors he could do for them but those who did not like him were afraid of the tremendous power he possessed in Dallas County. They were afraid to oppose him in any issue for fear that this man could, indeed, affect their professional careers. A good example is the charge, "Hold for Decker." This meant that when Decker wanted to talk to you or some friend of his disagreed with an arrest (without warrant), you were detained in the county jail until Decker wished to talk or release you. No attorney in Dallas County would dare apply for a writ of habeas corpus to secure your release.

Well, to get back to my "minor" problem, I finally found someone to call Decker for a reference and when he did Decker informed him that, "Mr. Craig had worked for me and I would not re-hire him and that is all I've got to say about Mr. Craig." So . . . I had worked for the Sheriff for eight years and yet, without a reference, it was as though those years had never existed. How do you explain this kind of situation to a prospective employer?

After many more exhaustive interviews, I found a company, on February 1, 1968, which had just opened a branch office in Dallas and was in BAD need of security guards to work in department stores where they had new contracts. When I applied for the job I told them of my background in law enforcement, leaving out the details of my separation with the Sheriff's Office. I only showed them the watch I was wearing, which is inscribed: Roger D. Craig, First Place, Sheriff's Department 1960. (The award was for Officer of the Year). They were impressed and with a sigh of relief I was hired without the customary background check.

My first assignment was a department store in East Dallas, where I held the very important position of keeping the shopping baskets out of the aisles. (Don't knock it—I was working 12 hours a day and making a whopping $1.60 per hour).

By this time my creditors were knocking on my door day and night. All of the furniture we had, which was not much, we lost and then "along came Jones."

I had contacted Penn when I arrived back in Dallas and after I lost the car he let me use his 1955 Ford, which he wasn't driving, and I was back in business!

Because of the crowded quarters at Molly's parents, we began to search for an apartment. We found many and were turned down every time. Some people said they did not want to rent to families with children. Others would accept us and then when we were ready to move in, they would say it was already rented and they had "forgotten." Finally, in mid-February we found a couple on Tremont Street, who were not afraid to rent to us. Oh, they knew who I was but they said it did not matter— they had kept up on the assassination.

Our only outlet for our tensions were the Sunday trips we made to the Penn Jones home in Midlothian, Texas. During these visits I would try to bring Penn up to date on the latest from the Dallas Police Department and Sheriff's Office. I was able to give him some help from time to time because I could keep in touch with these offices through officers there who were still friendly toward me. It was fun and relaxing to get together with Penn and his wife L.A., who is a delightful person with a great sense of humor. The two of them made you feel as though the whole world was right there.

On one of these visits Penn told me he was going to appear on the Joe Pyne show in Los Angeles and asked if I would go with him. Needless to say, I owed Penn Jones much over the previous months and if I would be an asset, I was certainly prepared to go, I told him. I got a leave of absence from my employer, Penn made the arrangements and we were off to Los Angeles.

The Los Angeles trip was a success as far as I was concerned, especially when we spoke to the young people at U.C.L.A. They were very concerned about the assassination and were kind to Penn and me. The only disappointment came in the form of Otto Preminger, who was sitting in for Joe Pyne that night. I think his statement to the audience speaks for itself. He said that he believed whole-heartedly in the Warren Report and when I asked him if he had read the Warren Report, he said "no"! After a week of appearances on television and radio my lungs were beginning to give me trouble and I returned to Dallas with Mrs. Jones, while Penn went on to San Francisco.

After a few weeks back on my important job of keeping the shopping carts in line I found that at a dollar and sixty cents an hour I had too much month left at the end of the money. We were behind on our rent and, oh well, back to the want ads.

We found a couple who were looking for someone to live in and care for their elderly mother, rent free. After all this time there was something free? Getting settled did not take very long—with just a few clothes. This worked out fairly well. I worked twelve hours a day and Molly did all of the washing, ironing, cooking and cleaning—in addition to caring for Terry, Deanna and Roger Jr. (Who had been staying previously with his grandmother). Did I say free?

In the meantime, Penn had returned from San Francisco and during a visit to our house he told me he could get me a job in Midlothian working at an oil refinery and that the pay was $500.00 per month. I hated to give up the prestige of my present position but money was money. I gave my employer notice and on April 15, 1968 I started work at the refinery. This was not crude oil but used motor oil—we re-re-processed it. The work was new to me and I had never re-refined used motor oil before. I found that I was a little soft. I had to dump three thousand pounds (50 fifty-pound bags) of clay into hot oil every morning and pump it back into the still which cooked it. This whipped me into shape quite rapidly. I was not concerned with the physical work involved for I knew that I had a chance to support my family and that was what counted.

The work went smoothly until the second Thursday of May, 1968 when, while trying to start an engine at the plant, I slipped and broke my arm—"good ole lady luck." I had my arm set and missed one day of work. On Monday morning I returned to work, knowing I could not live on workmen's compensation, which was about $40.00 per week. I painfully continued to work with the arm in a cast for the next six weeks.

During this six-week period my boss had offered to let me move into a house he owned in Midlothian so that I would be closer to work. I took him up on the offer because I was driving sixty miles each day to work and back and Molly was worried about me driving and working with the broken arm and—again I was being followed.

During this time a Dallas Sheriff's car stopped me and asked where I was going. I had known this deputy for several years and there was no reason for his behavior. Molly's health was getting worse. She had serious stomach disorders and the strain of past events had not helped—so we moved. Now we were in Midlothian and I was driving four miles to work and back.

During the time I was still driving back and forth from Dallas to Midlothian—or the job—I noticed that I was being followed by a blue and white pick-up, occupied by a white male. One day, after being followed by this truck for several days, as the truck was approaching the driver stuck a revolver out the window and was about to fire, when another car pulled up behind me and he withdrew the pistol. My hours were never the same two days in a row but this man seemed to know the precise hour I would leave work. Penn Jones and I tried to set a trap for this man but, he, apparently knew it and got away. I never saw him after that.

It was six weeks since I had broken my arm and this was the day I was to have the cast taken off. I felt good as it had been quite a burden. On that morning I reported for work and started preparing the pumps and tanks for cooking the oil when lady luck smiled down on me once again. I started to light the furnace and it blew up, burning my face and a good deal of hair and my arms. This was around the first of July, 1968. After the doctor treated me, he advised me that I would have to wear the cast another two weeks because he was afraid that I would get an infection in the burned area if the cast were removed. I do not want to leave the impression that my conflict with the Dallas establishment was the direct cause of these accidents. However, had the door not been closed to me in Dallas, I would not have had to turn to work with which I was not familiar.

In August of 1968 (while living in Midlothian) I received a visit in the middle of the night from a man in his fifties who said he was out of gas. I was already in bed and Molly was catching up on some of my court records when this man came to the door. Molly told him I was in bed with a sprained ankle and would not be able to help him. She directed him to the neighbors down the road. He went straight to his car, which was parked beside our house, got in, started it right up and drove off! Apparently, he was not out of gas but wanted us to know we could be found. This was about the time Penn was printing some pretty hot editorials in his paper with information I had supplied. I guess someone didn't like it.

I made some friends in Midlothian and was getting along fairly well. I had a job, a place to live and was able to purchase a used car.

The City Council was taking applications for a city judge. After talking it over with Penn Jones and some of my other friends, I went before the council for an interview, and, I must say, it was somewhat of a surprise when they appointed me. The future was beginning to show some promise. I continued the work at the refinery and pursued my new duties at city hall.

On August 5, 1968, Bill Seward, the only other employee at the refinery, was discussing a better way to process the oil with Dale Foshee, the owner. They were going to try something new in an attempt to obtain a better quality of oil. Dale purchased a new type of clay which would absorb more waste from the used oil as it cooked. Neither of these men told me that this new clay contained a substantial amount of some sort of acid. This meant that when I dumped it (the clay) into the hot oil tank, as I did every morning, and did not wear any sort of breathing devise, I inhaled a great deal of the dust from this new product.

Shortly after I started cooking the oil, I noticed I was having trouble breathing. I did not pay much attention to it and finished the day's work. That night the acid really got to me and I found myself passing out. I tried lying my head right in the window to get enough air—but still could not. Penn Jones came to the house and he and Molly rushed me to the hospital in Mansfield, Texas, about ten miles from Midlothian. I stayed under an oxygen tent for two days. On the fourth day I felt much better and was released from the hospital.

I had learned, about a week before going to the hospital, that the Justice of the Peace in Midlothian was resigning and I was persuaded by friends to seek that position. I had talked with the county commissioners before I went to the hospital and they made their final decision on the day I came home from the hospital. I was sworn in as Justice of the Peace on August 8, 1968. I would be an appointee until the November election. Now I was working at the refinery, holding the position of City Judge and also Justice of the Peace. The city paid me $50.00 a month and the Justice of the Peace position brought in about $50.00 a month. I was not getting rich but look at it this way, I was the entire establishment in Midlothian!

The business for the city was very routine and went rather smoothly. However, the Justice Court was another matter. I was having to correspond with the surrounding counties and they were all cooperative, with one exception (you guessed it), Dallas County. Some warrants, citations and subpoenas were sent to the Dallas County Sheriff for service. Needless to say, they were returned "unable to locate"!

So, the door was still closed to me in Dallas—even in matters of the law which these officials were sworn to uphold. Now, also Decker knew where I was and it was not long before my creditors, with whom I had been trying to make arrangements to pay a little to each month, had obtained judgments against me in the Dallas courts and I had been served with the papers. Now there was no hope of clearing my credit without paying everyone in full, which was impossible (I'll bet his glass was really shining). The next few weeks I managed to avoid my contact with the Good People of Dallas, hoping that they would forget about me—a fat chance!

In October 1968, my oldest son (Roger, Jr.) wasn't doing well in school and he decided to run away from home. I was, of course, very concerned about him—he was only fourteen years old. I contacted the Dallas Morning News to see if they would print his picture. I might have just as well invaded Russia. My name was immediately connected with Jim Garrison and before I could say stop the press, my name and connection with Jim was all over the newspaper, UPI, radio and television. I was getting calls from all over the country.

A couple of days later we received a call from the sheriff in Texarkana, Arkansas. He had Roger Jr. We went to Arkansas and retrieved him as quietly as possible. He had been working for one day on a ranch.

On October the seventh I reported to work at the refinery at which time my boss handed me a check marked, FINAL. He told me he was cutting down on production due to a slowdown in business and he wouldn't need me anymore. Now where have I heard that before?

Being Justice of the Peace, I wasn't without influence in Midlothian. I soon secured a job at a gas station changing truck tires. Not much prestige but a lot of hours and I quickly commanded the respect of every tire tool in the place.

A few days later, my former employer came to me and said that I would have to move out of his house because he wanted to use if for a week retreat to get away from Dallas.

By this time I was beginning to suspect the periodic publicity I had been receiving through the years, might have had something to do with my trouble finding jobs and housing. I guess I am a little slow—especially when this former employer hired someone to take my place at the refinery. He let him move into the house where I lived—as I found out sometime later. So now I had to work 12 hours a day and try to find a place to move my family. The election was coming up. This would not have been important except for the fact that being Justice of the Peace served as a deterrent from harassment by certain people, whose names I need not mention.

It was November and I still had been unable to find a house to rent. Midlothian was a very small town and there were just no houses to rent.

Anyway, the election was over and I had won by twenty votes. No doubt, twenty people who did not read the paper or watch television. I continued working at the gas station and living in my former employer's house. The election had done at least one thing for me. Dale still wanted me to move but was not pressing as hard. The days which followed were hard—we had rain and some sleet and working in this was beginning to affect my health. Molly was ill and Deanna, who had suffered from chronic bronchitis since birth, was not doing any better than we were. December was on us before I knew it and Mr. Roberts, the owner, decided to retire from the gas station. This meant, of course, that I was back on the street.

IV

Our President is lying up there cold beneath his flame

He is calling out for vengeance and to do so in his name

To keep the peace forever and erase our nation's shame

His dream goes marching on

This time there were no jobs to be found. However, business in the Justice Court was somewhat improved due to the opening of a substation in Midlothian by the Highway Patrol. I could not pay the rent or meet the bills but the increase was enough to buy groceries. I had resigned as City Judge so that there would be no conflict of interest between the two positions (City and County Court).

It was at this time that I was notified by District Attorney, Jim Garrison, that he would need me in the upcoming Clay Shaw trial—another wrench in the machinery. The night after I was notified of this, I received a telephone call and the voice asked if I was going to go to New Orleans. When I answered, "yes," he just said, "get a one-way ticket" and then hung up. I brushed this off as just another crank. I'd had those calls before. However, the next day I received another call. This time it was a different voice. This one asked if I were going to New Orleans and when I said, "yes," all he said was, "Remember you have a family" and hung up.

I must admit this worried me. After that I would get up during the night and check the family and house—not a very pleasant way to live.

During this turmoil I at last had a prospect of getting back into that illusive pastime called "employment"—it was again Penn Jones to the rescue—and I say this with the greatest respect and admiration! Penn had been corresponding with a friend of his in Boulder, Colorado, regarding helping me find employment out of Texas, which seemed the only thing left. The friend suggested to Penn that I make a trip to Boulder to check into some leads so the Jones family made the arrangements and I was off to Boulder. This was in January 1969.

I arrived in Boulder and was met by members of the Students for a Democratic Society, whose names I will not mention. (J. Edgar Hoover should not have his work made so easy). They took me from the airport and arranged for my lodging. The next three days I filled out applications at various places, including the Boulder Police Department and Sheriff's Office because those were the positions I was most qualified for and I believed I could be a cop and still have compassion for my fellow men. If they would not accept me that way, I could always quit—after all, I was an expert at being out of work.

After I had exhausted all possibilities, I thanked the people who had been so kind to me and returned to Midlothian, Texas to wait. I had been home about one week when I received word from the Boulder Sheriff's Department that there would be an opening soon and if I wanted the job, it was mine. Satisfied that the out of Texas bit was going to pay off, the Penn Jones, bless them, financed the trip back to Boulder. This time the family went with me. We drove straight through from Midlothian to Boulder. The second day in Boulder we found an apartment or two we might be able to afford until I started getting regular pay checks. I felt good about having a chance at a new start as I went to see Under Sheriff Cunningham.

When I arrived at the Sheriff's Department, Cunningham took me to his office, asked me to sit down and closed the door. It was then that I began to get that feeling I'd had so many times before when I was about to get the purple shaft. Sure enough, I had managed to lose a job before I even started. Mr. Cunningham began to ask me about my background with the Dallas Sheriff's Department (which he already knew from my previous visit) and the reason for my termination. Then he brought out his big gun, "What about Jim Garrison?" Well, knowing I'd been had, I told him I was going to have to testify in the Shaw trial (which I'm sure he already knew).

I'd heard about every excuse there was for not hiring me but he should have handed me this one in a gift-wrapped "surprise" package. "Mr. Craig," he said, (I had been Roger until then) "we've had a little situation here" and he went on—it seemed that one of their jailers had seduced a sixteen-year-old girl while she was in their custody—WOW—and with that and my connection with the Garrison probe, the heat would be more than they wanted to handle. He was sorry. So was I—all the way back to Texas.

When we arrived back in Midlothian, we were all exhausted and very disappointed. Molly had the flu, Deanna a bad cold and the strain of the past few weeks had taken its toll on me. I was having trouble with my stomach and lungs and was down to 138 pounds. It was February 1, 1969. We had just enough money left from the trip to perhaps rent a house and buy a few groceries. Dale Foshee was pressing me again to move and I had nowhere to go and no prospects of a job. Like a wounded animal, I could only think of returning to familiar surroundings—the place that I had spent most of my adult life.

We drove to Dallas and by some streak of luck sneaked by a property owner and managed to rent a house. Before this poor, misguided soul could change his mind, we gathered up our belongings in Midlothian and moved back to Dallas, where I again applied my trade of looking for work.

I spent the following days filling out many applications and some of the interviews were even promising. I was very careful not to mention any part of my involvement in the assassination.

However, on February 13, 1969 I was summoned to New Orleans to testify in the Clay Shaw trial. On the 14th when I finally took the stand the defense tried very hard to discredit me by saying that I worked in New Orleans and was, in fact, still working in that city under an assumed name. Failing to discredit me, they accomplished the next best thing, the distorted version appeared in newspapers and wire services throughout the country.

When I returned to Dallas on February 16, 1969, I was to realize the full impact of this distorted news story, for when I contacted the job possibilities I had before I testified, I found all doors closed. On March 4—after several days of no openings, or being told that I was not qualified, or that they would call me, which they never did—I found a job with Industrial Towel and Uniform Company of Dallas. This was a rental company and they needed men so that all I had to do was pass a polygraph test to prove I was not a thief, which I passed!

Now I was a Route Salesman. Ponder that awhile—a Judge reduced to picking up dirty laundry. Oh, well, work is work! Still weak and underweight from being sick during January and February, I was determined to make it on my new job.

I left home at 5:45 a.m. and arrived at the plant a little after 6:00 a.m., put my route slips in order, loaded my truck and started my deliveries. I got back to the plant about 4:30 p.m., unloaded the dirty linens, turned in my money and charge slips and got back home around 6:30 p.m. This was the season for cold, rainy weather—wouldn't you know? I had been to a doctor who gave me some medication for the chest infection I had developed and the medicine kept me going until March 14—when I, literally, ran out of gas.

On March 18, Molly called Penn and told him that I was not any better. Penn began to make arrangements for me to be admitted to the Veterans Hospital, where he was to meet me. By this time, I was out of it and Molly called an ambulance. I had completely passed out by the time it had arrived. I knew that I was going to the V.A. Hospital but when I woke up a short time later, I knew I was not at the V.A. Hospital. Those dirty bastards had taken me to Parkland Hospital, which has a reputation for saving people comparable to my employment record for the past two years. I gathered what strength I had, got off the stretcher and staggered down the hall.

Molly had reached Penn, who was waiting at the V.A. Hospital, and he was madder than hell as he hated Parkland Hospital even more than I did. So, I finally wound up at the V.A. Hospital via Penn's car, where I spent the next ten days. I was released from the hospital on March 28, 1969 with instructions not to work out in the weather until my lungs had improved. This, of course, eliminated my job as a route salesman.

I knew an inside job was going to be hard to find from my experience during the past two years. First of all, I knew that when my references were checked Decker would not give me a favorable recommendation—if he even gave one at all. Second, my unstable employment record during the past two years had resulted in a disastrous credit rating. Eight years of experience in various responsible duties at the Sheriff's Office were gone. They had, indeed, done their work well!

After many weeks of search, I still had no job and was again behind on the rent. At this point we took two cameras, one 8 millimeter movie and one Minor still, our projector and screen and sold them for enough to rent a cheaper house. We moved into a three-room house on Gurley Street which wasn't much but it kept out the rain!

One day I got a wild idea. I would go down to the Federal Building and apply for a government job—those people will hire anybody—well, almost anybody. I passed the civil service test and was told they had a job coming up in the office and I was qualified for it. I was to go back in two days to begin work. Things were certainly looking up. I went over to my father-in-law's and drank all of his beer to celebrate.

The two days passed and I headed for my government job, which was to be handling correspondence from other government agencies—they do a lot of writing to each other. Well, when I arrived, I was ushered into one of those cubby hole offices AGAIN, where I was told that they had received a memo telling them the budget was being cut and my job was being eliminated (I hadn't even started). Oh, well, at least I was losing "more important" jobs now.

On June 1st I answered an ad for an Assistant Manager's job at a liquor store, where the only qualification was that I pass another polygraph test, which I did, proving that I had not yet turned to stealing. The next day I reported for work to find that I was a delivery boy again. My job was restocking private clubs throughout Dallas who bought merchandise from the store. I soon made friends with all the club owners, and every time I would make a delivery, they would insist on buying me a drink. I was making $1.87 an hour. I wasn't the highest paid delivery boy in town but after a few stops I was probably the happiest!

In the meantime, being out of work from March until June 1st, I was again behind on the rent as well as the car payment on my used 1965 Buick. The landlord had asked us to move. I tried to explain my situation and the fact that I was now working and would try to catch up on the rent but he didn't care—I had to go. It was two weeks before I received a pay check. I don't know how we made it but we did. Molly then found a house for us to rent and I paid the first month's rent. I didn't worry about the car payment any longer for two days after I started to work the bank repossessed the car. We then again went back to driving one of Penn's cars.

During the slow periods of the weeks which followed I was always searching the paper and talking to people—trying to find a better paying job with a little security. I was working eleven hours a day, six days a week so it took me some time to locate one and I also had to be careful not to let people know too much about me because the general attitude in Dallas was not to get involved in the assassination. (A little late for Dallas).

On September 18, 1969 I applied at Peakload, Inc., a temporary employment service, who was looking for a dispatcher. The job consisted of taking orders from companies which needed temporary help for a few days, selecting the men from the hall who were best suited to the customer's needs, then seeing that they were delivered by our driver and picked up promptly after work. Al Nagel, the office manager, was from Minnesota and knew little of the events in Dallas and nothing of the people involved in the assassination so I slipped by and was hired. Now I was doing something which I enjoyed and the pay was $500.00 a month with time and one-half for over 48 hours. The next few weeks went by swiftly. I was working six days a week and making enough money to pay the rent, buy groceries and clothes for the kids.

On November 10, 1969 I was taken to the V.A. Hospital again. This time with neuritis, which the doctors said was caused by a vitamin deficiency over a long period of time, and bronchial pneumonia. This time I was not too concerned because Al Nagel liked my work and I was sure that I had a future with Peakload regardless of this temporary setback.

Well, after twenty-four days of what seemed like endless injections of vitamins, penicillin and streptomycin (one hundred and twenty-eight in all) I was sent home on December 4, 1969. The next day I called Al Nagel to tell him that I would return to work in a couple of days—when I got my strength back. Al informed me that I no longer had the job— that I had been replaced.

My final check from Peakload paid the rent for a month and bought a few groceries but Christmas was coming and I had managed somehow not to let the kids down—up until now. While I was in the hospital Penn Jones brought a letter he had received from Madeline Goddard. She had, apparently, read much on the assassination and sent her best wishes and support to us. Also, in the letter was the answer to this Christmas. Madeline had enclosed a check for $100.00.

She did not realize it, I'm sure, but that kept us from throwing my hands up in the air and giving up. The next few weeks were a repetition of earlier days—no jobs, no money, no prospects (there must be a song in there somewhere). Our only means of eating those days was Madeline Goddard's generosity; God bless Madeline and her generous heart.

Penn Jones had a few acres of land in Boyce, Texas, a short distance from Midlothian and he had persuaded us to move into the smaller of two houses on this land. We decided to go so that I could recuperate and regroup my thoughts. By this time, January 24, 1970, I was very depressed and ready to throw in the towel.

Penn and his son, Penn III, moved our belongings into the small three-room house and I must say that the fresh air and freedom from Dallas and its citizens was a welcome change. After a few days I felt better and began exploring our new surroundings. Penn had seventy-eight head of cattle on the place and I was feeding twenty bales of hay to them every morning. As my strength came back I also tackled various small, clean up jobs around the farm. It was the least I could do—the rent was free and Penn paid the light and water bills. We bought what butane we had to buy for heat and cooking. How about this—in 1948 I ran away from home at age 12 and spent the next four years working on farms and ranches in the west and northwest—now twenty-two years later I was back on the farm! There were days, however, when the rain and sleet would keep me inside, only venturing out when I had to (mostly to feed the cows).

The highlight of each day was when the mail man came as we were now corresponding with Madeline Goddard regularly and always looked forward to her letters. I do not know what we would have done if it hadn't been for this wonderful person. If I live to be a hundred, I couldn't repay her!

Roger Jr. was sixteen now and living with his grandparents in Dallas. Terry and Deanna were going to school in Waxahachie, seven miles away. They had to walk about three quarters of a mile to the school bus stop so in bad weather we would drive them to school. This was no easy job in the 1955 Ford of Penn's, which had seen better days. I certainly do not mean to sound ungrateful—Penn Jones and his wife were wonderful to us—we will always hold them close.

It was April when the larger house on the land in Boyce became vacant and Penn said that we could move into it. We needed the room and I would be closer to the stock and the feed for them was also in the barn near that house. Living in the bigger house was much easier and it was about this time that Penn decided to try to raise Holstein calves. There were no jobs in this small county and maybe we could make some money on this venture.

Molly, Terry, Deanna and I drove Penn's Travelall truck to Cleburne, where we picked up the calf Penn had bought on a pilot project. At three days old, the calf was a big baby at 80 pounds or more. Every morning at 7:00 a.m. Molly fixed the calf's bottle and we took turns feeding him until he decided that Molly was his mother. Cute—but something she wasn't ready for!

We continued taking care of the cattle for several weeks and during this time two calves were born. We named one, a little bull calf, "Jones" and the other a heifer calf, Deanna named "Susie." They became her only playmates. However, I wasn't making one red cent and the only help we received was from Madeline who, God knows, was carrying the burden of feeding my family.

On May 15 a decision had to be made. It was apparent that the calf project wasn't going to materialize and Penn was talking of selling some of the land and cattle. It looked as though Penn was having financial problems and I did not want to add to them. So, Molly and I talked and decided the best thing for us was to drive to Dallas and make arrangements to stay with someone and for me to try one more time (there's that song title). We talked to my mother, who said we could move in with her until I found a job and a place to live.

As we drove back to Boyce, we spoke of our apprehension about moving, but when we drove into the yard we knew it was the thing to do. The front door of the house was standing wide open. I knew what was gone even before I got out of the car. I was right. The 30-40 Krag rifle (the only one I had managed to hang onto), Terry's 30.30 Winchester, which he had received as a gift, his 410 shotgun, and the 12 gauge automatic shotgun Penn had loaned me were all missing. These were our only means of protection in this place so far in the country with no telephone or close neighbors. Now we had been stripped of that. Coincidence? Maybe. I was very uneasy and the sooner we got out of there, I felt, the better.

It took two days and two sleepless nights to arrange the move but we did it and were back in Dallas and staying with my mother. By this time my physical health was somewhat improved and my mental attitude was back to normal. This was due to the words of encouragement I had received from Madeline and others who had written to us over the past months to let me know that there were people in this country who cared. I was ready for any opposition from the Political Monster which ruled Dallas and even the very lives of those so-called Business and Civic leaders who did not have the guts to stand on their own two feet! As I thought over the past years, I was even amused that I, a man of limited education and no social position in this City of Purity, had struck fear into the hearts of its great leaders by just speaking to them on the street!

Although I had not worked steadily since my termination from the Dallas County Sheriff's Department, I did not forget my obligation as an American. Thus, when asked by certain critics of the Warren Report to help, I did what I could. Imagine the turmoil it will cause when and if the Dallas Police read this and find out I have copied and turned over to a certain editor several names, addresses and telephone numbers of people connected with the assassination of John F. Kennedy which were locked in the files of the Dallas Police Intelligence Division. Not to mention the files which were photostated and smuggled out of the Dallas County Mail under Bill Decker's nose (all after I left the Sheriff's Department). Even though I have not made any money in the past few years, I hope I was able to help those who have spent so much time investigating the assassination, who certainly haven't made any money either!

The last week of May, 1970 I got lucky. The ad in the newspaper read, "Wanted Dispatcher for temporary labor company". The Company was Peakload. I quickly made a call to the chief dispatcher, with whom I had worked previously, and found he was working sixteen hours every day. He was so happy to hear from me, because of his workload, that he offered to come and get me so that I could go to work that day. The company had a new office manager, Jim Morris. I went in immediately to apply—at the urging of the chief dispatcher, Bill Funderburke—and for an interview with Jim Morris, the manager. He was from Ft. Worth and knew more about the assassination and me than I would have preferred (from the questions he asked me concerning Bill Decker, Jim Garrison and others who had made the news). However, the office was in trouble as they had not been able to keep an evening dispatcher for more than three or four weeks at a time since I worked there in 1969.

With a word of caution as to my activities, Jim put me to work. This made Bill very happy as the pressure was now off him. I knew the work, the customers and most of the men I would be dealing with so Peakload did not have to worry about breaking in a new man. The rest of May and early June passed uneventfully but around the middle of June Molly went into Baylor Hospital, through the clinic as we could not afford a private doctor or the high rate of regular hospital services (I had only worked a short time and we still had a balance owing on Molly's surgery in August 1969). On June 26th, Molly underwent major surgery. She had been under a tremendous strain the past years and was physically and mentally exhausted.

During this period, I had managed to gather enough money to buy a 1962 Ford from a friend. It was not the best car in the world but it was only a hundred and fifty dollars and it did run. I paid $50.00 down and was to pay him the rest in a month or so. I also rented a small apartment and it seemed good to once again be by ourselves in our own home. But our new found Wealth was short lived.

Shortly after this, a self-professed private detective in Dallas, by the name of Al Chapman, had written a story about new evidence in the assassination which he had sold to the National Enquirer. In this article he quoted me as saying that I had given certain information to him and had personally identified a picture of a man and car saying it was Lee Harvey Oswald and his accomplice.

The entire story, with reference to me, was completely false. I had never been interviewed by this man and had at no time seen the picture to which he referred. Al Chapman, prior to the assassination, was a custodian for a church in Oak Cliff. There is a good deal of mystery about him for he will not reveal his business or residential address. Nor is the name of the church available. Although he is a part-time private investigator, he has no license.

The story was all over the office and Jim was concerned as he had been keeping up on anything written involving these events. Before long the

F.B.I. and the Dallas Police were making regular visits to the office on the pretext of looking for "Jim Jones" or "Tom Smith" or any excuse they could use to let me know they could also read! The heat was on. Jim was constantly there—every time I looked up—which was unusual. This leech, this skid row bum, and I am referring to Al Chapman, in his lust for money, not caring whom he hurt, had not only sold his story but my future with Peakload as well.

On July 17, 1970, I reported for work to find another man doing my job. I was told by this "replacement" that Jim wanted to see me. As I sat in Jim's office, I knew what was coming. Jim said, "Roger, you've done a good job but it is time for a change." I asked him for an explanation but all he would say was that it was time for a change and he was sorry!

Bill Decker died in August. The County Commissioners appointed his executive assistant, Clarence Jones, to fill the job until November, when he had to run for election (with the backing of the Democratic Party).

For the first time since Decker's reign, the Republicans nominated someone to oppose a Democrat for the office. The man was Jack Revel, former Chief of the Dallas Police Intelligence Division. This meant that the voters had the choice between two evils. Well, Clarence Jones was elected—his campaign signs and posters read, "Elect Clarence Jones— In the Tradition of Bill Decker"! It would be nice if Jack Revel would be upset enough over his loss of the election to make public some information—but this is very wishful thinking indeed.

Meanwhile, I am still out of a job (but still looking). I would like to think that the people of Dallas will change and rise up against the dishonest and irresponsible tyrants who govern in their name—but I do not see it happening in the near future. Dallas is my home but I will always feel like an outsider because I simply will not adjust to the idea that for Dallas, for Texas, for America this must serve as democracy.

A Few Odd and Interesting Facts

Allen Sweatt, Decker's Chief criminal investigator, let me know that he was aware of my friendship with Hiram Ingram and that he did not like it one bit.

Before I departed the Sheriff's Office for good Allen Sweatt and I talked a couple of times and he revealed to me that he knew Lee Harvey Oswald. He also told me that Oswald worked for the F.B.I. as an informer, that he was paid $200.00 a month and his code number was S 172.

ROBERT PERRIN AND NANCY PERRIN RICH

When Penn Jones wanted the records of Robert Perrin, the ex-husband of Nancy Perrin Rich, I had to find a new source of information. (I won't release this name for obvious reasons.) It seems that Nancy Perrin was connected with Jack Ruby, Clay Shaw and Lee Oswald at about the time of President Kennedy's death.

Robert Perrin was reported to have committed suicide in New Orleans, La. The autopsy showed no visible scars, marks or tattoos and Penn knew that Perrin had been arrested in Dallas and wanted me to get the records of the arrest along with his description. After some doing I finally obtained the record. It showed that Perrin had several tattoos and part of his right index finger was missing. None of this information showed up on the autopsy report. It would be interesting to know who WAS buried in Robert Perrin's place and where Robert Perrin is now, wouldn't it?

ADDENDUM

The favorite pastime in Dallas

Is a game they call murder with malice

They don't ask your leave

But not to deceive

To tell you would be—well, too callous

CAR ACCIDENT

On Wednesday, October 27, 1970, I went to downtown Dallas to Jack Revel's campaign headquarters to pick up some campaign signs. The headquarters were not open and I decided to visit a friend who works at a restaurant across the street. While talking with my friend the conversation turned, as it so often does, to the assassination. He and I had discussed this in the past.

During the course of our conversation a man who I had not met before entered into the conversation. He, of course, did not know me (not to my knowledge). I told him that I was from out of town and that I was interested in facts that hadn't been printed and in persons that had known Jack Ruby and Lee Oswald. This man said, "I knew Oswald and Ruby. I can tell you anything you want to know about them."

At this point I became very interested and I told him again that I'd sure like to know firsthand what they were like. He said, "I knew Ruby well— I had seen Oswald a couple of times in Ruby's place." I then said, "Well, in Ruby's business—the night club—I imagine a lot of people were seen there." He sort of chuckled and said "Huh—Jack Ruby's business was spelled Mafia." He then said, "I can show you a used car lot where Ruby collected a lot of gambling money over on Ross Avenue" (it was the 4600 block of Ross Avenue). So I offered to drive him over there and he said, "No—do you have your car here?" I did. He said I should follow him, which I did. I parked my car on the same side of the street as the car lot, a short distance down and walked back to his car. I opened the door of his car on the passenger side and he pointed to the car lot and said, "That's where a lot of the money comes in from the gambling operation and Jack picked it up here."

He said, "If you really want to know what's going on in Dallas you have to talk to someone who's been around—and I've been around in those circles." Then he said, "Just leave your car parked there and come with me—I'll show you something that's REALLY interesting." He drove me to 300 1/2 South Ewing in the Oak Cliff area to an apartment that had been a family dwelling and was converted into apartment units. I should mention here that Jack Ruby's address at the time of the assassination was 323 South Ewing.

The apartment at 300 1/2 South Ewing is upstairs and when we walked into the apartment there was a distinct feeling of an unlived-in atmosphere. The furnishings were bare. There was a couch, chair and coffee table—no lamps, no ash trays, nothing on the walls. The man had been smoking so it was odd that there were no ash trays. He said, "How about a cup of coffee?" We went into the kitchen, he opened the cabinet and said, "Oh well, I guess I'm out of coffee." He was also out of everything else as there was nothing in the cabinet.

The arrangement of the apartment was unusual as you had to go through the bedroom to the kitchen, which was very small. The closet door was open in the bedroom. However, there were no clothes in it. At that time, I became slightly nervous about the situation.

We went back into the bedroom from the kitchen. While in the bedroom he said, "I want to show you something." He opened the top drawer of the dresser and pulled out a shoulder holster—there was a 32 revolver with a three-inch barrel in the shoulder holster. He pulled the 32 out of

the holster and said, "what do you think about that?" I remarked that you don't see many 32's with a barrel like that. He put the 32 back in the drawer and went around to the side of the closet which was not visible when you went into the kitchen. At that time, he produced two rifles—one was a bolt action which looked like a 30.06, the other was a high-power automatic which appeared to be a 257 caliber.

I remarked that they were nice rifles and I would like to have a good deer hunting rifle. He then laid those two on the bed and he said, "You haven't seen anything yet." He then got down on the floor and he pulled 5 more rifles from under the bed. Each of these were equipped with scopes. He then pulled a cardboard box about 13 inches long and 10 inches deep also from under the bed. The box was closed and on the side was printed "Ammunition—Handle With Care." He then slid the rifles and ammunition back under the bed. I said jokingly, "What are you gonna do—start a war?" He said, "Could be."

At that time, he looked at his watch and said "excuse me just a minute, I have to go down to the landlady's apartment and make a phone call—I promised some people I would call them" (there was no telephone in the apartment). He was gone for about ten minutes. During this time, I made a mental inventory of the apartment. After he returned, he asked me if I was ready to go back to my car. There was a pay phone on the corner from the apartment and I asked him to pull over so that I could call the people who owned the car (I had told him that it was borrowed while I was in Dallas), that I wanted to let them know that the car was okay. From the pay phone I called my wife and gave her the man's name and address and told her of the situation. His name—as he gave me is A.E. Allen, 300 1/2 South Ewing, Dallas, Texas.

Before we went to his apartment, or the apartment, I told him being from out of town that I didn't know much, but that I had heard that Ruby was in the gun running business. He said that Ruby wasn't actually buying and selling weapons. That people in higher positions made the arrangements for the buying and selling of weapons. That Ruby was mainly the go-between for delivering the money and making arrangements for the storage of the weapons until they were shipped out.

During the course of the evening he made the statement several times that, "if you want to stay healthy, don't say anything to anybody in Dallas about the assassination unless you're damn sure you know who you're talking to."

He then said that there were a lot of people in Dallas who were out to "get" him because he knows too much.

One of the strangest things that he did was to drive on East Jefferson to a used car lot and stop. There were two men inside the office and he went in and talked to them. I stayed in the car and could see them through a window of the office. He was in there only a few minutes. His car was a light blue Oldsmobile 66 model. When he came out of the office, he got into a gray Olds sitting on the lot, and he drove it onto the drive stopping just before he entered the street—he motioned to me—I was watching him. I got out of the blue Olds, and he took me back to my car in the gray Olds.

On the way to my car across town, he kept repeating there's a lot more to this (the assassination) than they'll ever know. In taking me to my car he cut across to Ft. Worth Avenue. While driving slowly along he pointed out certain private clubs—saying that he wasn't allowed in one or the other. My first thought was that he was trying to give me the impression that he was knowledgeable about the workings of the Dallas underworld. However, it really seems that he was using a delaying measure—since it took from 10:00 p.m. until 11:15 p.m. to drive me to my car—an ordinary 15-minute drive at that time.

When I got out of his car at mine, he said, "I'll call you tomorrow." Earlier in the evening he had implied he was going to give me more information. I had given him a number to reach me by. Needless to say, I did not hear from him after the incident that followed!

I had locked my car when I parked it. When I got into it, I turned the key over to start the engine. At this point there was a muffled type explosion and then smoke came out the sides of the hood. The hood had a double latch and didn't blow. Fire was coming through the air vents under the dash and a pillow was burning inside the car.

I jumped out of the car and raised the hood. The engine, hoses, firewall and even under the bell housing was all ablaze. Several persons came up and someone called the fire department. A man named Bill Booken was walking by at about the time it happened. The fire department used 2 cans of chemical to extinguish the fire. This was one of the hottest fires I had ever seen. There was no smell of gasoline before or after, there was no back fire as the car had not started and afterwards the gas lines were checked and there were no leaks. There was an air breather on the car and in fact, there was no mechanical reason for the explosion.

This happened at 4625 Ross Avenue. Mr. Booken took me to Anderson's Restaurant at 4909 Ross Avenue where I called my wife and she arranged for my brother Duane to come after me. I didn't know that I had been injured until I felt the warm blood running down my shirt after my brother picked me up. I had lost quite a lot of blood by the time I went to the emergency room. I was there for three hours. A police report was made. I had received 5 puncture type wounds in the chest area. One vein had been severed and had to be tied and stitches taken in the wounds. X-rays were also made. I went to our family physician the following day and had the stitches removed the following Monday. It was never completely determined what hit me. Another close call! The doctor at the emergency room said I was lucky the wounds had not been lower and our family physician said I was lucky the wounds were not in the neck. So . . . I suppose I'm just lucky all the way round!